Regards from the DRAGON *Seattle*

Taky Kimura

Compiled By David Tadman

To Taky.

You are the greatest

Bruce Lee

Regards from the DRAGON

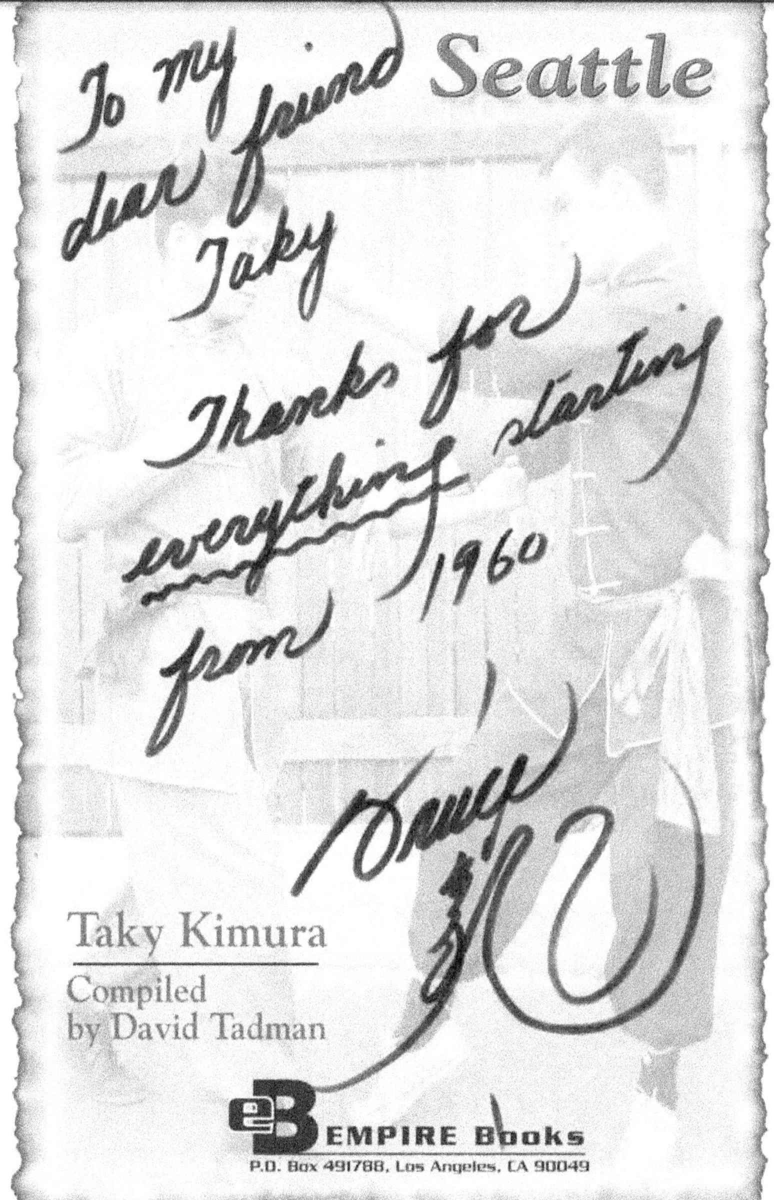
Seattle
To my dear friend Taky
Thanks for everything starting from 1960
Bruce
Taky Kimura
Compiled by David Tadman
EMPIRE Books
P.O. Box 491788, Los Angeles, CA 90049

DISCLAIMER

Please note that the author and publisher of this book are NOT RESPONSIBLE in any manner whatsoever for any injury that may result from practicing the techniques and/or following the instructions given within. Since the physical activities described herein may be too strenuous in nature for some readers to engage in safely, it is essential that a physician be consulted prior to training.

First published in 2009 by EMPIRE BOOKS LLC.

Library of Congress Catalog Number:
ISBN-10: 1-933901--45-9
ISBN-13: 978-1-933901--45-9

Empire Books
P.O. Box 491788
Los Angeles, CA 90049
(818) 767-79 00

First edition
09 08 07 06 05 04 03 02 01 00 99 98 97

Printed in the United States of America.

Library of Congress Cataloging-in-Publication Data

Kimura, Taky.
Regards from the dragon- Seattle / by Taky Kimura ; compiled by David Tadman. -- 1st ed.
p. cm.
ISBN 978-1-933901-45-9 (pbk. : alk. paper)
1. Lee, Bruce, 1940-1973. 2. Martial artists--United States--Biography. 3. Palmer, Doug--Interviews. I. Tadman, David, 1965- II. Title.
GV1113.L44K56 2009
791.4302'8092--dc22
[B]
2009019380

Foreword By Linda & Shannon Lee

BRUCE LEE'S
TAO OF
CHINESE GUNG FU
振藩拳道

以無限爲有限

以無法爲有法

This is to certify that
Taky Kimura

fourth

If Bruce were here, he would have many things to say to his friend Taky Kimura. Bruce often talked with me about Taky, so I know without a doubt that he would want Taky to know the following sentiments. I have taken the liberty of using Bruce's voice to express his thoughts:

"Taky, I am grateful to you for your loyal friendship from the time I met you until I had to leave in 1973. You were my best friend because you were always real and genuine. No pretense, no guile, no ulterior purpose. Just genuine love, respect and appreciation between us.

"I am grateful to you for seeing and understanding the value of my life's work and for dedicating your life's work to spreading my message far and wide around the world. But, my brother, it is your life that I celebrate because you were the one who really "got it," who had the knowledge and the will to apply it to your own life. From there you have gone on to generously share with untold thousands of students and fans your example of following the path to personal liberation.

"You speak often about how knowing me changed your outlook on life, how your self-esteem suffered from the internment during the war, how you felt the prejudice of the community and could not find meaning for your life after those experiences. Well, my friend, that's all very nice of you to say, and I know that your life did change after we met, but it was always a two-way street with us. Reflect on how much you helped me from the time I arrived in Seattle, green behind the ears. Even though the confidence I exuded was genuine in many respects, I still had a lot to learn about living in America. You never treated me like I was "fresh off the boat," you never made fun of my imperfect English, you only helped to show me the way in my new home. And then in the last years of my life, when things were pretty crazy for me in Hong Kong with many people seeking my favor, I could just pick up the phone and call my friend and know that the words you spoke were true and selfless. I want you to know how much that meant to me.

"Thanks, too, Taky, for looking after my family all these years. Linda, Brandon and Shannon knew they could turn to you, my friend, if they ever needed anything—and you've always been there for them. I'm grateful you've kept my big family together too--all the students I taught, then all the ones you have taught and the thousands of people who have been fortunate enough to receive your gift of wisdom and graciousness. Thanks for looking after my gravesite, and that of my dear son Brandon, all these years. I know you meet lots of people at the cemetery, and you take that opportunity to talk about my philosophy and art. You have touched the hearts of many, not just because you talk about me, but because you live your life by the beliefs and principles we discussed so often.

"Taky, you're the best friend a guy could ever have had on this earth and in the hereafter. We will meet again, but I can wait. The world is a better place because of YOU."

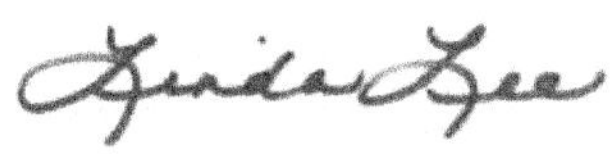

Contents

My Father By Andrew Kimura

I am most grateful and fortunate to be the son of Taky Kimura. When I was young it was hard to share him with his many students and friends, in which he was surrogate father figure to. As I grew older, it became easier for me to accept his role as teacher, friend and father, and I realized he was doing for them as Bruce had done for him so many years before.

Taky Kimura is a wonderful man with a giving heart and generous soul, I am forever indebted to SiGung Bruce Lee and his family for their influence in my father's life. For if my father had never met Bruce Lee, surely he would not have become the man he is today. Not only did Bruce Lee hand down the precious gift of Gung-Fu that has enriched our lives, but he also restored my father's confidence, pride and humanity which was taken from him in a dark chapter of our countries history in the internment of the Japanese Americans, during the Second World War. During those years and after the war, my father endured much hatred and racism, but never forgot who he was, it just took a good friend (Bruce Lee) to remind him. With the rich heritage of my father's parents and the philosophies of the Japanese people, and in reflect of the way the samurai lived their lives, he was able to overcome these obstacles.

Taky Kimura is kind, unselfish, humble and the strongest man I have ever known and I am honored to call him father and Sifu as well as my best friend.

In having to write this foreword I am at a loss for words. There are no words that would adequately describe this man I am so proud of. Anyone who knows him, or has met him, or has spent any time with him, can attest to the fact that we are all blessed to know him and are better people for it. For there is a quiet strength and wisdom that you gain from meeting and talking with him as he gives so freely of himself in hopes that he may graciously impose some small bit of knowledge and understanding about the world, so you may be enlightened. So as the words fail me, I will relate some stories about him in the hope that you, the reader, will understand in just what a wonderful human being Taky Kimura is. He is the man who has always put friendship and family above all else, always trying to help others as friend and Sifu.

My earliest memories of me and my father were of us at the Gung Fu Club playing martial arts, putting the gloves on and sparring together, letting me hit him and feeling like I always got the better of the exchanges, except when he would hit me hard one or two times to remind me to keep my guard up and let me know he was really the boss and in control. Later, I found out it was to make me tougher for the challenges he knew life would present me in the years to come. Like Bruce Lee said "life is combat".

For six years, my father drove me to school, an hour drive each way and we would have discussions about many things, or he would quiz me as to what I learned at school that day. Sometimes we lis-

tened to music and we would sing along to our favorite songs. Other times he would let me shift the gears to the car when he was driving. I played soccer, baseball and basketball for seven years and in all that time he never missed one practice, always given me encouragement during half time. When I played football during high school it was the same thing, he would cheer me on and encourage me to do my best and no matter how the outcome of the game, or my performance, he was always proud of me, telling me what I did right and what I could work on to do better within the next game. These are only a few of the precious memories I have of my father and I shall never forget them and will pass them on to my son. It was these lessons learned within sports, or in the Gung Fu Club that have helped me to be strong throughout the years of my life, and I can never thank him enough for his teachings.

My father and I have always had a ritual of words that we say to each other every night; he says "UN! " and I say, "BEATABLE!", meaning, that he and I together are UN-BEATABLE. Not a night has gone by as long as I can remember that we do not say this to one another, even by phone if we are not together. The strength in our father and son relationship has made me a better human being.

I now uphold the tradition and continue to pass this same ritual on to my son Brodie, every night. "UN!"..."BEATABLE!"...Doing this with my own son has made me come full circle. If I can only be half the man my father is within my lifetime, then that is the only mountain that I have to climb. Taky Kimura is my father, my Sifu, my mentor, my higher power and my strength, but most of all, Taky kimura is my hero.

Andrew Kimura

Kimura Acknowledgements

A Special Thanks to the Bruce Lee Foundation: Linda Lee and Bruce Cadwell; Shannon Lee and Wren Kessler; Tammy Ledda; Chris and Dustin Ledda.

Brodie, you are destined to carry on the Kimura legacy. With your keen mind you are on the cutting edge of accomplishing all the things many people can only dream about.

Peggy Comin, thank you for everything you've done for me, I am forever grateful.

Monica Kimura, I cannot express how much value you have brought to our family.

Adam, you have the potential to accomplish all that is meaningful to you.

A very special "thank you" to Henri Liedke, who rented a house to my family after WWII, while others would not give us the time of day do to our ethnicity you gave us a place to live and prosper.

A special thanks to the Kimura Family: My father, Suejiro Kimura. My mother, Haruyo Kimura. My siblings: Minoru, brother; Eiju, brother; Terry, sister; June, sister; Mary, sister; Fumiko, sister.

Thank you to our Senior Students who have given me so much over the years:
Abe Santos, Michael Hilow, Scott Lindenmuth, Joanne Duvall, Anne Harrington, Julie DonTigny, Alain De Preter and Veronique Costermams

We would like to thank our UK students: Martin Sterling, Martin O'Neill, Tony, John, Luca and his wife.

Abe, Tsuyoshi
Agbalog, Michael and Sprint
Alberg, Bob
Allen, Mark
Alvord, Tracee
Amaya, Sergio
Amiss, Matt
Anderson-Droke, Cal H.
Andrews, Justin
Angelo, Elisa
Anurodh, Safya
Arnold, Thomas Jon
Arnone, Lance and Mary Ann
Arnsberg, Mark
Arsenian, Troy
Atuja, Raymond
Aubochon, Kathy
Averill, Linda
Baad, Lawrence
Barber, Holly Beth
Barker, Holly
Barnett, Michael
Barnett, Steve
Barry, Debbie M.
Barry, Jim
Bateman, Scott E.
Batson, Bob
Beardsley, Lary E.
Beerman, J. Kelly
Belenski, Bill - Special Thanks!
Bell, Larry James
Bellone, Aaron
Belo, Nathaniel
Bemis, Matt
Benedict, Kit
Bennett, Mike
Bennett, Tim
Bevins, Ralph
Bhanu, Vivek
Bigelow, Brinton
Bitte, Eric
Bland, Ed
Bökel, Christian
Bollen, Victor
Bowman, Michael
Bracelin, Ray
Bracelin, Sander
Brassard, Thomas M.
Brewer, Lewis E.
Brill, Bill
Bristol, Dustin
Broadbent, Doug
Brodsky, Sasha Rudi
Brown, Robert V.
Buermann, Heather
Burk, Gregory D.
Burke, Mary Ann
Burnham, Peter
Burnham, Will, Petey and Peter
Cabalquinto, Michael B.
Campbell, Shawndra
Canon, Anne Marie
Carlson, Jeff
Carmell, Kevin - Special Thanks!
Casey, Chris
Castelli, Luca
Chan, Eric C.
Chan, Mike
Chan, Sue and Harry
Chen, Tina
Childs, Ed
Chin, Kathy
Chin, Y. Ken K.
Chinn, Kevin
Chiu, Clifton L.
Cocanaver, Paul
Cole, Karen
Conn, Steven
Contoravdis, Sam
Cornelius, Shane
Coulter, Reverend Roy
Cowled, Marcus

Cramer, Ellis
Cramer, Greg
Croson, Fred
Crowley, Michael and Breon
Cruse, Thomas
Currit, Marie
Curritt, Steven
Daigneault, John
Daigneault, Richard Karl
Daniel, Russell
Dao, Hoan T.
Davis, Kai
Davis, Mike
Delange, Henri
DeLight, Gary
Deselle, Alain
Diessner, Dan
Digel, Jon E.
Dill, Josh
DiSalvo, Enrico
Donaglia, Vincent
Donnelly, Peter
Dougherty, Elizabeth
Ducay, Arthur A.
Duffield, Herman
Dunn, David L.
Duong, Son
Duvall, Ken
Duvall, Theresa
Ekblad, Karen
Elder, Dena
Elder, Mark
Emery, David P.
Emery, Debra
Eng, Daryl
Engh, Dale A.
Euster, Wayne
Eyth, Reza
Fast, Michael D.
Fay, Lance P.
Ferris, Tom
Filipovitch, Natasha
Finch, Lotez
Fischl, Paul
Fleming, Theresa
Flores, Frank
Forbes, Shannon E.
Forman, Larry
Foster, Gary
Foster, Scott
Frank, Wyley
Franz, Dana
Freel, Tony A.
Fujita, Toshihiro
Fukushima, Yoshiko
Fulton, John
Galipeau, John
Garber, Michael B.
Garcia, Gilbert
Gass, Thomas John
Gendreau, Todd O.
Gerber, Jeff and Hillary
Giannaros, Costas
Gibbs, Donna G.
Gilge, Craig R.
Glaser, Bryan
Go, Allen and Jeanne
Godwins, Peter, Kerry, Tyler, Connor and Devon
Goldman, Stephen
Golecz, Feliks
Gonzolez, John "Gato"
Goodwin, Chris
Graham, Jeffrey
Granoados, Ivan
Grant, Ed and Joe
Green, Leon J. II
Green, Randall Wayne
Greene-Bialic, Russell
Greka, Niko
Grunkemeier. Stephan & Rachna
Gurdian, Augusto & Felix
Gustafson, Albert K.
Guth, Dick
Gwin, Frank
Habel, Sue
Hagwood, Bryan
Haigh, Andrew
Halliwell, Kevin
Hamlett, Darnell
Handman, Scott
Haney-Scott
Haney-Scott, Rosh
Hankins, Kevin
Hansen, Brian
Hanson, Calvin
Harris, Spencer
Harris, Spencer
Harrison, Sharon and Mike
Hart, Bob and Tyler
Haugen, Grant
Hawley, Jennifer
Hayden, James, Calvin
Hedner, Norm
Heitmuller, Robert
Hengstebeck, David
Henry, Adam
Henry, Marshall and Lisa
Herschel, James
Hickles, Domonique
Higoshi, Toshi - deceased
Ho, Louis Siu Ping
Hoff, Ken
Hoffman, Paul A.
Hohlbein, Rex, Wes, Ruth & Family
Holland, Clifford R.
Hollingsworth, Alrick
Hollingsworth, Roy and Linda
Horgens, James
Hostetter, John D.
Huynh, Minh
Jacobs, Al
Jacobs, Dan
Jacobs, Paula
Jahn, Ryan
James, Charles
James, Thomas
Janacek, Larry J.
Jenne, Dean
Jensen, Tara
Johanson, Shary D.
Johnson, Cydney
Johnson, Mark R.
Johnson, Wayne E.
Johnston, Zack
Jones, Jeremy
Julianne, Yates
Kahl, Tom
Kaldestad, John
Kaneko, Norm and Dale - came to class in Seattle from Portland every Monday night for a year. Close family friends and students.
Kanpp, Galen
Kawahara, Yugo
Keiffer, Nigel L.
Keller, Randy
Kelley, Jesse C.
Kelly, Mike
Kendall, Alison R.
Kessler, Sylvia and Joe
Ketchum, Gary
Ketchum, Sylvia
Khou, Srun T.
Kilmer, Patrick C.
Kindall, Ron
Kino, Terry L.
Kinsfather, Robert, Jason and Andrew
Klein, Doug
Knauer, Jack A.
Koeman, Constantyn
Kohanek, Clark O
Kreng, John thank you for help, the journey continues
Kumar, S. Reji
Kuniyuki, Todd
La Chine, Thomas L.
LaChine, Thomas and Karin
Lalo, Carrera
Lam, Rodney K.
Lam, Tuan Anh
Lash, Daniel
Lau, Lai
Lau, Terence Kien-Wa
Lawrence, James
Lawyer, David Glenn
Lee, Alex
Lee, Anton
Lee, David
Lee, Michael
Lee, Ray C.
Lemmon, Mike
Lenon, Alvin A.
Leo, William L.
Letson, Russ L.
Lim, Makara
Linden, June
Lipton, Greg
Lishner, David
Liu, Alex
Ljunggren, Janice Ann
Lo, Shuen Shyang "Henky"
Locicero, Daniel "Frenchy"
Locicero, Mark and Mike
Lone, Betty
Look, Michael Joseph
Lopez, Angel
López, Juan
Lorrain, Michael V.
Loucks, Maggie and Mason
Louie, Camilla
Lowndes, Mark K.
Luckenbaugh, Harvey M.
Luk, Lewis
Lundberg, Roland
MacDonald, Molly
Maduzia, Bob
Maes, Michael John
Mahloch, Roxianne
Maier, Gabby
Mallouee, Eugene
Manning, Willie
Mark, Shelley
Markham, Kelly

Marks, Lou
Marshall, Betty Lu
Martin, David
Matsu-Pessot, Craig
Matthews, Cash
Mayberry, Mitch
Mayfield, Mark J.
McCallister, Big Mike - thanks for the great looking lawn!
McCallister, Randy
McDaniel, Gregory E.
McDonald, Bruce Lee
McDonald, Gregory E.
McGruer, Rory
McVay, Steve
Michaels, Michele
Michel, Greg
Miller, Brian
Miller, Robert
Miller, Scott W.
Milroy, Steve
Mitman, Don
Mitman, Mark
Mizuno, Kumiko
Moebes, Robert J.
Moneymaker, Laura
Morris, Evan
Murrary, Luke
Mutz, Ron
Nakashima, Stu
Nash, Bob
Nesbitt, Dennis
Nevitt, Matt
Nevitt, Tyler
Nichols, Sharon
Ninomiya, Satushi
Noback, Keith
Nolon, Tom
Norrell, George
Nye, Jeff
O' Higgins, Mark
O' Wery, Shannon "Brown"
Oakley, Gretchen
Octavo, Bien
Oda, Kazuyo
Odem, Michael
Ogdon, Jeffrey
Okomoto, Jim
Olsen, Teddy
Olson, Heidi
Ong, Martin
Ormand, James
Ortega, CaryAnne
Osborne, Mike
Otaki, Jane
Paige, Jim
Palmer, Colin
Palmer, Scott
Pang, Douglas
Parimley, Jason
Park, Ryan
Pawelke, David
Peehl, John
Peterson, Frank
Phelps, Rod
Phenicie, Joseph
Phenicie, Joshua
Piche, Rebecca Lynn
Pine, Clark
Pirrie, Scott
Poletaeva, Lena
Pon, Arthur
Pratt, Bryan
Prencipe, Joseph
Prentice, Larry
Prim, James
Quenneville, Teresa
Quinlan, Ben
Radin, Sandra
Ramirez, John Michael
Ramirez, Rodrigo
Ramos, Becky
Ramos, Claudio
Raulston, Kelly
Reed, Susan
Regan, Robert
Rhen, Tonjia
Rieber, Maria
Roberts, Joseph
Roeber, Jon
Rogers, Bob Sr. and Jr.
Rogers, Jo
Romero, Nilka
Rosen, John
Rosen, Phyllis
Rue, Bruce
Ruvelson, Jason
Saito, Wayne
Sanders, Terry
Sandvigen, Craig
Santiago, Joe
Santos, Chris
Santos, Emmie and Arrianna
Santos, Roderick "Rod"
Santwire, Ryan
Sato, Chris
Satterlee, Richard
Saul, Bill
Scheffler, Ben
Scheffler, Larry
Schley, Enffie
Schmitt, Joanne Marie
Schrader, John
Schreier, Janis
Schryvers, Bob
Scott, Dai
Seng, Bruce
Sergieva, Ralitsa
Shepard, Dave
Sherman, James
Shigcoka, Yukihurn
Sibonga, Martin
Siciliano, Alan
Silas, Pete
Silverstein, Cindy
Silverstein, Steven
Simpson, Eddie - Special Thanks!
Simpson, Mike
Skartvedt, Brad
Smith, Art
Smith, Horton
Smith, Marley and Rayne
Smith, Matt "Smitty"
Snow, Ron and Chiemi
Spaulding, Robert
Spears, Elisa
Stanphill, Norma
Statesman, Guy
Stearn Terry
Steerman, Shawn
Stefurak, David
Stephens, Fred - deceased
Stephens, Jenn
Stephens, Robert
Stevens, David
Stevens, Lloyd Jr.
Stevens, Mike
Stewart, Terry
Stockland, Tanya
Strom, Grant
Stuart, Ken
Suleman, Jamil
Sullivan, Riley and Otie
Sutter, Ed Jr.
Suzuki, Takashi
Swanson, David
Tabor, Peter
Taraviras, George
Tashiro, Victor
Tateishi, Masami
Taylor, Andy
Taylor, James
Taylor, Shan
Taylor, Stewart
Temkova, Daena
Temples, Bob
Teng, Thomas
Tew, Dixon
Thal, Alan Todd
Thomaier, Tyana
Tillman, Charlie
Tippie, Terrence
Tooles, Brian
Touliatos, John
Toutoungi, Abdullah
Tran, Phan
Trebon, Ron
Truesdell, Jeremy
Truong, Dang-Thao N.
Truong, Tam
Truong, Tan
Tseng, Kien Wei
Tsuruds, Jay
Turney, Neil Jr.
Uchizono, Takaaki
Underhill, Rusty
Utarnachitt, Rich
Valicova, Jitka
VanDamme, James
VanDroof, Kurt
VanEkstrom, Ron
Vehara, Yukitoshi
Vold, Ryan
Vontver, Jason
Vontver, Ross
Voyles, Christina
Waddell, Andrew
Wagner, Johanna
Ward, Brian
Watanabe, Kazuhiro
Weber, Marcus
Weitzel, Kerry
Whittaker, Warren
Wickland, Stephen
Wiedemann, Sylvia
Wiley, Jeff
Williams, Cyril
Williams, Jason
Williams, Steve
Wilson, Jimi
Win, Mikol
Womack, John
Wong, Adam
Wong, Kwok
Wong, Sue
Woo, Charlie - deceased
Yanak, Chuck
Yango, Henry
Yango, Herminio
Yonezawa, Glenn
Young, Ed
Young, Pat Ly-Au
Yuen, Ray
Zang, Matthew
Zelinsky, Donald
Zhu, Yuming and Aaron
Zwiebel, Bob

Foreword By Dan Inosanto

It is my honor and privilege to write this foreword for my friend and SiHing Taky Kimura.

I was introduced to SiHing Taky by our late instructor, SiFu Bruce Lee, in 1964. I still consider, to this day, one of the greatest compliments I have ever received, was when SiFu Bruce told me, "You have a personality just like Taky." I can think of no one I would rather be compared to. SiHing Taky was the closest friend SiFu Bruce had and the person he trusted the most when I met him. His trust and affection for SiHing Taky stayed true until SiFu Bruce's untimely passing.

I remember when our friend SiHing James Lee passed away, SiFu Bruce told me, "Now there are only the two of you, (myself and Taky) that I have to trust and teach, and keep my art alive. Always remember, SiHing Taky is your senior and always pay respect to him and ask his advise. You two are the only ones I have."

When I think of SiHing Taky I can't help thinking of the "Boy Scouts", trustworthy, loyal, helpful, friendly, kind, courteous, reverent - I could go on but I think you understand. SiHing Taky is a one of kind, humble and modest man. A man I admire and a true role model for anyone, in or out of the field of martial arts.

For all of you who are fortunate enough to meet and train with SiHing Taky, I know you will treasure the experience.

Dan Inosanto
Founder and Head Instructor
Inosanto Academy of Martial Arts

Jun Fan Gung Fu Institute
振藩國術館
0001
Aug. 10 1965
This is to certify that
Taky Kimura
fourth

Foreword By Tsuyoshi Abe

I am very excited to hear that SiFu Taky Kimura is finally coming out with his book. Well, it is about time. My good friend David Tadman on the tenuous task in helping Sifu Taky to compile and produce the material and the endless information he has collected throughout the years of friendship he had with SiJo Bruce Lee and put it into book form.

The years of training and friendship SiFu Taky shared with SiJo Bruce Lee is very special and valuable, and it is also wonderful that now, he has decided to share his memoirs with the many old and new Bruce Lee fans on the rise. SiFu Taky's life is unique and wonderful! From his youth in the interment camps during World War 2 and the struggles afterwards, then befriending Bruce Lee, SiFu Taky's story is one of happiness and pain. Throughout SiFu Taky's life, he has taken care of many people like his brothers, sisters, cousins, and son Andy and daughter-in-law Monica, his grandson, friends, students and many more.

The Seattle years of Jun Fan Gung Fu / Jeet Kune Do are just a small part of SiFu Taky's life. However, it is a deep and precious story filed with wonderful memories and material treasures. This book will highlight the memoirs and musings SiFu Taky shared with SiJo Bruce Lee that will now be handed down to you, the readers, who will surely see Bruce Lee in a new light, Taky Kimura's best friend. I hope after reading this book, that you, the readers, will get to know Taky Kimura on a deeper level as his family, friends and students already do.

I am personally cerebrating this opportunity to see SiFu Taky Kimura's life put to paper into book form. I will forever deeply appreciate him for his true friendship and being a wonderful mentor and of course one of the greatest teachers ever in and outside the martial arts. I also pay tribute to him for introducing me to my other SiFu in Jun Fan Gung Fu / Jeet Kune Do, SiFu Dan Inosanto who has helped me realize my true potential in countless ways over the last twenty years. SiFu Taky Kimura and SiFu Dan Inosanto made me who I am as a teacher, mentor, man and human being. Without them, I am no one.

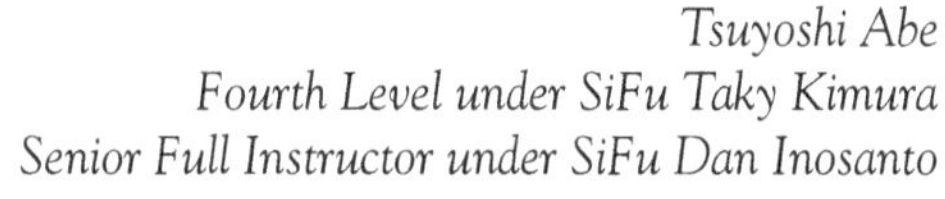

Tsuyoshi Abe
Fourth Level under SiFu Taky Kimura
Senior Full Instructor under SiFu Dan Inosanto

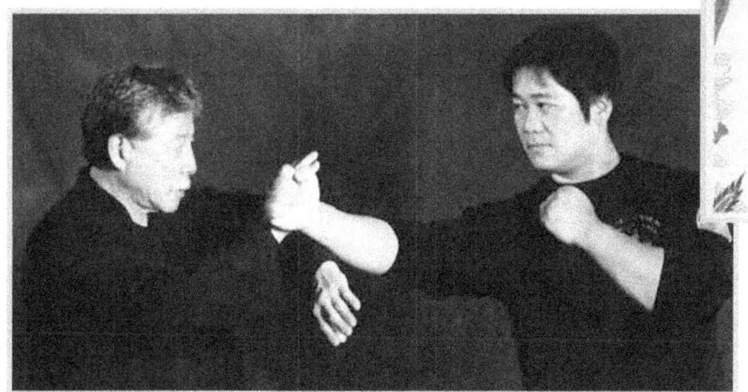

Authors Acknowledgements

I would like to thank the following people for all their help in making this book come to life.

Firstly, to my wife Allison who has endured many lonely days and nights, but with understanding, while I was working diligently in creating this book. To my nine year old boy Max who I am so proud to be the father of, your love and support through this journey has made this experience an incredible one. To my parents and sister, thanks for putting up with me through this time, the end result speaks for itself. Thanks for your guidance dad in making me a better writer.

To Linda and Shannon Lee, thank you for your interest and enthusiasm in seeing this book come to life, your love for Taky Kimura and his family have been proven time and time again. You both are strong with a wisdom that transcends in how we all know you. Your love and understanding for others and your vision for greatness is something to be admired by us all. Shannon, you truly are the keeper of the gate.

To Dan Inosanto, it is an honor to have you associated with this book. Your martial arts and philosophy of life are what Bruce Lee would be pleased with you. You have again and again selflessly given of yourself, putting others before you so they may achieve their goals. You are the keeper of the flame, Bruce Lee was proud to call you his friend.

To Kris Storti, it's good to know that Linda and Shannon Lee can rely on someone who really cares and gets the job done. You are the blood in the veins. Thanks for your support, always.

To Monica Kimura, let me just say this, you are a true mother figure to everyone, a wonderful person, a peace keeper and optimistic person who is a fighter on all levels. Thank you for your help, I am honored to know you.

To George and Mary Lee, my family up North. You inspire me every day and as I did with you and the Oakland Years book, I now work along side Taky Kimura with his book while you both are in my heart and mind, pushing me to do the best job I can do. I am honored to call you my friends.

To Doug Palmer, thank you for helping in making this book a better one. Your musings of the times you shared with Bruce Lee are both historic and enlightening. Thank you for being a part of this tribute to both Bruce and Taky.

To Shuzo kato, your participation in this book gives new insight into what Bruce Lee was achieving at that time. He respected you as a teacher and a man. Thank you for being a part of Bruce Lee's legacy.

To Cheryl Chow and family, thank you very much in taking the time in sharing yours and your parents memories of Bruce Lee. Much has been said about the time Bruce Lee came to live with your family and to have your historical story within this book, makes this book a better one.

To Julie DonTigny, you have helped me on many levels with this book, taking the time to coordinate, research and help compile certain materials, making this book an even greater journey to have encountered. Your love for Taky and his family and the legacy of Bruce Lee is evident in your heart as well as your actions. Your photographic eye in capturing Taky is unsurpassed. It has been an honor working with you.

To my close friend and Sifu Tsuyoshi Abe, your knowledge about Bruce Lee and his martial arts legacy is unsurpassed. Your guidance over the years within our friendship has helped me on many levels. Respect, honesty and honor are your creeds and you are not only a good influence on me, but everyone who has encountered you. Thank you for everything since 1994.

To Steve Kerridge my close friend and literary partner in the Bruce Lee world, you once again have pushed me into completing yet another project. Your help and enthusiasm has kept me going when things got dark. Here is to the many projects ahead that you and I are collaborating on, with you involved, a good book will become a great one.

To Steve Walling, you have been there by my side from day one, the traveling, the meetings with the ones who knew Bruce Lee the best, our journey has been locked together, you're a good and honest friend.

To Curtis Wong, your guidance and influence has made me wise and open-minded. You have taught me that in this business there is no time for problems, only problem solving. Your positive outlook on the way you look at life has trickled down to me; you are truly a great teacher.

A special thank you to Barrett and Vic Lepejian, you have been there from the beginning in helping me create the wonderful images I have used in countless Bruce Lee projects. The skill and artistry your ISGO photo labs have are unsurpassed and one you're late father Isgo mastered and cannot be matched. Your father's vision and humanity have influenced us all.

To Perry Lee, "The biggest Bruce Lee Collector in the world"! Your knowledge of Bruce Lee's Seattle years is truly eye opening. Thank you for your help in securing interviews with the Ruby Chow family. The materials given by you to me for use in this book truly highlight the feeling and moments in time surrounding the Ruby Chow era. Your help was greatly appreciated.

To John Kreng, the journey continues. . .

To Jose Fraguas and Michael James, thank you for puttying up with this long journey and the ones to come. Your belief in me and the overall vision in what I am trying to accomplish is the backbone within me. You both are great and have gone above and beyond your call of duty, in helping me and others in every way possible. I am proud to call you my friends.

To Tom Jenner, thank you for your photography and in taking the time to help our vision come to life.

Special thanks for the photographic imagery compiled at the Seattle Jun Fan Gung Fu Institute. All images captured at the school in recent years are owned by Julie DonTigny and Tom Jenner.

And to all the old and new fans on the rise who keep Bruce Lee's legacy alive! This book is also for you...

David Tadman

Note

It has been an honor for me to know Taky Kimura for many years now. He is a man who is truly humble, honest and righteous. Sifu Taky is a man who takes the time to listen to the individual and help them through their ups and downs. I was first introduced to Sifu Taky through my close friend and Sifu, Tsuyoshi Abe who holds both a high-ranking level with Sifu Taky Kimura as well as Sifu Daniel Inosanto. From my first meeting with Sifu Taky, it was evident that this man carries a historic view of the years he shared with Bruce Lee. Not only has he schooled me in many things related to Bruce Lee, but he has also taught me many things within the philosophical realm and about the human condition. To this day, every time we speak in person or via the phone / computer, he always shares with me the wonderful stories that made up his and Bruce Lee's close friendship.

When I first started this book, Sifu Taky felt that there was not an general interest out there to hear his story about his best friend and the years they knew one another. After convincing him, he gave me permission to view and extract from his personal archive, the materials to use to make up the book. In the course of my investigations of Bruce Lee in Seattle, I discovered numerous memorabilia that I knew from first look, would be considered historic by the masses. So, then we started the long journey in piecing together the pieces of the puzzle. Each step of the way, I realized more and more in how important Taky Kimura was to Bruce Lee, not only as his top instructor for the Seattle Jun Fan Gung Fu Institute, but also how important he was to Bruce Lee, as in his own words, "being his best friend". They both relied on one another with respect and gratitude. They shared their most personal feelings with each other about family, friends and the world at large. To Bruce Lee, Taky Kimura was an older brother / father figure and to Taky Kimura, Bruce Lee was his mentor, Sifu and closest friend who was philosophically and spiritually far beyond his physical years.

Upon completion of this book, I realized that it was going to be a very important one in the eyes of the reader on many levels. For one, this book is filed with incredible pictures that mark a special time in history with Bruce Lee. Second, the personal letters and hand written notes within this book were until now, only meant to be seen by two people, Bruce Lee and Taky Kimura. The letters and notes Bruce Lee wrote truly describe in detail his friendships, martial arts, acting career and general musings about family. This book gives an insight to who Bruce Lee was as a human being and how he relied on others to help further his vision in the world. When reading through this book, you get a real sense of being a part of those times as if you were there in a tangible way. And in fact, it is our hope, that you the reader, will feel you were there and a part of those great times.

Working along side Taky and Andrew Kimura has been a wonderful experience for me. They are people who love other people, and take care of them, making sure justice comes to the ones who deserve it. They fight for the underdog and always look at life, no matter how difficult it can be, in a positive light. I have learned much from Taky and will take what I have learned with me upon my own personal journeys.

So, in your journey while reading this book, remember this, it is not about the superstar in who we like, nor is it about the artist we want to emulate, or the preacher that makes us want to follow him, it is about looking inside and finding all of those things within us that makes us the superstar, artist and preacher. We all have the ability to change and rock the world and in the words of Sifu Takayuki Kimura handed down to him by Bruce Lee, **"It is not the destination, but the journey that defines us, my friend".**

Peace, Love and Brotherhood
David Tadman

In Memory

In 1979, George Foon, a close friend to me and the world of Bruce Lee, came to Seattle with Dan Insanto and Richard Bustillo to tour and document the places Bruce stayed and frequented while he lived in Seattle in the early 1960's, for a book Dan Inosanto was writing called "Jeet Kune Do: The Art and Philosophy of Bruce Lee." It was both an exciting and heartfelt time-sharing our memories of our SiFu for that project. The most memorable time was when we all visited SiFu Bruce's gravesite, it was both happy and sad for us, but we knew it was important to highlight and document us paying homage to the one who brought us to that point in time in our lives. One of Bruce Lee's gifts to the world was the ability to bring others together to celebrate life and on that day back in 1979, that's exactly what I, Dan and Richard did, we celebrated our SiFu who gave us and the world so much.

(Top) Taky Kimura, Dan Inosanto and Richard Bustillo pose in tribute to their SiFu Bruce Lee in Seattle in 1979.

(Bottom) From left to right, Taky Kimura, Richard Bustillo and Dan Inosanto at Bruce Lee's gravesite, paying tribute to their SiFu in 1979.

Reflections of My Family

I am forever in debt to my parents for their loving attention and for sacrificing themselves to make sure that my 2 brothers, 4 sisters, and I were provided for, even when they went without.

Suejiro Kimura, my father, came to America before the beginning of the 20th Century. He arrived at the age of 16 with the intention of making his fortune and one day returning to Japan to retire in comfort. Like most other Japanese immigrants of the day, it did not work out that way. Instead, he went back to find his bride, my mother Haruyo, and returned to the States to continue in searching for his fortune. That was a common story for Japanese immigrants of that generation. Most immigrants decided to stay permanently once they had children who were natural American-born citizens. I am happy to say I am one of these children.

My father worked in a crew of Asians as a Section Hand, eventually becoming Foreman. Their job was to maintain railroad tracks, insuring that the locomotives could transport huge virgin timbers to lumber mills, and then on to be used in the homes and buildings that became the cities we live in today. It was one of many low paying and backbreaking jobs Japanese and Chinese men (Coolie Labor) were imported to do, as Americans did not want to do them. Colloquially, they were called "Gandy Dancers."

In those years, my father and all other Asians were looked down upon and mostly called Japs and Chinks. In the early days, my father suffered from loneliness and after realizing he was not able to make friends with white people due to language and cultural barriers, he befriended Indians living on the reservation near to his Montana jobsite. He enjoyed the Indians camaraderie and their Pot Latches where they would sing Indian songs, dance, and eat meals made from parts of the animals that the white men didn't want to eat. My father and the American Indians though a world apart, discovered a precious bond of true and genuine humanness that to this day, gives light to the great concerning cause of true and fair understanding with all in this ever frightening and changing modern world. We can put people in outer space; we have placed man on the moon, but still, we cannot find true respect or love for each other. The stories behind the Indian "potlatches" is a great and interesting one of racial harmony and human dignity. Philosophically, it brings to light the precociousness of human pride and all of its "commonality", survival and the will of finding the sacredness of humanity regardless of race or ethnicity. I was reminded of these stories years later when Bruce would take me to Chinese Restaurants in the International District in Seattle, Washington where the restaurant-owners who were friends of his would prepare us special authentic dishes that also included unusual cuts of meat.

I was lucky in a sense, because my father really took to me and I have many fond memories of our relationship. We would go fishing and on many occasions he would take me to work with him when he had jobs he would do alone. He had a three-wheel pump car that we would ride on.

My mother was a quiet and tiny woman - no more than four feet eight inches tall. She was small but she was mighty and she possessed a soothing, healing and loving power that triumphed over all pain and fear. She was always there for my siblings and I, in sickness and in health and when she counseled us, we would listen quietly and respond positively – BECAUSE SHE WAS ALWAYS RIGHT!

During prohibition, my mother made rice wine for my father and the American men he worked with. We were raided periodically and the government men would frighten the hell out of us by threatening to put our parents in jail. My parents were not selling the wine, so there was never really any problem with the authorities.

My family grew and in time became a household of seven children, 3 boys and 4 girls. One of my sisters, Fumiko, who was born with a bad leg was at home one day, assisting my mother in starting a fire in the kitchen stove to prepare all of us for the evening dinner. She accidentally leaned over the firebox and caught her dress on fire. She was burned over a third of her body. Sadly, she spent several days in the town hospital and soon had to be transferred to Seattle to another facility. Sadly, she passed away as the burns were too severe and at that time there was no medical means to keep her alive. She was only eleven years old.

Our family life continued in the small town of Clallam Bay in the State of Washington up until 1942 when during the Second World War, we were committed to Tule Lake California, where we were put into an internment camp for a little over a year and then transferred to another camp in Idaho for 4 years. After that, we were freed following the end of the war. The first camp, Tuley Lake, was South of Oregon, right on the border. The camp had 72 blocks in it and everyone was of Japanese ancestry. The camps were flimsily made and they contained army cots for us to bed on. It was funny in some ways, they gave out clothes that looked like riding pants that the soldiers used in WWI. The government gave them out to us and we all wore them to our horror. They looked like riding britches and we also had to wear crazy looking hats. Everything in the camps was run like a little city. The food was driven and delivered by us to the mess halls. No one had a garden and it was very sandy everywhere. There were these big storms that blew sand into the buildings all the time and it made it hard to do daily chores. We were as positive as we could be; there was nothing we could do about it. We just kind of rode it out and in the last year many of the young men had volunteered for the service while others helped the farmers that were having trouble with their crops. They came into our camps and recruited us to work in their farms. One summer, I worked in Oregon on a farm, weeding the garden and I had to bend over working these 1,000 foot rows of onions for over 10 hours a day, killing my knees and back. We had to buck bales of hay that were really heavy, throwing them over our heads. It was hard work and we were paid next to nothing. My brother Eiji was a staff sergeant in the 442nd and I also volunteered for the military, to prove my loyalty like all the others, but in the end, the government didn't trust us. We made so much fuss about it, they finally gave us a chance with a battalion out of Hawaii. The same battalion fought in the African campaign through Italy and into Europe and lost more soldiers than everyone else, while at the same time, gaining more citations for their bravery. I tried to join, but my eyes were too bad and they wouldn't take me. After I got out of the camp I couldn't get a job, and the military still wouldn't take me. I don't feel bad about it, it's just something that happened and if you are angry about it now you are only hurting yourself. It was something that was not right, but what are you going to do. When things got me down I would reflect about the times in the camps and the times I practiced Judo for a while. I trained with top-notch Judo players who taught me well. There were tournaments for us to participate in and it helped us greatly as a motivational pastime. There was one Judo tournament I was in as a white belt. I threw the guy in 1 second and I beat him. I was so quick they put me up against a black belt in the 2nd match. My opponent was a short guy and he got under me to try to do a shoulder throw. He didn't execute it perfectly, so I fell on my shoulder and broke my collarbone. There wasn't really anything they could do for me medically, I just had to suck it up and wait for it to heal. The war finally ended as abruptly as it began and in an instant, they said they were closing the camps and everyone has to leave. It was incredibly frightening due to being released with no place to go, no home, no food, and no possessions.

After the war my brother Minoru searched for lodging for our family in Seattle. It took him 2 weeks to find living quarters for us all. He found a place where a German man by the name of Henri Liedke was living in a big house all by himself. Mr. Liedke was worried that we would ruin the house and did not want to give us shelter. My brother Minoru camped on his doorstep for a week or more until he agreed to rent to us. He had a 1-bedroom house for renting and my brother wanted to live in this house with all 9 of us. After living there for some time, Mr. Liedke built on an extra room to make us more comfortable. We stayed in his house for a little over a year. In the meantime, I finally found a job after a month as a helper for a landscaping gardener.

My whole family looked for work, everywhere was hiring, but no one wanted to hire us because we were Japanese. Finally, my brother who was a staff sergeant in the military came back from the army and was lucky in obtaining a job because of his background. My brother was well respected and he put a good word in for me at a foundry where he had found work himself. My job was to shovel sand into a furnace and while working there over a period of time, the harsh conditions damaged my lungs.

Eventually, my family ended up finding a small grocery store that was run by an old Greek couple. The husband was quite the ladies man and he was playing around on his wife, the stress of that made her go crazy and they had to put her in the Harborview mental clinic. When she got out, she kicked her husband out and began running the store on her own. She had 6 cats running around the store and they were running amuck. Times were tough for her and she was getting desperate. She decided to sell the store because she was only getting 20 dollars a day in business. A friend of my fathers loaned us the money to buy the store. After a while we were making 300 dollars a day compared to her 20 and when that happened, the lady who owned the store and her friends started getting jealous of our success, so they started talking to each other and took us to court to sue us. The judge looked like a giant who was going to kill you and we feared he would take her side, because of 3 young guys against an old lady before the judge type of thing. To our surprise, the judge said that the women there didn't fool him and they were trying to scam us, so he threw her out of the court and we won to our very big surprise. After all we went through, the injustice of the camps, finally, an honorable judge ruled in our favor. We were truly happy.

A few years later, my father Suejiro Kimura passed away. He was the type of person who would work through his pain, no one knew his agony. One example of this from my childhood was one day he came home from work and handed me his work glove, telling me to cut out the middle finger and I did so, only to find his middle finger tip at the end of the glove. He had cut it off in between 2 train rails. He finished that workday without a complaint like nothing happened. Another time we went out, just the two of us, to get a Christmas tree. This particular year, he went by himself and I happened to pass him coming down the mountain, with a tree over his shoulder, while my friend and I were going up. We chatted with him for a little and he headed off down the mountain. He never said anything, but later I found out he had fallen and a large splinter had gotten jammed up under his armpit and logged there. Despite the stoicism and roughness of my father, we were always very close. My father was my hero, my strength. He worked hard for his family with little or no pay off. I am proud to have been his son.

While running our store, some Caucasian customers talked to us about selling Japanese Mandarin Oranges. My older brother thought that was a great idea and started a campaign that took 20 years. He worked with senators Magnuson and senator Jackson, as well as many others in order to get the oranges imported into the U.S. The oranges in Japan had citrus cankers, so we had to take precautions against this problem. The government had created a ban because of this, so it took my brother 20 years to get around that law and finally after 200,000 dollars later, the government said we could bring the oranges in, but only to Washington and Oregon. After 15 years we expanded to another few states.

A few years later, I had suffered the loss of both of my brothers. My middle brother Eiji who received his discharge from the army as a staff sergeant in the 442 infantry was hired by an Olympic foundry which lead to my being hired there as I have mention above. Eiji was a big husky guy, he was about 5' 8" 170lbs stocky, bigger than both me and my other brother Minoru. He was very athletic, played high school sports and he had a very colorful way about him with a great sense of humor. He got along with everyone.

Eiji use to run laps at the YMCA and one night, he was running with a friend who he would run with a couple nights a week. He had just finished running a mile when appeared to hunch and his friend thought he was stretching after his exceptionally fast mile. But actually, Eiji had suffered a massive heart attack, falling onto the track where he was running and passed away at the age of 47. Not even two months after Eiji died, Minoru passed away from leukemia at the age of 51.

My brother Minoru was very tenacious; he died of leukemia and fought the entire time. Trying anything that might let him last longer. One time, I brought him watermelon or something people had told me would make him better. And even though he was very sick and couldn't eat anything he would try for me. He fought to the bitter end. That's the kind of person he was, a warrior who never gave up. After suffering the devastation loss of my brothers, I found myself running the store and continuing their dream of importing Japanese oranges. I miss them dearly.

Canada was bringing in a lot of citrus oranges, they had bigger distributors and eventually started bringing their fruit into our area. They wanted to do business in a way I wasn't ok with. Both the Japanese and the Canadians wanted to push me out of the business. Finally, I talked to the Japanese and said that I spent 20 years to get them into the country and if you guys aren't going to be respectful and faithful, then I am not going to work with you anymore. I just didn't want to do business like the way they wanted no matter how much money there was to made.

I met Peggy my wife to be who had shopped with us for a while at the store. We became good friends and I would go to visit her sometimes. We started dating and the relationship grew from there. We got married and then had our son Andrew Minoru Kimura on September 17th, 1971, but little did we know a divorce would soon follow a little less than two years after.

After having my son Andy, I was in the grocery business for years. We were open 6 days a week and closed Sundays. Sunday was my day I would take our 2 dogs out to the beach house for some fresh air and relax from the hard work week.

My dear mother Haruyo Kimura was a short person, not a big speaker. A gallant person, never took kids to task. We always knew never to get on her bad side, she was a very quiet person who always cared and loved us. She passed away at the age of 92, she never, ever said anything about not feeling well in her whole lifetime, but some point near the end I took her to the hospital upon finding out that she felt ill, I remember two nurses that were trying to stab a needle into her vein that they couldn't find and my little 75 pound mother threw them across the room. She was very tough. They said the cause of death was most likely diabetic complications, combined with age and Alzheimer's. My mother was the glue who kept us together, she loved her husband and children deeply and sacrificed it all for us. My mother, father and siblings who have passed will always remain in my thoughts and prayers until one day we all meet again.

You the reader, now know about my family who raised me. For me, family is an important thing to be shared with everyone who reads this book. I have not made it a point to talk about my upbringing for many years for various reasons, but as I am exposing myself to the world within this book, I find it necessary to include not only my friendship with my best friend Bruce Lee, but also the history in how I got to that point. Through the love of my family and the bonding friendship of Bruce Lee, I will leave you now with these important words from the master himself; "If you love life, don't waste time, for time is what life is made up of."

Taky Kimura

GROCERY

Reflections of Bruce

I met Bruce Lee shortly after he arrived in Seattle. I was 38 and almost old enough to be his father. He was 17 years old at that time and came to stay with Ping and Ruby Chow who were long-time friends of his father and who owned a restaurant where Bruce worked as a waiter. I met him through Jesse Glover who was Bruce's first student in Seattle.

My first impressions of Bruce were, that he was full of energy and somewhat flamboyant, but on the other side he was a typical teenager. He spoke English with a British accent and at that time he stuttered a bit, which made it difficult at times for him to express himself properly. No one ever made fun of him about that, because it would have been a disaster! In fact, a good friend of mine stuttered also. I introduced him to Bruce and my friend began to stutter. Bruce was looking at him and began tensing up because he felt my friend was making fun of him. Thank God my friend quickly said, "I stutter too!" Bruce realized the whole situation and we all laughed.

Bruce and I became very good friends right away. We were both Asian and they say that "blood is thicker than water." I guess he needed someone that he could trust and depend on for more than simply gung-fu training.

I went through a lot of very hard situations in my life, and at that time I had no respect or regard for myself. Bruce made me realize that I am a human being and I have equal rights. He changed my way of thinking and looking at myself. He told me I'm just as good as anyone else and I began to believe in myself. In the gung-fu school he took me aside, under his wing, and helped me to develop self-confidence.

Bruce Lee outside Ruby Chow's on a Sunday afternoon about to venture into sightseeing around Seattle with his best friend and assistant instructor, Taky Kimura.

THE TEACHER AND THE STUDENT

Bruce was traditional on many levels, but was never held down by those beliefs. I do believe though, he kept a lot of things for himself, but I also know that he was very open with me. I understand that the traditional teachers do not teach 100 percent of their knowledge and that they keep things for themselves in case some students turn on them. I can honestly say that if he felt you were trustworthy, he was very unselfish about his teachings. If you were sincere, honest and dedicated, he would teach you without holding anything back. He didn't care what race or nationality you were, but at times that attitude brought him some problems with some Chinese masters who felt uncomfortable with him teaching non-Chinese people.

When Bruce first taught me and his other original students, his nucleus was definitely the Wing Chun system, but taught us a modified version of it. Of course he was familiar with many other Chinese Kung-Fu styles such as Praying Mantis, Choy Lee Fut, Hung Gar, etc., but I think he really identified himself with the Wing Chun method. The realistic approach to fighting that he used later on to create the art of Jeet Kune Do was always taking form within him.

One time during a demonstration, I was badly injured in my right eye. Bruce was demonstrating the principle of a straight punch, telling everyone that he wanted the force of the punch to penetrate through the target. He looked at the group and at the same time he threw the punch. His fist connected to my right eye, broke my glasses and cut my eyeball. We went to the hospital where the doctor took all the glass splinters out of my eye and scolded me for wearing those glasses during such a violent physical activity.

Bruce really scolded me for moving! I was sure as hell I didn't move, but I wasn't going to be one telling him I hadn't!

ENTER JEET KUNE DO

Bruce's principles of simplicity, directness, and efficiency were already the guidelines during his time in Seattle. He was evolving and being very creative. His knowledge was limited at that time, but the basic principles of economy of motion, simplicity and directness that he was teaching in Seattle were the same that he taught later on in the Oakland and Los Angeles schools. The difference was in the delivery systems of the techniques and the training methods that he developed after being exposed to other arts such as Boxing and Western Fencing. For instance, his straight punch was pretty much the same but the footwork he was using in Los Angeles was from Fencing. He realized that he had to be able to punch and hit targets from a longer distance than a classic Wing Chun man - he wanted to be more mobile as well.

The art of Jeet Kune Do was developed by Bruce while he was living in Los Angeles. I can say that it was the product of many years of martial arts research. Probably because my close relationship with him as a

friend, I am the only guy in Seattle that saw the JKD level that he was into whenever he came up here. His approach was very revolutionary in the mid-'60s and many people weren't ready to understand what he was talking about. The training emphasized contact sparring with headgear, gloves, and shin guards - that was something very uncommon then. He was talking about "liberating" the martial artist when a lot of people didn't understand what it meant "to be slave to a style". I can compare the art of Jeet Kune Do to a beautiful sculptured object. The final product is awesome but how did he do it? I think it's important to go through the pieces that he discarded, study them, and learn them to get up to that point, because it was an ongoing process of "shedding away the nonessentials." Sometimes there are things that we don't understand today, but will became increasingly clear to us in time. Unfortunately, I have seen the effects of exploitation and inadequacy in Jeet Kune Do and rarely, if ever, do many gain more than just a physical understanding of what JKD all about.

Bruce used to come to Seattle because Linda's mother was living here. He used to call me in advance so I could take time away from work to be trained in the new things he was discovering martially. I was very fortunate that he didn't forget me and was willing to share his knowledge. He was very perceptive as a teacher, because he knew that I was only capable of assimilating a certain amount of information at any given point, so he never threw a bunch of stuff at me at once. He paced himself as a teacher, according to my capabilities as a student.

At one point, Bruce called me and said that Chi Sao was not the focal point anymore, as we had thought earlier. I was shocked. He probably realized the limitations of certain aspects of Wing Chun when trying to practice "sticky hands" with someone like Kareem Abdul Jabbar. I have to say that at that time I didn't understand what Bruce meant, but now I do. I guess this was part of his "liberation" as a martial artist. He didn't mean Chi Sao was useless, but only that it was not the nucleus of what he was teaching in Los Angeles, He realized that it was a important part of the totality in combat, but not the only part of it as he emphasized during his days in Seattle where he taught Wing Chun. For a wing chun man, Chi Sao is probably the most important aspect in training and it dictates the students' approach to fighting. He didn't have the tunnel-vision approach of the classic gung-fu man. The Wing Chun that I know is the modified version Bruce taught me and I guess its structure takes away a lot of the impractical things that you can learn in other systems. But don't misunderstand me, I don't want to take anything away from anyone else.

THE STUDENT BECOMES THE TEACHER

I'm not here to teach people how to fight. If what I'm sharing with them can help them to feel good about themselves, then I'm happy. I don't make instructors, and I don't certify people. I'm not here to tell students that what we have is better than this style or that style. I'm just interested in being in my little corner. At one time, Bruce and I were talking

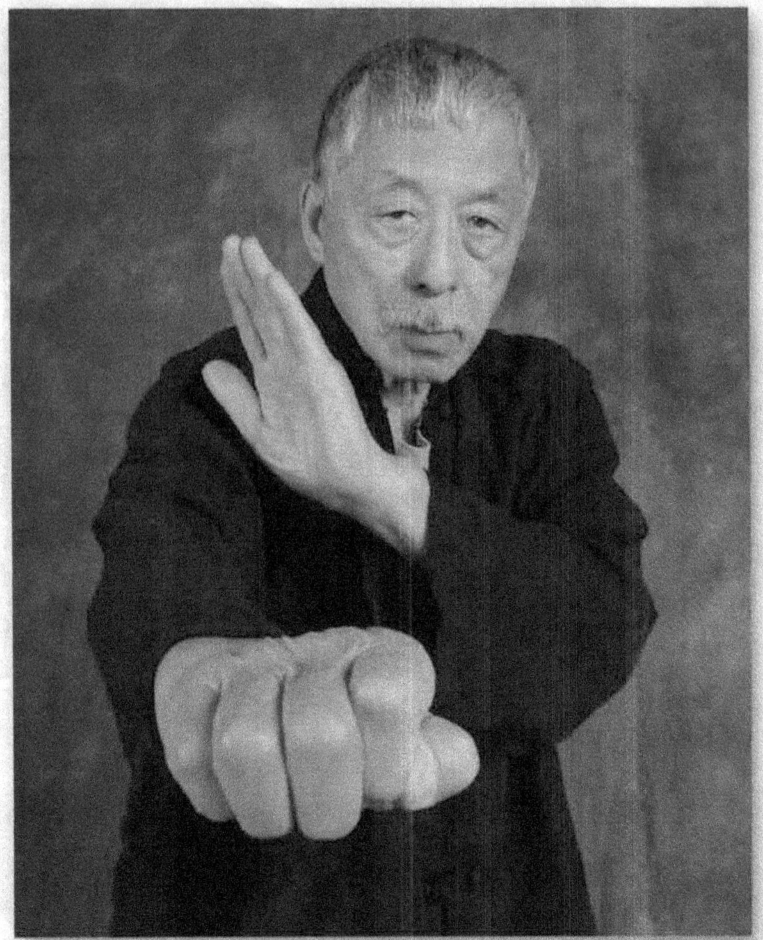

about starting a chain of schools in United States, but later on we decided against it. I still remember what he said: "What is really important is that you have a few close friends around, and work out a couple of times a week, and go down to Chinatown to have a cup of tea."

Bruce said and it is my thought process as well, to become a good fighter you have to be trained to be a good one and so to become a good teacher you have to be trained and taught to be a good teacher as well. Definitely, if you can use what you know in a fight, then later on as an instructor, you'll have direct experience to pass onto your students. But don't be mistaken - you may fight many times and not learn anything from those experiences, and in the end you won't have any direct experience to pass on.

I am a private person and like to stay in the woodwork. I don't think I have that much to offer because my knowledge is limited, but I feel secure with what Bruce taught me. I kept the school out of respect for Bruce. It's a private club. I don't feel the need of being in the public eye and I really enjoy sharing with a small group of people what I learned from Bruce. I don't look for students, they find me. I do it in honoring Bruce. I don't think I can ever pay him back in what he did for me as a friend. So, I do my best to keep his memory alive.

THE STAR SHINES SO BRITE

When Bruce decided to take the path of an actor, it was obvious this is what he was meant to do. Bruce told me about his childhood and teenage film career many times, but it was not until I saw him as Kato in "The Green Hornet" that I knew then he was destine for greatness. Bruce would constantly fill me in on his progress with his acting career, both here in the states and when he was abroad, becoming a huge international star in Asia. He would write me, or have Linda do it if he was very busy, or I would get a surprise call from him out of the blue.

At times, I could sense Bruce was lonely for his friends back home and the security he felt back in the States. He found it hard to trust anyone in Hong Kong for a variety of reasons and wanted to come back badly and start his own production company in Hollywood and I believe he was in the beginning stages of doing just that. Bruce really enjoyed his success in Hong Kong, but longed to bring that success to the States and be accepted here.

All Bruce's friends enjoyed his success to and we were all in support with what he was trying to accomplish. When Bruce released each film, we all celebrated along with him, even though we were thousands of miles away from him.

PLAYING THE GAME

When Bruce asked me to be a part of his film "The Game of Death", I was first horrified that I might make him look bad with my two left feet, so at first, I tried to decline. But, being that Bruce was my closest fiend and my SiFu, I could not refuse in the end and began to prepare for my departure to the Far East to become one of the guardians of the Temple Floor levels. Bruce promised me he would make me look great on film as a master of the Praying Mantis Gung Fu style.

After a couple of postponements of filming, one do to Bruce stopping production on to film "Enter the Dragon", the date was officially set for me to come and the plane tickets were in my hand, but unfortunately, Bruce passed away and the film was never completed. It still pains me to this day to talk about the loss of my best friend, but I know it is important to keep Bruce's legacy alive through the memories we all have of him and so I will do my part until my last breath.

Though Bruce confided in me that he was not happy with many of the scenes he shot within "The Game of Death", he had plans to re-shoot and re-structure some of the ideas he had to make that film the best-ever and I believe, had that film been completed, it would have been a masterpiece.

A STAR HAS FADED

When I got the news that Bruce had passed away, I was devastated to say the least; it was surreal to me as it is to this day. How could such a strong man, both physically and mentally, and so healthy, be taken away from us all. In the words of Linda his wife, "I have learned to live with

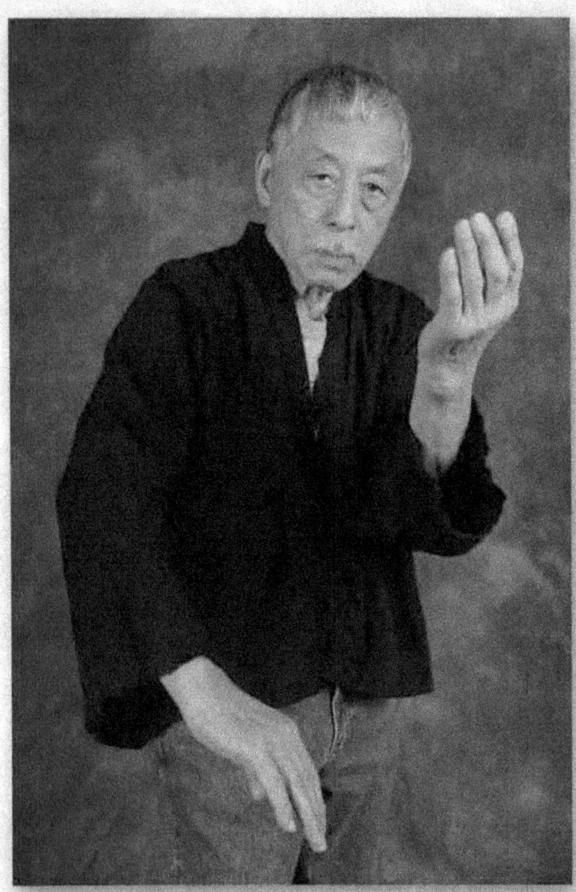

remembering Bruce in how he lived and not how he died". We must remember the great accomplishments in what Bruce lee brought to the world and how he brought us all together under one roof to celebrate his ideas and ideals. By celebrating Bruce through books like this, or documentaries and re-living his greatness through his films, we pay homage to the man, the myth and the legend.

MY BEST FRIEND

From the first time I met Bruce Lee, or friendship grew everyday. At first, one could sense that me being older than him was like me being a father figure to Bruce, or an older brother and at many times, Bruce would come to me for advice. Bruce and I trusted each other completely and confided in one another all the time. Through his letters and phone calls to me, he would tell me that I was his best friend and I would also reciprocate to him those same feelings as well. I can still remember when Bruce and I were early on into our friendship, when I did not think so highly of myself and my moral was down do to my imprisonment in the Interment camps, Bruce one day grabbed me and looked strait in my face and said to me, "Do you think because I am Chinese that I am a better man than you?" Bruce said this to me because he was fully aware about the Japanese invasion into China / Hong Kong in his father's era and that many Chinese and Japanese did not like each other, but Bruce was willing to show me that I was a good man and that circumstances should not dictate the outcome of one's life unless they are welcomed circumstances.

Bruce is the reason in why I was able to lift my head up in pride and he is also the reason in why I have strived to better my life every day. I instill those positive philosophies Bruce left me into my son Andrew and my grandson as well. The best legacy I can leave the world is to perpetuate the legacy of my best friend, Bruce Lee.

THE PHILOSOPHICAL JOURNEY

I have found that martial arts discipline has always put me through psychological changes and I honestly believe that anything that puts you up against yourself is going to be beneficial, because you'll be more aware of

whom you are and eventually you'll transcend yourself. Let's face it, all martial arts styles have ego to them. How well you punch or kick, how powerful your actions are, how good your form looks, are all driven by the ego. The idea is to use the arts to transcend ourselves by letting our spirit come through. That is the reason why I always believed and related martial arts discipline to mental discipline. Martial arts teaches you discipline, both mentally and physically. It takes a certain amount of discipline to push your body to operate in a specific and unusual and well-coordinated way. The pursuit of perfection in all aspects of martial arts is not a bad thing and that is what we are attempting. In short, used in a proper way, I believe martial arts are a great way to help us grow as individuals.

THE MENTAL

You must always try to develop your mind; you can be very strong, fast, and fit but if you lack a strong mind your physical aspects will mean nothing in a real situation. Your mind is the trigger of your body. On the other hand, those interested in the arts should accept the fact that there are no short-cuts. Hard work is the main thing and there is no substitute. Bruce always taught us to train with the idea of ending a real confrontation as quickly as possible by defeating the opponent in the minimum amount of time. But he always advised us that fighting is the very last resort.

For those teaching the art I would like to mention there must be a difference between teaching and practicing, since many people mistake the two. Teachers shouldn't think that their teaching is a substitute for their own training. Self-training is extremely important in order to keep teaching properly. It is like a university teacher - after the classes he goes home and does more research, trying to keep up with new ideas and theories.

YOUR JOURNEY

Thank you for choosing this book to read at this point in time in your life, it honors me that you would celebrate along side me, my reflections and musings of my close and dear friend, Bruce Lee. It is my hope that this book will give you an insight into not only Bruce Lee the martial artist, or Bruce Lee the actor, it is also my hope that this book will show you who Bruce Lee was as a good human being.

If this book can move you to your own self-discovery and to find the truth behind your being, then this book would have done Bruce Lee's legacy justice. So let this book not just be another one that sits on your shelf and passed by time to time, let this book embark you, the reader, on your own personal journey and liberation. In Bruce Lee's own words, I will leave you with this my friends, PEACE, LOVE AND BROTHERHOOD…

Taky Kimura

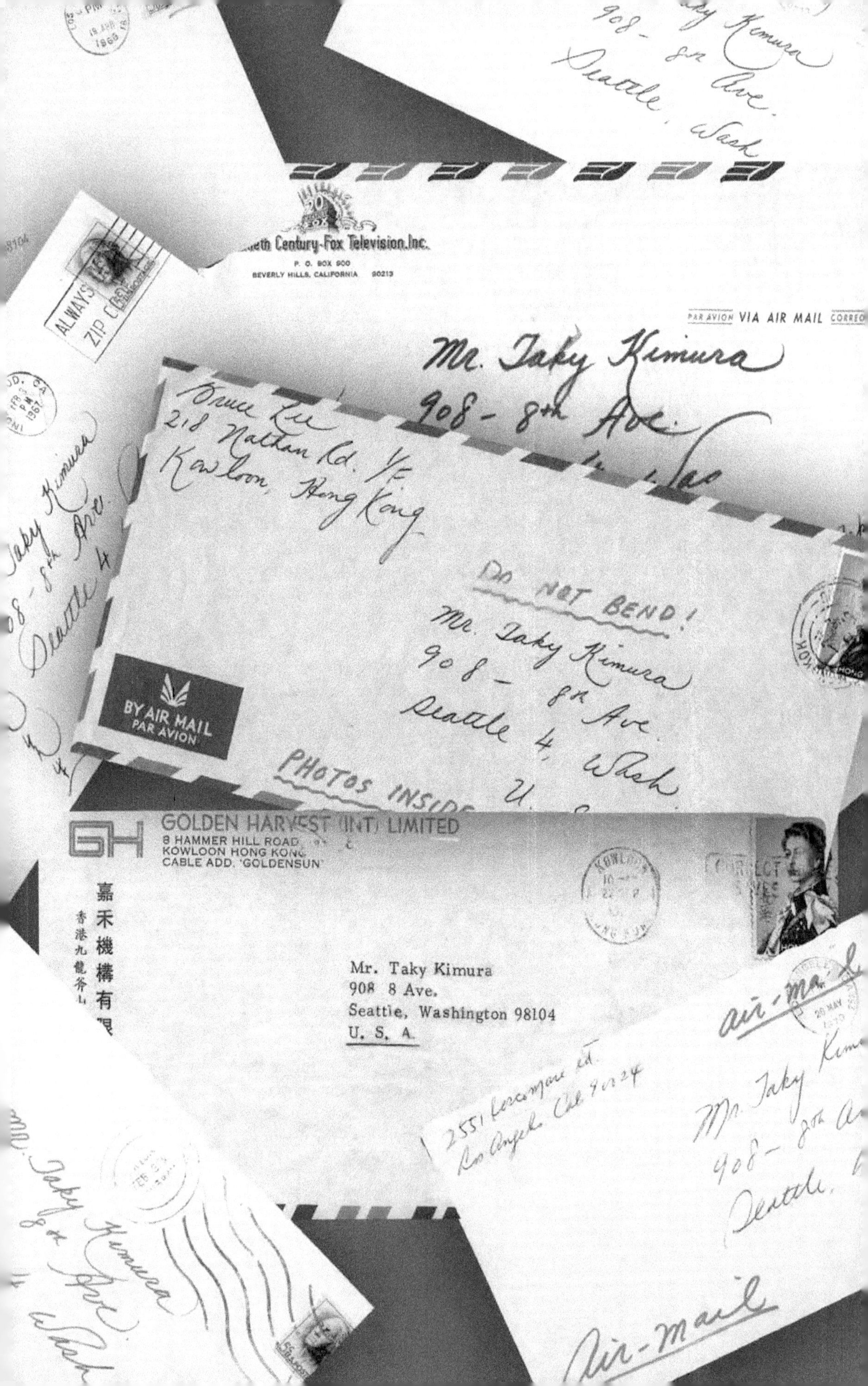

Twentieth Century-Fox Television, Inc.
P. O. BOX 900
BEVERLY HILLS, CALIFORNIA 90213
PAR AVION VIA AIR MAIL
Mr. Taky Kimura
908 - 8th Ave.
Seattle, Wash
Bruce Lee
218 Nathan Rd. 1/F.
Kowloon, Hong Kong
DO NOT BEND!
Mr. Taky Kimura
908 - 8th Ave.
Seattle 4, Wash.
PHOTOS INSIDE
BY AIR MAIL
PAR AVION
ALWAYS USE ZIP CODE
GOLDEN HARVEST (INT) LIMITED
8 HAMMER HILL ROAD
KOWLOON HONG KONG
CABLE ADD. 'GOLDENSUN'
嘉禾機構有限
Mr. Taky Kimura
908 8 Ave.
Seattle, Washington 98104
U. S. A.
2551 Roscomare Rd.
Los Angeles Cal 90024
air-mail
Mr. Taky Kimura
908 - 8th Ave
Seattle, Wash
Air-mail

Letters of Appreciation

Throughout our close friendship, Bruce Lee would send me letters, touching on everything from family, friendship, his acting career and mostly, his martial arts and philosophical vision. People say that Bruce is no longer among us, I don't agree. Every morning I awake, I think of him and the times we shared and then when I see the letters he wrote to me, I know he is still with me, the pen was only the extension of his soul and that soul and energy for me lives on.

When you look at his television and film career, books, posters people influenced by him, and a whole slot of new projects coming out on him, how can one say he is gone? There is a whole new generation of people who are learning about Bruce Lee and if this is the case, he is still teaching us all to this day. Yes, physically he is gone, spiritually, he is among us all and through the letters within this book, you will see not just Bruce Lee the "STAR", but most importantly, you will see Bruce Lee the man on a journey creating himself step by step.

From just the normal musings within this section to the poignant views of a great martial arts master and actor, these letters will allow you, the reader, to experience first hand what I did so many years ago.

Within all these letters, you will find historic information, but what is more important, is that to me, these letters symbolize a friendship up until now has never diminished, because through these letters, Bruce Lee lives on.

A small sample of the personal correspondence from Bruce to Taky.

Letter 1

Description of Letter No. 1

Just another "ongoing" psychological teacher to student pep talk to get me off my bottom and keep the "tempo" going. I understood his psychology, but when the "in the set" gold glitter is no longer present and is gone unknowingly, there becomes a decline of on going intent. However, I did my utmost best to keep the fire in our bellies.

Transcription

Dear Taky,

Happy to have received your lengthy letter and hear that ACTION is coming along to re-construct the Institute.

You are most qualified to be the head representative of my Institute. Though I time and again stress the word ACTION, by no means do I ask you to be over-aggressive to hard pressure your client. When I stress ACTION, I mean action on you so that you will go ahead and start the wheel rolling, following YOUR own plan. My constant word of ACTION is to instill ACTION into your mind so that you will go ahead with your plan with definiteness of purpose.

First of all, you are doing as well if not better than James and Dan. Actually, I am not starting a sort of contest; what I really want is to have my instructors know my principle and aim and that the instructor will sit down and organize his campaign and follow his own plan and fulfill it bit by bit EVERYDAY (that's what I mean by ACTION)

As long as you do not let yourself down, you will NEVER let me down. I do not wish you to be an aggressive promoter to the client, I do wish, however, you be an aggressive promoter of your own thoughts and plans. Also, I fully realize that nothing can be accomplished in one night, but I do know something are achieving everyday toward its accomplishment, though be even planning in your own mind sitting down. Set a goal (saying 40 for time being) and work toward it as close as you can.

When I said to get in touch with Dan and James, I only mean to exchange points of view in your spare time. Remember always that you are the head of Seattle Jun Fan and you are a separate unit, and as far as your role in Jun Fan, you are senior to all the rest. Never mind comparing outcome as to production, but be productive in your mind.

List the school under your name and conduct YOUR own institute as of 1967.

Take care,

Bruce.

Dear Taky
Happy to have received your lengthy letter and hear that ACTION is coming along to re-construct the Institute

You are most qualified to be the head representative of my Institute. Though I time as the again stress the word ACTION by no mean do I ask you to be over aggressive to hard press your client. When I stress ACTION I mean as on you so that you will go ahead and start the wheel rolling following YOUR plan. My constant word of ACTION is instill ACTION into YOUR mind so that will go ahead with YOUR plan with of purpose.

First of all, you are doing a if not better than James and Dan I am not starting a sort of contest I really want is to have my institute my principle and aim and that will sit down and organize his comp follow his own plan and fulfil it bit EVERYDAY (that's what I mean

As long as you do not let yourself down You will NEVER let me down. I do not wish you to be an agressive promoter to the "client", I do wish, however, you be an agressive promoter of your own thoughts and plan. Also, I fully realize that nothing can be accomplished in one night but I do know something are achieving everyday toward its accomplishment through the even planning in your own mind setting down a goal (saying 40 for the time being) and work toward it as close as you can.

When I said to get in touch with Dan and James, I only mean to exchange points of view in your spare time. Remember always that you are the head of Seattle Jun Fan and you are a separate unit, and as far as your role in Jun Fan, you are senior to all the rest. Never mind comparing outcome as to production, but be productive in your mind.

List the school under your name and conduct YOUR own institute as I

(Left) Taky and assistant instructor Charlie Woo standing side by side posing for a picture at the Jun Fan Gung Fu Institute in Seattle. (Right) Taky Kimura in kicking form posing for the camera at the Seattle Gung Fu Institute.

Letter 2

Description of Letter No. 2

John Newman was helpful in terms of assisting me in certain aspects of the curriculum. Bruce also talks about he sending a picture for the school. This was a traditional thing to do in all martial arts schools back then and even to this day. The students bow in and out to their head instructor whose picture is framed and hanging on the wall. This is a mark of respect and also promotes the school's lineage.

Transcription

Taky,

On the reminder of the first page of John's lesson pan, only one item that has not been fulfilled, and that is to send one of my picture for the bulletin board in the gym.

So here it is.

Bruce

Bruce Lee sent this picture and others like it for us to hang on the wall in the Seattle Jun Fan Gung Fu Institute. When a student bows in and out they would pay respect to the picture of their SiFu / SiQung, on the wall if he was not present.

ASTOR TOWER HOTEL 1300 NORTH ASTOR STREET CHICAGO, ILLINOIS WH 3-1111

Taky,

On the reminders of the first page of John's lesson plan, only one item that has not been fulfilled, and that is to send one of my picture for the bulletin board in the gym. So here it is.

Bruce

MAXIM'S
CHICAGO
PARIS

Letter 3

Description of Letter No. 3

Bruce was a very good businessman. There was always a psychological side to what he was doing either in the martial arts, acting, or structuring a business. He knew what it took on all levels to make that business succeed. He truly was a self-made man and for a young man at that time, to have that kind of mindset, well, there were few and far between, like him. He was great at what he did.

Transcription

Taky,

Enclosed you will find fifty contracts of the Jun Fan Gung Fu Ins. which you can use for the gym up in Seattle. There are three copies of each contract, one (the original one!) for your record, one for the student and the last one is supposed for the collecting agency, which I doubt if the student can't pay we are not going to get anything. However, these contracts serve to bind the student mentally if not at all legally.

The minute a student signs up for the lessons he is in for three months, $27 down ($10 for initiation) and balance $34 to be paid with in two months in two or even three installments. Enclosed you will find one sample contract which I'm sure you will know what to do.

After the baby there will be brochures, business cards (for you), promotional letters printed and as soon as they are ready I'll send them to you. They will be real subtle with honest commercialization for bigger increase of business.

I have to go to the class now.

I've been taking charge of the class full time. I teach Mon., Tues., Fri., and Sun., plus four more hours of private lessons.

Take care my friend,

Bruce.

Taky,

22. Jan., 1965.

Enclosed you will find [illegible] contracts of the Jun Fan Gung Fu Ins. which you can use for the [illegible] up in Seattle. There are three copies of each contract, one (the original one !) for your record, one for the student and the last one is supposed for the collecting agency, which I doubt if the student can't pay we are not going to get anything. However, these contracts serve to bind the student mentally if not at all legally.

The [illegible] for the [illegible] is for three months, $27 down ($10 for initiation) and the balance $34 to be paid within two months in two or even three installments. Enclosed you will find one sample contract which I'm sure you will know what to do.

After the baby there will be brochures, business cards(for you), promotional letters printed and as soon as they are ready I'll send them to you. They will be real subtle with honest commercialisation for bigger increase of business.

I have to go to the class now and because has been working swing I've been taking charge of the class full time. I teach Mon., Tues., Fri., and Sun., plus four more hours of private lessons.

Hope to see you soon.

Take care my friend

Bruce Lee

Bruce.

Bruce Lee at the Los Angeles Chinatown School during the first opening day class, teaching his students his philosophy on Jeet Kune Do.

Letter 4

Description of Letter No. 4

This letter is another example in how Bruce was helping me structure the Gung Fu class I was teaching at the school in Seattle. Bruce was always on top of things, but he also stressed that I give the school the touch of my own individuality. He also designed all emblems / symbols as well. At times Bruce would have James Lee make the Seattle school some training equipment as shown in this example below. Though Bruce was gone and I was acting Sifu in Seattle, Bruce's influence was always there.

Transcription

Whether success or failure, you always have my help and trust. walk on toward your own thinking and aim, all's well.

I'm in the process of getting a printing machine; as soon as I get it, I'll mail all the necessary stuffs to you, including those you request in the letter. In brief, here are some of the answers to your questions.

1). after 3 months beginners should get the 1st blank rank ~~~~~just let me know the name and rank number of student should issue membership card after the 3 months period along with promotion

2). I am still finding a cheap tailor for the outfit. Ask that Mrs. Mar to make the rank symbol with arrows on the outside. I think she's good and economical.

3). Drawings

James will send these to you as soon as he makes them.

Take care and have fun.
Bruce

Here is an example of some equipment that James Lee made for Bruce. It's kind of like a wooden dummy (Mook Jung) crossed with a humanoid robot. You can see examples today of similar machines that the UFC fighters use, like the full human shape dummies, etc. Bruce felt it important to get as close as you could to practicing full force on human shapes, so when you are in a situation and have to use self defense, then it won't seem so foreign to you when executing the technique.

whether success or failure, you always have my help and trust. Walk on toward your own thinking and aim, all's well.

I'm in the process of getting a printing machine; as soon as I get it, I'll mail all the necessary stuffs to you, including those you request in the letter. In brief, here are some of the answers to your questions.

1). after 3 months beginner should get the 1st blank rank [scribble] just let me know the name and rank number of student [scribble] should issue membership card after the 3 months period along with the promotion

2). Am still finding a cheap tailor for the outfit. Ask that Mrs. Mar to make the rank symbol with arrows on the outside. I think she's good and economical.

3).

Jamie will send these to you as soon as he makes them.

Take care and have fun

Bruce

Letter 5

Description of Letter No. 5

Another "carrying" and psychological step in keeping students interested and loyal. He was "constantly" trying to share the psychology in Seattle that he was expressing and using while living in California.

Transcription

Taky,

Quarterly card for winter (Sept. 21 ---------Dec. 21 1967)

Fill in the rest with TYPEWRITER and sign your name on (INSTRUCTOR)

Bruce

STUDENT NAME

PERMANENT MEMBER NO.	SEX	RANK	YEAR	QTR	BRANCH	1-SUMMER 2-AUTUMN 3-WINTER 4-SPRING

MEMBER

NOT TRANSFERABLE

JUN FAN GUNG FU INSTITUTE

振 藩 國 術 館

THE UNDERSIGNED IS A REGULARLY ENROLLED STUDENT AT THE JUN FAN GUNG FU INSTITUTE FOR THE QUARTER AND YEAR INDICATED ABOVE.

SIGNATURE (NOT VALID UNLESS SIGNED IN INK)

CARD EXPIRES

MEMBERSHIP TERMINATES IF NOT RENEWED

(INSTRUCTOR) Bruce Lee (PRESIDENT)

Example of the student cards that Bruce Lee developed that highlights rank, season and student. The cards came in many colors. Bruce also experimented in many other colors that he never used. Those cards must be a collectors dream now!

TAKY,

Quarterly Card for WINTER (Sept. 21 → Dec. 21 1967)

Fill in the rest with TYPEWRITER and sign your name on (INSTRUCTOR)

Bruce

Letter 6A

Description of Letter No. 6

This is a detailed comprehensive explanation of what Jun Fan Gung Fu is when broken down. Bruce broke it down for me in simple terms, so I could understand it better. He also broke down the historical roots / lineage of the system. Bruce did something special for me by doing this, so I could understand it completely. As far as the rank he gave me, I was humble and thankful to him for giving it to me as I personally felt I did not deserve such an honor. On the other hand, recognizing that he was looking at, and judging me, in respect to the others, he was headstrong in his decision. I am still humble by it to this day.

Transcription

Taky, 5/23/1966

Thank you for letter plus dues; this time, the dues really come in handy due to postponement of shooting.

First of all, our school's name is 'Jun Fan' Gung Fu, after my Chinese name. Though I'm grateful for Wing Chun, the fact remains that the Jun Fan is yet several steps ahead of the Wing Chun System. Where Wing Chun ends, Jun Fan starts----not to add on, but to see the isness with freedom and in its totality. One thing must be stressed that without Wing Chun, I would never have arrived at this stage. The three basic structures of the Jun Fan System are:---(1) Sticking to the nucleus---Wing Chun idea, though I've expand on it. (2) Liberation from the nucleus-----my idea of non- confinement, to see things totally. (3) Returning to original freedom-----the circle without circumferences---direct expression.

As for history of Wing Chun, here are the chronological order-------though Yim (last name) Wing Chun was taught by Ng Mui, a nun from Sil Lum, Wing Chun is the founder of this new system. She taught it to her husband Leung, and Leung taught it to two Chinese Opera actors, Wong Wa Bo and Leung Ye Taie, for exchange of a set of swords and a set of staff. Wong Wa Bo then taught Leung Teong. Leung Teong taught Chan Wa Shun and Chan Wa Shun taught my instructor Yip Man. Five generations (not including the present) altogether.

You are the second generation of the Jun Fan system and as well as the highest rank holder of that system at the present time. This system will be the "it"----not in the past 4 thousand years has there been a "live" system of totality without any classical confinement. The Jun Fan consists all roots of all system yet having a unique characteristic of its own.

Your request of film on techniques cannot really be fulfilled without actual demonstration to you personally. However, I'll send you some forms for classical teaching. I'll try to draw you the Tai Chi with explanation. I hope to fly up to Seattle the first chance I have. So at that time I'll devote some time to you. In the mean time, think of your problems and jot them down and wait for my trip.

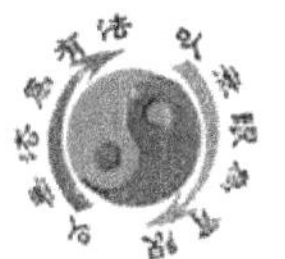

5/23/1966

Taky,

Thank you for letter plus dues; this time, the dues really come in handy due to postponement of shooting.

First of all, our school's name is 'Jun Fan' Gung Fu, after my Chinese name. Though I'm grateful for Wing Chun, the fact remains that the Jun Fan is yet several steps ahead of the Wing Chun System. Where Wing Chun ends, Jun Fan starts----not to add on, but to see the isness with freedom and in its totality. One thing must be stressed that without Wing Chun, I would never have arrived at this stage. The three basic structures of the Jun Fan System are:---(1) Sticking to the nucleus---Wing Chun idea, though I've expand on it. (2) Liberation from the nucleus----my idea of non-confinement, to see things totally. (3) Returning to original freedom----the circle without circumferences------direct expression---------------

As for the history of Wing Chun, here are the chronological order-------though Yim (last name) Wing Chun was taught by Ng Mui, a nun from Sil Lum, Wing Chun is the founder of this new system. She taught it to her husband Leung, and Leung taught it to two Chinese Opera actors, Wong Wa Bo and Leung Ye Taie, for exchange of a set of swords and a set of staff. Wong Wa Bo then taught Leung Jeong, Leung Jeong taught Chan Wa Shun and Chan Wa Shun taught my instructor Yip Man. Five generations (not incliding the present) altogether.

You are the second generation of the Jun Fan System and as well as the highest rank holder of that system at the present time. This system will be the "it"----not in the past 4 thousand years has there been a "live" system of totality without any classical confinement. The Jun Fan consists all roots of all system yet having a unique characteristic of its own.

Your request of film on techniques cannot really be fulfilled without actual demonstration to you personally. However, I'll send you some forms for classical teaching. I'll try to draw you the Tai Chi with explanations. I hope to fly up to Seattle the first chance I have. So at that time I'll devote some time to you. In the mean time, think of your problems and jot them down and wait for my trip.

Actually, I prefer a stance that is between a straight stand up style and the low crouch style, with knees slightly bend and the back left heel raised. The body incline slightly forward, weight distribution, 40% front and 60% back. Wait till I see you and I'll show you perfectly. This is a most flexible stance for attack and defence

A young Jun Fan standing side by side with master Yip Man, outside Yip Man's flat in Hong Kong.

Letter 6B

Description of Letter No. 6

This is a detailed comprehensive explanation of what Jun Fan Gung Fu is when broken down. Bruce broke it down for me in simple terms, so I could understand it better. He also broke down the historical roots / lineage of the system. Bruce did something special for me by doing this, so I could understand it completely. As far as the rank he gave me, I was humble and thankful to him for giving it to me as I personally felt I did not deserve such an honor. On the other hand, recognizing that he was looking at, and judging me, in respect to the others, he was headstrong in his decision. I am still humble by it to this day.

Actually, I prefer a stance that is between a straight stand up style and the low crouch style, with knees slightly bend and the back left heel raised. The body incline slightly forward, weight distribution, 40% front and 60% back. Wait till I see you and I'll show you perfectly. This is a most flexible stance for attack and defence.

Enclosed you will find your rank certificate authorized by me. Those stupid fool omitted the word 'promoted' in the sentence------well, what is done is done and if there are some new corrected ones coming, I'll replace it for you. So far, there is one 4th rank holder, one 3rd rank (James Lee----Charles passed away), and I don't know how many 2nd rank holder are 1st rank holders. Therefore, it is my wish that in order to be a true member of the Jun Fan Institute, each member must have a membership card plus a rank certificate. Without either one of the two documents no member is recognized as the official member of the Jun Fan Institute. So if you like your qualified student to be in, send me their cards (in the case of promotion) and I'll issue their certifcate authorized by me. Then you will have to sign your name on the instructor blank to make it complete. This way we can really start a good group and any past undesirable characters can be casted out. So report those that need rank certificates and those that have lost their cards-------there is no way for replacement on that and has to be replaced by another card with the last number written over the already printed number. So tell the student to take good care of that card. How is the girl class coming along? What are the age range? Simplicity and realism must be stressed and on top of that, no rhythmatic training, use broken rhythm.

Enclosed you will find your rank certificate authorized by me. Those stupid fool omitted the word 'promoted' in the sentence------well, what is done is done and if there are some new corrected ones coming, I'll replace it for you. So far, there is one 4th rank holder, one 3rd rank (James Lee----Charles passed away), and I don't know how many 2nd rank holder or 1st rank holders. Therefore, it is my wish that in order to be a true member of the Jun Fan Institute, each member must have a membership card plus a rank certificate. Without either one of the two documents no member is recognized as the official member of the Jun Fan Institute. So if you like your qualified student to be in, send me their cards(in the case of a promotion) and I'll issue their certificate authorized by me. Then you will have to sign your name on the instructor blank to make it complete. This way we can really start a good group and any past undesirable characters can be casted out. So report those that need rank certificates and those that have lost their cards-------there is no way for replacement on that and has to be replaced by another card with the lost number written over the already printed number. So tell the student to take good care of that card.

How is the girl class coming along ? What are the age range ? Simplicity and realism must be stressed and on top of that, no rhythmatic training, use broken rhythm.

Bruce doing Chi Sao with Master Yip Man in 1963, shortly after his arrival back to visit his family after 4 long years.

Letter 7

Description of Letter No. 7

This was the last letter to me in regards to martial arts in Seattle. He was always very diligent in keeping my positive attitude up and my spirits high. He believed in my ability to carry on what he broke ground with. I was constantly striving to maintain a level of positiveness in relation to his teachings. He was always keeping me excited with new things related to his martial arts. That kept my spirit content as well as my teaching ability. Bruce was a great teacher and he always inspired me to become a better student and teacher as well. Bruce knew that men and women had different needs within the martial arts, so he was always comprising custom plans for both genders, so they both could make the best out of the curriculum.

Transcription

Taky,

Received registered letter and the dues. thank you. The new of Don Lindsley is most shocking. Disregard of what happened he has my thought & moral support. Every man is entitled to one mistake. I hope you will call Don's mother for me or better yet, give me her address and phone number. Also, be sure to keep me informed on this terrible matter.

Enclosed you will find three certificates, one for Tosh, one for John & the third one for Marc. I hold Chris's certificate because I like to hear from you of his progress and dedication. 3rd rank is pretty high and he should qualify for it. Is he showing up regularly? earnest & diligent? Let me know. In the meantime, I'll hold on.

As for equipment for the girl class, I suggest a football shield (for kicking mainly-----you can tied it around groin area, or hold it) and a thick plastic welding glass (for Bill Jee). Enclosed you will find some cards of the institute that you can use. (will send separate)

By the way, be sure to fill in the membership number and sign your name on the empty space below marked INSTRUCTOR. Also, I put in one for you because I've secured the correct print now. The omitted word "promoted" is filled in.

Be sure to let me know if any new ideas regarding the expansion come up. Think of expanding & maintaining the class as I have plan for you after the series make the hit.

Jesse asked me (when I was in Seattle) if he can open a school. I said it's okay as long as Gung Fu is not involved. Write & let me know how things are and let me know of your program for girls and I'm sure I can add on & expanding that program systematically.

Bruce

P.S. will you send me the information's of the file on John, Chris, Tosh. And let me have your file so I can duplicate one.

Taky, Received registered letter and the dues. Thank
you. The new of Don Lindsley is most shocking.
Disregard of what happened he has my thought
& moral support. Everyman is entitled to one
mistake. I hope you will call Don's mother
for me or better yet, give me her address
and phone number. Also, be sure to keep
me informed on this terrible matter.

Enclosed you will find three certificates,
one for Tosh, one for John & the third one for
Marc. I hold Chris's certificates because I like
to hear from you of his progress and dedication
3rd rank is pretty high and he should qualify
for it. Is he showing up regularly & earnest &
diligent? Let me know. In the meantime, I'll
hold on.

As for equipment for the girl class, I suggest
a football shield (for kicking mainly----- you can
tied it around groin areas, or hold it) and a
thick plastic welding glass (for Bill Jee)

Enclosed you will find some cards of
the Institute that you can use (Will send separate)
By the way, be sure to fill in the

...embership number and sign your name on
... empty space below marked INSTRUCTOR. Also
... put in one for you because I've secured
... correct print now. The ommitted word
"...moled" is filled in.

Be sure to let me know if any news
... regarding the expansion come up. Think
...panding & maintaining the class as I have
... for you after the series make the hit.
Jesse asked me (when I was in Seattle)
... can open a school. I said it's okay
... as Gung Fu is not involved, but I
... know he's going in with Demile —
...haracter I can't stand. What is your
...aling his martial art academy? Of
...one knows better not to fool around
...

...rite & let me know how things are
...me know of your program for girls
...sure I can add on & expanding
...program systematically.

Bruce

P.S. - Will you send me
the information of the
file on John, Chris, Tosh
and let me have your file so I can duplicate one.

(LEFT) *Bruce Lee demonstrating on Taky Kimura as the Seattle class looks on.*

(RIGHT) *Students and close friends to Bruce Lee, Doug Palmer and Sue Ann Kay, show the class their technique as Taky Kimura looks on.*

Letter 8

Description of Letter No. 8

Another sign of our enduring friendship, keeping me appraised of his success and goings on.

Transcription

Taky,

This coming Thursday I'll start the Gung Fu class (public sort of) in Chinatown. There will be no signs outside. So far around 25 signed up officially; by the end of the month I will raise to at least 35 if not 40.

I'll be the grand marshal of the Chinese New Year Parade down in Chinatown here in L.A.

Still unable to find a tailor that will make the uniform from the type of material I want ~~~ am keep trying.

How's things going on up in Seattle? Been reading those books?

The stuffs I've printed from Hong Kong will be ready in around a week ~~ will send them to you as soon as I get them.

Take Care and have fun.
Bruce

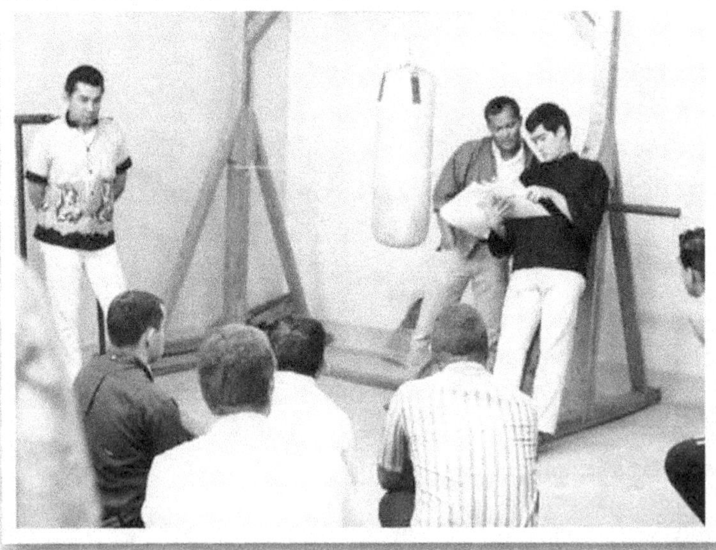

Opening day at the Los Angeles Chinatown School in 1967. Bruce Lee and Dan Inosanto go over the classes training program as the students look on.

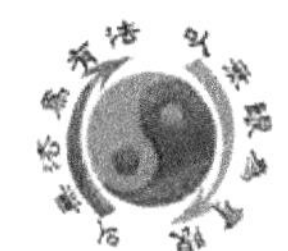

Taky

This Coming Thursday I'll start the Gung Fu class (public sort of) in Chinatown. There will be no signs outside. So far around 25 signed up officially, by the end of the month I will raise to at least 35 if not 40.

I'll be the grand marshal of the Chinese New Year parade down in Chinatown here in L.A.

Still unable to find a tailor that will make the uniform from the type of material I want — am keep trying.

How's things going on up in Seattle? Been reading those books?

The stuffs I've printed from Hong Kong will be ready in around a week — will send them to you as soon as I get them.

Take care and have fun.

Bruce

Opening day at the Los Angeles Chinatown School 1967, as students and friends look on and listen to Bruce Lee's Jeet Kune Do philosophy.

Letter 9

Description of Letter No. 9

This letter is great, because it shows Bruce's business side. He was such a positive innovator and the way he promoted his martial arts, as Bruce Lee's method was brilliant. Bruce used these great analogies to get his points across and as you can see here, he never ran short in ways of doing just that. From Jun Fan Gung Fu, to Bruce Lee's Fighting Method and then Jeet Kune Do, Bruce was a true innovator on all levels.

Transcription

Dear Taky,

Thank you for your letter plus the money. I agree with what you've stated in your letter, and I've come up with the right solution for the school. A better lesson plan for both the advance and the beginning class. Also, a lot of "sizzles" has been included to make the Bruce Lee's method much more attractive. In fact, a sort of combination sales and instruction manual will be made for you. In short, we've been selling the steak (which is the fact ~~~~ the "law and "theory" etc.) and not the sizzles, which are emotional exciters ~~ like the "bubbles" in champagne, the "foam" on the beer, or remember the frosted mug for the root beer we take? The frosted mug is the "sizzle". Or it is the way the hat is tilted (sizzle); the hat is for protection against rain (fact). To sum it up, seldom can a cold fact get a sale underway as fast as a sizzle that thrills the other person. Our class will be full of sizzles and our cold "Bruce Lee's method" will back it up. Have no fear, the 100% refined Bruce Lee's method is here. Tell the class I'll be there personally to give a lecture on the "Bruce Lee's method" and "what is the difference between this method and other martial arts." To be sure, they will be Bruce Lee's style conscious after the lecture. Of course, the one week training with you will equip you with the ability to conduct and teach the method.

I'll see you on the 24th and am looking forward on our training.

Take care
Bruce

Dear Tady,

Thank you for your letter plus the money. I agree with what you've stated in your letter, and I've come up with the right solution for the school. A better lesson plan for both the advance and the beginning class. Also, a lot of "sizzles" has been included to make the Bruce Lee's method much more attractive. In fact, a sort of combination sales and instruction manual will be made for you. In short, we've been selling the steak (which is the fact — the "law" and "theory" etc.) and not the sizzles which are emotional exciters — like the "bubbles" in champagne, the "foam" on the beer, or remember the frosted mug for the root beer we had! The frosted mug is the "sizzle". Or it is, a way the hat is tilted (sizzle); the hat is for protection against rain (fact). To sum it up, seldom can a cold fact get a sale underway as fast as a sizzle that thrills the other person. Our class will be full of sizzles and our cold "Bruce Lee's method" will back it up. Have no fear, the 10% refined Bruce Lee's method is here. Tell the class I'll be there

ersonally to give a lecture on the "Bruce Lee's ethod" and "what is the difference between method and other martial arts." To be sure, they will be Bruce Lee's style conscious after the lecture. Of course, the one week ning with you will equip you with the lity to conduct and teach the method.

I'll see you on the 24th and am oking forward on our training.

Take Care

Bruce

(ABOVE) *Bruce solo and in action for the camera in what would become a photo shoot of many, for Bruce Lee's Fighting Method.*

(RIGHT) *Bruce along side his second in command, Dan Inosanto on a beach in Pacific Palisades California. This shoot was to be part of the Bruce Lee's Fighting Method book series. Bruce actually scrapped that idea and it was not too long after he passed away, Linda decided to release it worldwide.*

Letter 10

Description of Letter No. 10

During the course of opening the school in Seattle, Bruce was in constant contact with me, going over different lesson plans for me, my assistant instructors, as well as the students, both men and women. It was a hectic time for all of us, but we took Bruce's lead and eventually his vision was realized. Dan Inosanto also helped in developing lesson plans for the Seattle school. Bruce entrusted him greatly and work closely with him while in Los Angeles.

Transcription

Taky,

Enclosed find my answer sheet to the yellow sheet that you left me. Get together with Chris and John and read it in front of them. First read from the yellow sheet then read the correspondent answer on my sheet.

I'll submit John's lesson plan to Dan and have him write another one and between the two I'll come up with a standard lesson plan.

Enclosed also find information regarding dojo accident insurance ~~~ merely mention you have a small club teaching Karate or Gung Fu and do not mention my name. Make it sounds like a small usual Karate Club.

Am looking forward to the uniform and emblem.

Bruce

Bruce Lee demonstrates on Dan Inosanto in Los Angeles Chinatown, the basics of Jun fan Gung Fu.

Taky,

Enclosed find my answer sheet to the yellow sheet that you left me. Get together with Chris and John and read it in front of them. First read from the yellow sheet then read the correspondent answer on my sheet.

I'll submit John's lesson plan to Dan and have him write another one and between the two I'll come up with a standard lesson plan.

Enclosed also find information regarding Dojo accident insurance — merely mention you have a <u>small club</u> teaching Karate or Gung Fu and do not mention my name. Make it sounds like a small usual Karate club.

Am looking forward to the uniform and emblem.

Bruce

Letter 11

Description of Letter No. 11

In this brief letter, Bruce was accommodating me when I asked him about certain books / reference that he used to better his martial arts training. He kept those things very top secret, but shared them with me on a regular basis. Bruce had thousands of books in his library and at times would pick me books up from used bookstores. Then he would highlight the important parts of the book with his notes inside and then give them to me. I still treasure these books dearly.

Transcription

Taky,

Here are my experience in Gung Fu. Read it careful and ask Sheldon Wong for some of the Chinese character. However, do not let anybody else read it.

Bruce

Bruce Lee sitting with his amazing library of books that touched on everything from martial arts to philosophy, as well as the many religions around the world. Bruce was a well-read man, always investigating. He is in his office at his apartment in the Barrington Plaza building. This picture was one of many promotional shoots he did to promote himself as "Kato".

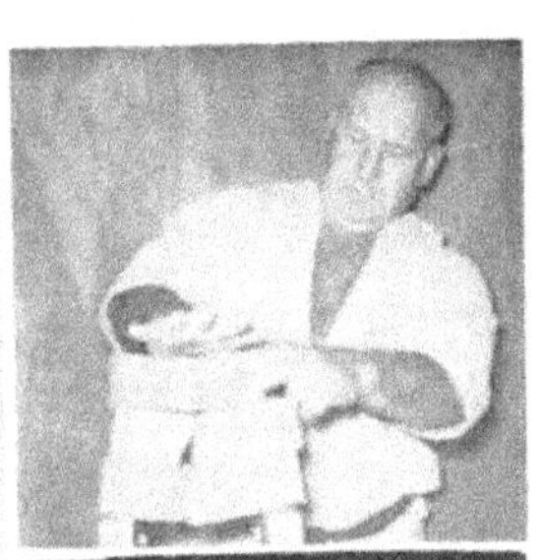

modern KUNG-FU KARATE

唐手功夫

BREAK BRICKS in 100 DAYS
fast, new, AMAZING system
DO IT NOW FREE literatures
only $5.00 cash, check, m.o.
Oriental Book Sales
P.o. box 1183 Oakland, 4 Calif.

CHINESE GUNG FU
The Philosophical Art of Self Defense
by Bruce Lee - $5.00

"Secrets of Chinese Karate" - By Ed Parker - $5.95

Modern Kungfu Karate - Iron Hand Training - $5.00

Modern Kungfu Karate - Poison Hand Training - $5.00

Oriental Book Sales P.O. Box 1183, Oakland 4, California

Secret Art of Chinese Leg Maneuvers
by Lee Ying Arng - $4.50
Karate by Nishiyama - $7.50
What is Karate by Oyama - $6.50
Way of Karate by Mattson - $5.50

Taky,

Here are my experience in Gung Fu. Read it careful and ask Sheldon Wong for some of the Chinese character. However, do not let anybody else read it.

Bruce

Striking Straw Mats - 18 at $12.50
Striking Straw Mats - 9 at $9.50
Striking Straw Mats - 6 at $5.95

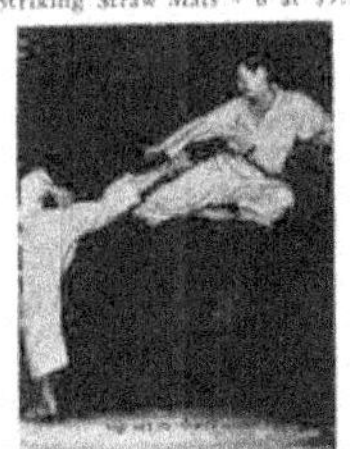

Kenpo Karate - By Parker - $6.25
Guide to Jujitso
Associated Art by - Moynahan - $2.75

All California Orders 4% Tax
All Sales Final, No Refund or Exchange

Letter 12

Description of Letter No. 12

Bruce sent me an illustration poster that outlined the T' Ai Kik form. Bruce wanted me to explore many different forms within the martial arts he was teaching me. This was just another tool that helped progress my understanding of Chinese Gung Fu.

Transcription

Taky,

Taky, just got back from Oakland to-day. (15 min ago, in fact!)

Enclosed you will see a detailed easy to follow T'Ai Kik form wall chart.

Follow it, and remember circles and continuation. Am rushing You to-day. If in doubt ask Sheldon. I doubt it though.

Will write to-nite.

Keep up the good work!

Bruce

P.S. Keep the chart in good form. I like it back. When you're through with it.

Bruce Lee in Oakland, California posing for the camera in what would be a shoot for a new Gung Fu book he was to do with James Lee, etc. Only a few of these images have been leaked out to the public. Unfortunately, this book never came to be.

Taky,

Just got back from Oakland [15 min ago, in fact!] to-day. Enclosed you will see a detailed easy to follow T'AI KIK form wall chart. Follow it. and remember circles and continuation. Am rushing you to-day. If in doubt ask Sheldon. I doubt it though. Will write to-nite.

Keep up the good work!

Bruce

P.S. Keep the chart in good form. I like it back. when you're through with it.

Letter 13

Description of Letter No. 13

This letter shows how Bruce was in the planning stages of developing the criteria for the Seattle Gung Fu School, which included making uniforms and the appropriate badges / emblems with the right rankings for the students and instructors. Bruce wrote me many times to follow up about the uniforms, it seemed so hard to get anything done when Bruce moved from Seattle, so he always had to check up numerous times to make sure the people we entrusted for these jobs would deliver what they promised.

Transcription

Taky,

Let me know if you've found out about the uniform.

If not, let me know if that Mrs. Mar still makes the vest & bages (somewhere else didn't you say?) At any rate, find out the total cost.

Thank you

How's everything

Bruce

Bruce Lee in James Lee's backyard in martial arts pose, Oakland, California.

Taky,

Let me know if you've found out about the uniform

If not, let me know if that Mrs. Mar still makes the vest & bags (somewhere else didn't you say?). At any rate, find out the total cost.

Thank you.

How's everything

Letter 14

Description of Letter No. 14

I tried with all my heart to fulfill his wishes but again I did not have the charisma to get those people to do things the way he could, if he were in Seattle.

Bruce flew me down to see him and come to his birthday in 1967; it was the last time I would come down to see him there. After that, Bruce would come to see me in Seattle many times. He truly loved Seattle, it was really his home.

Transcription

Taky,

Received 18 top jackets ~~~what happen to the pants?

Please advise the price for the whole jacket and pants so I can mark a price for sale.

Armstrong wrote and extend invitation to his tournament at the Seattle Arena on Oct. 22 (Sunday) I don't know but I might just come.

Still working on book and lesson plan. I'll stop now ---- let me know as soon as you can about the price for the whole uniform - when can we get pants.

Take care

Bruce

P.S. Plan on coming down for my birthday – I'll fly you down.

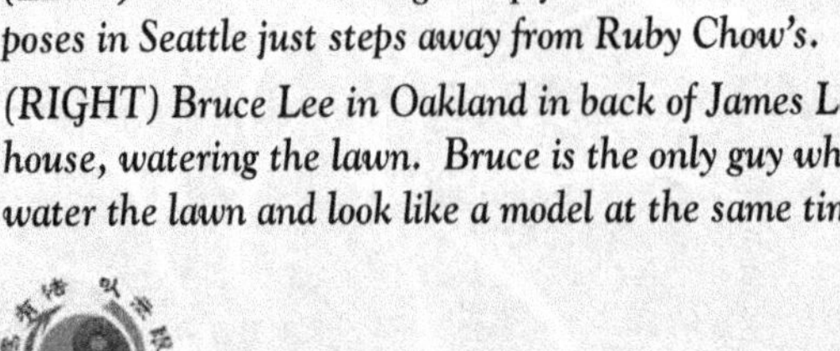

(LEFT) Bruce Lee looking sharp for the camera as he poses in Seattle just steps away from Ruby Chow's.

(RIGHT) Bruce Lee in Oakland in back of James Lee's house, watering the lawn. Bruce is the only guy who can water the lawn and look like a model at the same time.

Taky,

Received 18 top jackets — what
happen to the pants?
Please advise the price for the
whole jacket and pants so I can
mark a price for sale.
Armstrong wrote and extend invitation
to his tournament at Seattle Arena
on Oct. 22 (Sunday) I don't know
but I might just come
Still working on book and lesson
plan
I'll stop now — let me know
as soon as you can about the
price for the whole uniform
— when can we get pants

Take Care.

Bruce

P.S. Plan on coming down for my
birthday — I'll fly you
down.

Letter 15A

Description of Letter No. 15

Bruce was relentless in his demand to retain his requests with regard to the "martial arts" teachings with me. He constantly used demanding psychology to get me to respond to his fast "mind set". He did not comprehend the problems I faced trying to get his acquaintances to readily respond to his requests. There was a big difference with respect to certain students who loved and respected Bruce, and me who did not have the identity that Bruce had. Those certain students basically ignored me. I respected what Bruce had done for me, but the "glitter" and excitement that Bruce commanded in a room "vanished" to a large extent after he left Seattle.

Transcription

Taky, *Sept. 20 1967.*

Thank you for your immediate response to my last request.

At last, the lesson plan has completed, and I'm forwarding the official lesson plan along with John's proposed one. You will see, after you've read it carefully, that it is very "simply" arranged. Follow it closely and if there is any points not clear to you, write me about it. By following this plan, a student will be very sharp after six weeks. Try follow the lesson plan in your own home training, use one lesson plan in each training session in your case and speed it up. Get Tosh to join in, you will be able to improve just on these twelve lessons.

Make sure you can come down for my birthday and stay for the weekend as I have something important to discuss among the instructors and I like you to be present. Make arrangement for it now.

Back to the uniforms. Can you make some more, at least another eighteen jackets and pants (of course, do not forget to send eighteen pants to match the eighteen jackets you've already sent) Remember the pants should not be too baggy, and should follow the line of a regular loose workpants (maybe a bit looser). As for the length, leave it a little bit long so the females at home can sew it up for the desired length. By the way, they do not shrink too much, do they?

Also, have maybe five among the other eighteen uniforms made into large size.

If the whole uniforms cost $ 7.00 to make, material and labor, I think we should sell them at $16.50 each. This price is according to the Tokaido Karate – gi sell by Japan Karate Association. Of course, among friends so to speak, this is assistant or close group, we should have a fixed price to sell them, which we should avoid as once the official $16.50 is marked. But again there are always special considerations.

You yourself should have two made and charge it to the Institute. After all, with you, everything fits to you buddy.

One thing comes to mind, and that is with the karate gi, the price goes up as the size growths. In the case of the Tokaido brand, large is $17:00 and $17.50, extra large is $18.00, and dig this, super extra large is $19.00. So, we will wait and see if the tailor increases his price as the size increases. At any rate, we should charge the medium uniform $16.50 and the large $17:50. Let me know your thinking on this.

What's his name Armstrong is inviting me to come up to Seattle for the Oct. 22 tournament? I might come up with Linda, and I'll let you know ahead of time if I do.

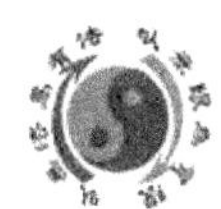

Taky. Sept. 20 1967.

Thank you for your immediate response to my last request.

At last, the lesson plan has completed, and I'm forwarding the official lesson plan along with John's proposed one. You will see, after you've read it carefully, that it is very "simply" arranged. Follow it closely and if there is any points not clear to you, write me about it. By following this plan, a student will be very sharp after six weeks. Try follow the lesson plan in your own home training, use one lesson plan in each training session in your case and speed it up. Get Josh to join in, you will be able to improve guts on these twelve lessons.

Make sure you can come down for my birthday and stay for the week-end as I have something important to discuss among the instructors and I like you to be present. Make arrangement for it now.

Back to the uniforms. Can you make some more, at least another eighteen jackets and pants (of course, do not forget to send eighteen pants to match the eighteen jackets you've already sent) Remember the pants should not be too baggy, ~~like~~ and should follow the line of a regular loose workpants (maybe a bit looser). As for the length, leave it a little bit long so the females at home can sew it up for the desired length. By the way, they do not shrink too much, do they?

...so. have maybe five among the
...teen uniforms made into large
...the whole uniforms cost $7.00
...material and labor. I think
...sell them at $16.50 each. This
...according to the Tokaido Karate-
...by the Japan Karate Association.
Of course. among friends so to speak, this
is assistant or close group, we should
have a fixed price to sell them, which
we should avoid as once the official $16.50
is marked. But again there are always
special considerations.

You yourself should have two made and charge it to the Institute. After all, with you, everything fits to you buddy.

One thing comes to mind, and that is with the Karate gi, the price goes up as the size growths. In the case of the Tokaido brand, large is $17.00 and $17.50, extra large is $18.00, and dig this, super extra large is $19.00. So, we will wait and see if the tailor increases his price as the size increases. At any rate, we should charge the medium uniform $16.50 and the large $17.50. Let me know your thinking on this.

What's his name Armstrong is ~~inviting~~ inviting me to come up to Seattle for the Oct. 22 tournament. I might come up with Linda, and I'll let you know ahead of time if I do.

One of the major reason for me

Letter 15B

Description of Letter No. 15

Bruce was relentless in his demand to retain his requests with regard to the "martial arts" teachings with me. He constantly used demanding psychology to get me to respond to his fast "mind set". He did not comprehend the problems I faced trying to get his acquaintances to readily respond to his requests. There was a big difference with respect to certain students who loved and respected Bruce, and me who did not have the identity that Bruce had. Those certain students basically ignored me. I respected what Bruce had done for me, but the "glitter" and excitement that Bruce commanded in a room "vanished" to a large extent after he left Seattle.

Transcription (continued)

One of the major reason for me to come up is my latest discovery that will definitely guaranteed to sharpen your kicking in no time. Wait till we get together, and this change of ability will occur in a matter of minutes, as you already have the hidden ability and training. So I'll probably see you either in Oct. or you will be flying down as my guest in November. An important meeting will take place at that time and as a senior member, you must be present.

Take care my friend and rush the uniforms to me at your earliest convenience.

Thank You

Bruce

Bruce Lee in Seattle in 1961, posing on the stairs, on the way to his room above Ruby Chow's restaurant.

to come up is my latest discovery that will definitely guarenteed to sharpen your kicking in no time. Wait till we get together, and this change of ability will occur in a matter of minutes, as you already have the hidden ability and training. So I'll probably see you either in Oct. or you will be flying down as my guest in November. An important meeting will take place at that time and as a senior member you must be present.

Take Care my friend and rush the uniforms to me at your earliest convenience

Thank you

Bruce

Letter 16

Description of Letter No. 16

On going "pep talk" to "bolster" the mind set and maintain the positive. Bruce was "constant" and philosophical in this regard all the time.

Transcription

Taky,

Received letter. Thanks

The demonstration was favorably received and as always each one adds to the experience of presentation.

Do not think that I'm an old woman, but I like to remind you once more on the uniforms and emblems.

Also, I myself have already set up 'two' lesson plans for the Jun Fan standard lesson plan. Dan Inosanto started work on the draft yesterday and he asked for two weeks time for completion. Thus, to speed matter up I, myself, as stated, have started on my own plan already. So as soon as Dan finishes his and together with Newman's plan, I will come up with a real efficient program of teaching for the Jun Fan Gung Fu Institute on Jeet Kune Do. We have to really form a strong private group. The success of Washington State's organization is in your effort. Thank You once more for your loyalty and sincerity.

No one has done more to me than you.

Take care and hope that you have once more gradually break into practice.

Bruce

Taky Kimura, Bruce Lee and friend and student Sue Ann Kay on a cold winters day, in Seattle Washington outside the University Way Jun Fan Gung Fu Institute.

Taky,

Received letter. Thanks

The demonstration was favorably received and as always each one adds to the experience of presentation.

Do not think that I'm an old woman, but I like to remind you once more on the uniforms and emblems.

Also, I myself have already set up 'two' lesson plans for the Jun Fan standard lesson plan. Dan Inosanto started work on the draft yesterday and he asked for two weeks time for completion. Thus, to speed matter up I, myself, as stated, have started on my own plan already. So as soon as Dan finishes his and together with Newman's plan, I will come up with a real efficient program of teaching for the Jun Fan Gung Fu Institute on Jeet Kune Do. We have to really form a strong private group. The success of Washington state's organization is in your effort. Thank you once more for your loyalty and sincerity. No one has done more to me than you.

Take Care and hope that you have once more gradually break into practice

Bruce

Letter 17

Description of Letter No. 17

Charlie and I responded "timely" and sent money to Hong Kong for our dummies. Bruce was very "responsive" to share our emotion with respect to the wait in receiving them. Besides, how could we complain to our SiFu, Bruce about having to wait so long before getting our "Mook Jung". Just Bruce's continued and "on going" keeping in touch with me was enough to appease the situation. Bruce shared his "emotions" with me, whether it was about the intimacy of his life, or mine. Everyone has to have a "true brother" to share their burdens and positions with and Bruce was mine.

Transcription

Taky, *Aug. 10 1965*

Received your letter plus feet measurement for Gung Fu shoes – will make you a pair plus a Gung Fu pants (good for work-outs) when I see the lady who makes them.

As for the dummy it will be best if you can send a fifty dollar bill (or money order though it is troublesome to have to cash by passport) and registered it and send it to me in your next letter. Instruct Charlie the same thing. The dummy will cost around H.K. $140 (price has raised since 1959) and the shipping cost is in the neighborhood of U.S. $23. Will show you the exact cost when they issue me the bill.

Enclosed find two photos of Brandon when he is a day before 6 months old. He had 4 teeth at 4 months old and at present has 6 teeth. He can sit real good and can grasp on the crib and stand up by himself.

Good idea to start a woman class ---- see what develop --- maybe it will grow and maybe you can find yourself a nice wife among the students (like I did).

In regarding the practice pants for the students of Seattle I'm afraid you have to get the length of their feet (width and waist size is not necessary) in order to order them. I'll see if I can get direct connection.

Bruce

Bruce on the Mook Jung (wooden dummy) in traditional form. Though Bruce later on develop the JKD sets for the dummy, he always stayed true to his traditional foundation of Wing Chun, without being held down by it.

Taky, Aug. 10 1965

Received your letter plus feet measurement for Gung Fu shoes— will make you a pair plus a Gung Fu pants (good for work-outs) when I see the lady who makes them.

As for the dummy it will be best if you can send a fifty dollar bill (or money order though it is troublesome to have to cash by passport) and registered it and send it to me in your next letter. Instruct Charlie the same thing. The dummy will cost around H.K.$ 140 (price has raised since 1959) and the shipping cost is in the neighbourhood of $ U.S. $23. Will show you the exact cost when they issue me the bill.

Enclosed find two photos of Brandon when he is a day before 6 month old. He had 4 teeth at 4 month old and at present has 6 teeth. He can sit real good and can grasp on the crip and stand up by himself.

Good idea to start a woman class — see what develop — maybe it will grow and maybe you can find yourself a nice wife among the students (like I did)

In regarding the practice pants for the students of Seattle I'm afraid you have to get the length of their feet (width and waist size is ~~all size~~ not necessary) in order to order them. I'll see if I can get direct connection. Bruce

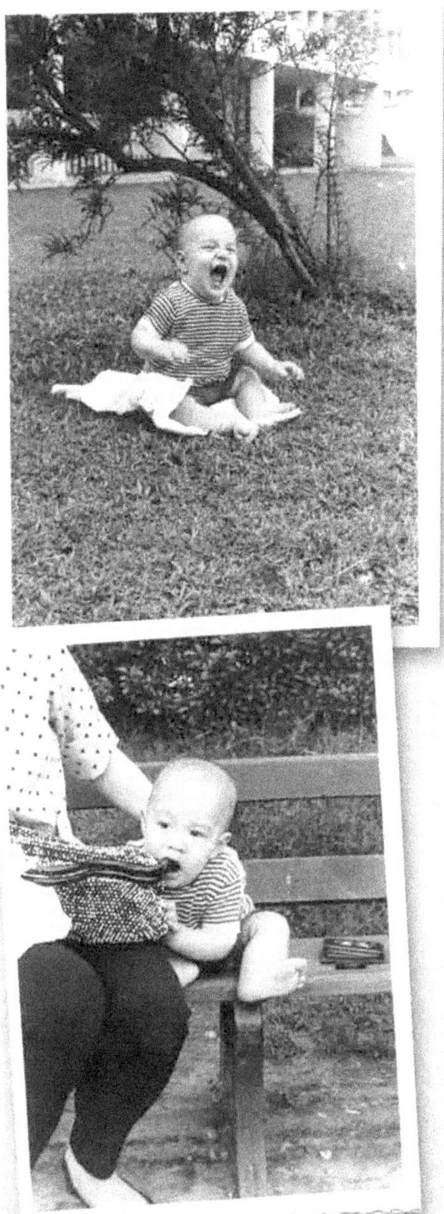

Linda with baby Brandon posing for the camera in Oakland, California.

Letter 18

Description of Letter No. 18

Bruce wrote me this letter while he was in Hong Kong. This letter reminds me of the progression in which Bruce was taking me within his martial arts training. He wanted us to have within the school, The Chinese Wing Chun Wooden Dummy so that our training would mirror exactly what he experienced within his training in Hong Kong, with Master Yip Man. Bruce also mentions he was going to film Master Yip Man and send over that footage for us to use as a guide tool and show where he received his knowledge. I still have those dummies today in a safe place.

Transcription

Taky,

Received your money orders of $150 for dummies plus $100 for Jun Fan; at this moment, you guys sent me each $25 too much. in my last two letters I told you and Charles the dummy total cost for each is only $50 (U.S.). When I see you and Charles I'll refund you.

Well, I ordered your dummies yesterday and according to the man it will take around 2 1/2 weeks --------figure around another month and a half for shipping.

As soon as they are ready, my mother will ship them for me because I will most likely be leaving on the 17th of this month (Sept.) I plan to come up to Seattle to see you.

If 20th Century Fox deal doesn't come out (It's 85% now) I have a contract here waiting for me. So I've to wait and see what's up. Brandon has been sick these past ten days and is getting a little bit better now.

Glad to hear you are coming along with the Gung Fu class is the girl class also showing progress?

How's Charlie's class out in Renten (?) coming along? Did you go there and see?

Am going to buy a nice 8mm. movie camera (already got a projector and screen) and shoot the 3 forms of Wing Chun, having my instructor as the demonstrator.

By the way, how's your mother ---do pay her my respect and regards.

When dummies are ready, will send them to your address, addresses to you.

Keep well,
Bruce

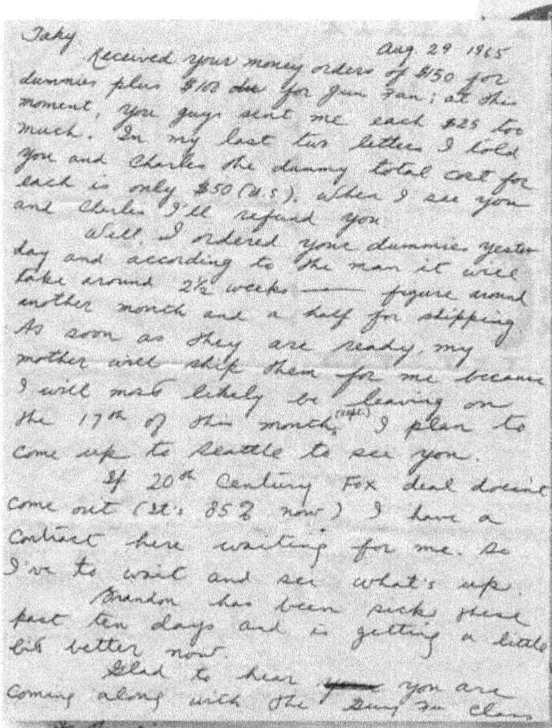

Taky

Aug 29 1965

Received your money order of $150 for dummies plus $100 due for Jun Fan; at this moment, you guys sent me each $25 too much. In my last two letters I told you and Charles the dummy total cost for each is only $50 (U.S.). When I see you and Charles I'll refund you.

Well, I ordered your dummies yesterday and according to the man it will take around 2½ weeks — figure around another month and a half for shipping. As soon as they are ready, my mother will ship them for me because I will most likely be leaving on the 17th of this month (Sept.) I plan to come up to Seattle to see you.

If 20th Century Fox deal doesn't come out (It's 85% now) I have a contract here waiting for me. So I've to wait and see what's up.

Brandon has been sick these past ten days and is getting a little bit better now.

Glad to hear you are coming along with the Gung Fu Class. Is the girl class also showing progress?

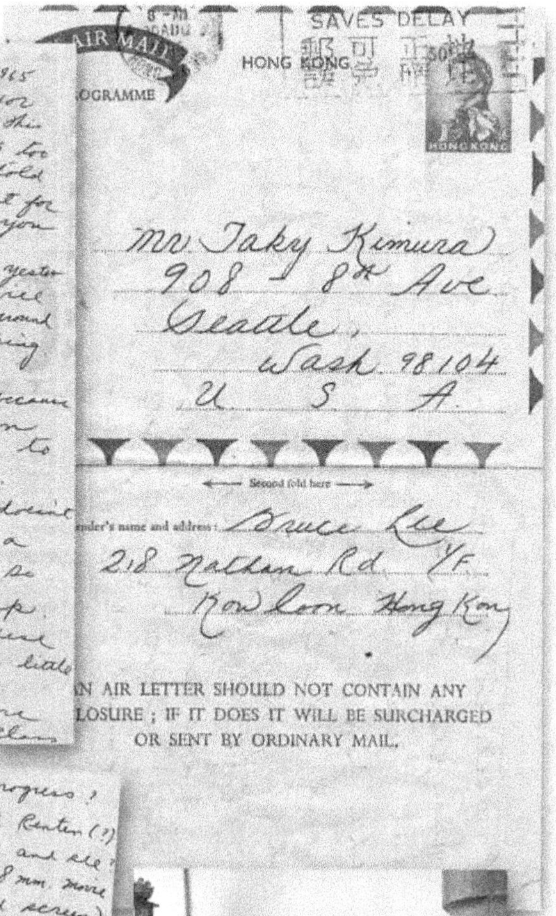

How's Charlie's class out in Renton (?) coming along? Did you go there and see?

Am going to buy a nice 8mm movie camera (already got a projector and screen) and shoot the 3 forms of Wing Chung, having my instructor as the demonstrator.

By the way, how's your mother — do pay her my respect and regards.

When dummies are ready, will send them to your address, addressed to you.

Keep well.

Bruce

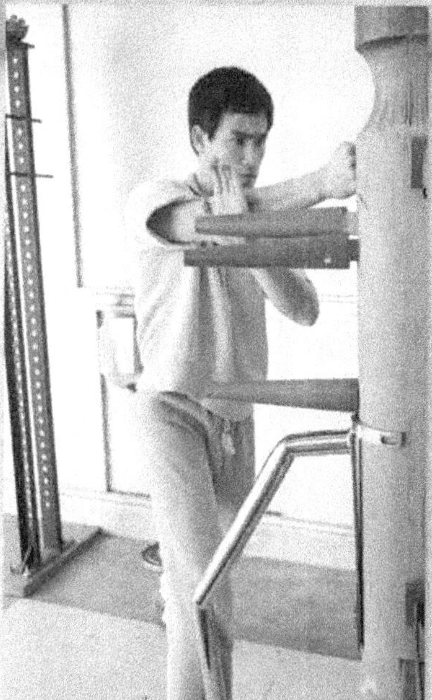

AIR MAIL

AEROGRAMME

SAVES DELAY

HONG KONG

Mr Taky Kimura
908 - 8th Ave
Seattle,
Wash 98104
U S A

← Second fold here →

Sender's name and address: Bruce Lee
218 Nathan Rd 7/F
Kowloon Hong Kong

AN AIR LETTER SHOULD NOT CONTAIN ANY ENCLOSURE; IF IT DOES IT WILL BE SURCHARGED OR SENT BY ORDINARY MAIL.

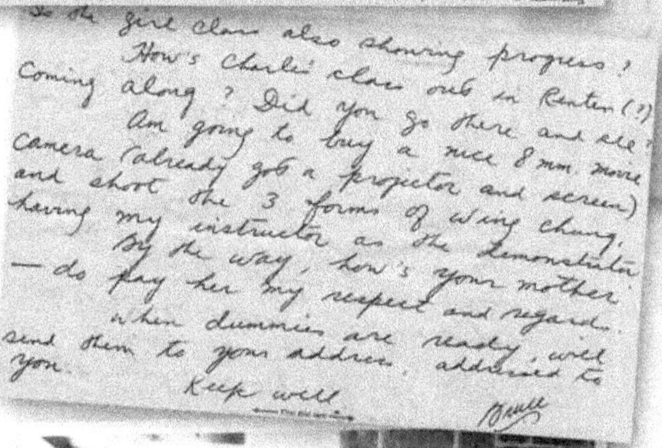

(LEFT) Phoebe Lee hovers over Bruce as they have Yum Cha (Dim Sum) at their family's favorite restaurant in Hong Kong in 1965, upon Bruce's visit back to honor his father after he passed away.

(RIGHT) Bruce working out on the wooden dummy (Mook Jung) 1967 in his garage.

Letter 19

Description of Letter No. 19

I respectfully appreciate the reverence, courtesy and friendship Bruce showed and shared with me through the journey of his life. Bruce was a giver and he gave me many things I carry close to my heart to this day.

Transcription

Taky,

My mother called me long distance last night to let me know that she is coming to the United States for a trip-----the reason: my sister is getting married. Of course, your dummy was definitely brought up and she said all set to go and will mail it tomorrow! Man, she is something else. I, too am waiting for some stuff's she's supposed to send like long time ago---

At any rate, it might take some time but I can assure you that it will come. I'm sorry for the long delay.

She is planning to come at the end of July. After visiting San Leandro, she is flying down to L.A.

Enclosed you will find some pictures taken long time ago. I'm sure you would like to have them as our beloved friend old Charles is in it.

Am waiting for some news like next week----I'll start some private lessons with the stars. $25 an hour. So far the prospects are Vic Damone, Paul Newman, Steve McQueen, Don Gordon, Lloyd Thaxton, etc. I'm planning to fly up to Vegas next month to meet Frank Sinatra. if he for it---I am in.

Among the things I'm waiting for my mother to send is the certificate of Jun Fan Gung Fu Institute. They are very well designed and as soon as I get them I'll issue you the certificate of fourth rank of Jun Fan Gung Fu. You can frame it up to show the friends. Of course, I have to issue to Chris and Tosh too. Who else is included?

Well man, drop me a line when you find the time.

Take care,
Bruce

Taky,

March 29 1966

My mother called me long distance last nite to let me know that she is coming to the United States for a trip-----the reason: my sister is getting married. Of course, your dummy was definitely brought up and she said all set to go and will mail it tomorrow! Man, she is something else. I, too am waiting for some stuffs she's supposed to send like long time ago---------

At any rate, it might take some time but I can assure you that it will come. I'm sorry for the long delay.

She is planning to come at the end of July. After visiting San Leandro, she is flying down to L.A.

Enclosed you will find some pictures taken long time ago. I'm sure you would like to have them as our beloved friend old Charles <u>is</u> in it.

Am waiting for some news like next week----I'll start some private lessons with the stars. $25 an hour. So far the prospects are Vic Damone, Paul Newman, Steve McQueen, Don Gordon, Lloyd Thaxton, ect. I'm planning to fly up to Vegas next month to meet Frank Sinatra. If he goes for it---I am in.

Among the things I'm waiting for my mother to send is the certificate of Jun Fan Gung Fu Institute. They are very well designed and as soon as I get them I'll issue you the certificate of fourth rank of the Jun Fan Gung Fu. You can frame it up to show the friends. Of course, I have to issue to ~~Cha~~ Chris and Tosh too. Who else is included ?

Well man, drop me a line when you find the time.

Take Care

Bruce

Agnes Lee's wedding in 1966. Linda far left, Bruce next to Grace Lee picture right.

Letter **20**

Description of Letter No. 53

When I look at these correspondence with Bruce I get choked up on many points, but the main one would be the fact that these were some, if not the last letters I would receive from Bruce before he passed away. Bruce asked me to be in "The Game of Death", but I refused because I felt I could not give the film justice. I told Bruce that I had two left feet and I would only make he film look bad. Bruce told me I was being ridiculous and too self-conscious and that he would make me look like a pro. Finally, I gave into his demands and agreed to show up for the shoot. Dan and Kareem had already shot their scenes so it was me next, but unfortunately as fate would have it, Bruce passed away and I never got a chance to use those plane tickets they had sent me. I do have those great memories though of Bruce updating me with the progress of his filming, it seemed things were going his way. Bruce stopped production on "The Game of Death" to star in "Enter The Dragon" and after that was completed, he wanted me to come to HK to do my part. Bruce sent me many of picture stills to show me the stuff he already shot with Dan and Kareem. I have to admit, being sent those telegrams from Golden Harvest and Bruce, made me feel as if I was a star myself. Those memories have stayed with me every day.

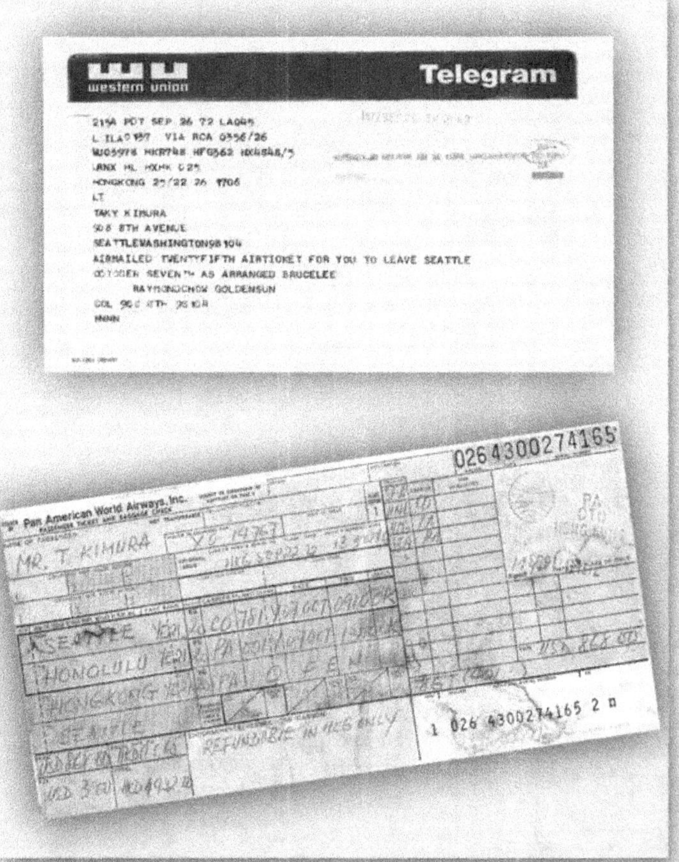

western union Telegram

2154 PDT SEP 26 72 LA085
HONGKONG
LT
TAKY KIMURA
908 8TH AVENUE
SEATTLEWASHINGTON98104
AIRMAILED TWENTYFIFTH AIRTICKET FOR YOU TO LEAVE SEATTLE
OCTOBER SEVENTH AS ARRANGED BRUCELEE
RAYMONDCHOW GOLDENSUN

Pan American World Airways, Inc.
0264300274165
MR. T. KIMURA
SEATTLE
HONOLULU
HONG KONG
SEATTLE
REFUNDABLE IN HCB ONLY
1 026 4300274165 2 0

(TOP) This was a reminder sent from Bruce Lee's office at Golden Harvest that my airline ticket was sent and for me to make sure I was on that plane.

(BOTTOM) This airplane ticket was sent to me by Bruce and Raymond Chow to come to Hong Kong and film "The Game of Death".

GOLDEN HARVEST (INT) LIMITED
嘉禾機構有限公司
8 HAMMER HILL ROAD
KOWLOON HONG KONG
TEL K-250138-9
CABLE ADD GOLDENSUN
香港九龍斧山道八號

Ref. No. 72-1447

[illegible], 1972

Mr. Taky Kimura
908, 8th Avenue
Seattle, Washington 98104
U.S.A.

Dear Mr. Kimura,

As arranged between Bruce and you, I am sending you herewith an air return ticket for you to come to Hong Kong. We have booked you on Continental Airline which will take you to Honolulu on October 7th, and then a Pan Am plane will take you from Honolulu to Hong Kong, arriving here on October 8th.

Please cable us should there be any change at your end on your itinerary. Our cable address is "GOLDENSUN HONGKONG".

Looking forward to seeing you,

Yours faithfully,
GOLDEN HARVEST (INT) LTD

Raymond Chow
Managing Director

GOLDEN HARVEST (INT) LIMITED
嘉禾機構有限公司
8 HAMMER HILL ROAD
KOWLOON HONG KONG
TEL K-250138-9
CABLE ADD GOLDENSUN
香港九龍斧山道八號

Mr. Taky Kimura
908 8 Ave.
Seattle, Washington 98104
U. S. A.

September 20, 1972

Dear Taky:

It was nice to hear your voice when I called you, and I am looking forward to very much getting together for a re-union in Hong Kong after all these years. During these years a lot of water has run past under the bridge.

I will refuse to express myself any more until I see you personally and, by the way, to be dramatic, do bring your old and blue classical Gung Fu uniform back, will you?

They say movies are land of make believe but, baby, you and I together we are going to create belief but beliefs of quality and about truth.

Aeroplane ticket is being sent. Shooting is scheduled for two weeks. If something comes up, I will call you personally. If not, I will see you upon your arrival on or around October 8th.

Take care and have fun.

Peace, Love, Brotherhood,

Bruce Lee

(RIGHT) This letter hits home for me. Bruce would always boost my ego and told me that he and I were going to do great things. Regardless of my worries in doing "The Game of Death", he kept on me in a praising light and in the end I wanted to do it. He told me he would take care of all aspects of making me look like a master warrior. I wish it all transpired.

(INSET) Bruce Lee and James Tien in pose for a picture, behind the scenes of "The Game of Death".

Letter 21

Description of Letter No. 21

On going "pep talk" to "booster" the mind set and maintain positiveness. He was "constant" and philosophical in that regard.

Transcription

Taky,

A brief note to thank you for your help in making my demonstration outstanding. More favorable comments are heard regarding it.

Do start on the uniforms and emblems as soon as you can.

Thanks again and hope to get together for a week in November,

Bruce

Bruce Lee demonstrating the Jun Fan Gung Fu basics on Taky Kimura at a local school in Seattle, while giving a demonstration as Linda looks on.

Taky.

A brief note to thank you for your help in making my demonstration outstanding. More favorable comments are heard regarding it.

Do start on the uniforms and emblems as soon as you can

Thanks again and hope to get together for a week in November

Bruce

Letter 22

Description of Letter No. 22

This might have been my last participating gathering at Ed Parkers Championships with Bruce, helping Bruce highlight his talents as a martial artist. I honor those times, they were both fun and insightful at the same time.

Transcription

Taky,

By now Ed Parker MUST have contacted you. So as soon as you make plane arrangement, let me know. James Lee will be coming down too and also Jhoon Rhee of Wash. D.C. will be staying as a guest at the house. So this coming week-end will be a lot of people at the house.

I'm looking forward for your visit. Also be sure to bring the sample uniform down. It should be ready by now; I wrote you a letter quite a while back asking for it.

So let me as soon as you can regarding your flights information plus the uniform.

See you,

Bruce

Left to right, Linda Lee, Bruce Lee, James Lee, Ed Parker with his son Ed Parker Jr. in Long Beach, California before Ed Parker's Internationals Karate Championships.

Taky,

By now Ed Parker MUST have contacted you. So as soon as you make plane arrangement, let me know. James Lee will be coming down too and also Jhoon Rhee of Wash. D.C. will be staying as a guest at the house. So this coming week-end will be a lot of people at the house.

I'm looking forward for your visit. Also be sure to bring the sample uniform down. It should be ready by now; I wrote you a letter quite a while back asking for it.

So let me as soon as you can regarding your flight ~~room~~ information plus the uniform

See You.

Letter 23

Description of Letter No. 23

This was for Ed Parker's Long Beach Karate tournament. I attended the 1964 and 1967 ones and as I remember it was always an honor to perform / demonstrate with Bruce. I was so honored that he told Ed Parker that he needed me to put on the demo with him. As they did not want to pay my ticket, but ended up doing so at the request of Bruce. It was an honor to be Bruce's dummy / fall guy at the expense of getting my butt kicked and uniform torn. I TREASURE THOSE MOMENTS!

Bruce Lee and Ed Parker pose for a picture at Ed Parker's house in Pasadena, California.

936 MEI LING WAY . LOS ANGELES CALIF 90012 . MA 6-1287

July 24, 1967

AIRMAIL

Mr. Taky Kimura
908 8th Avenue
Seattle 4, Washington

Dear Taky:

Looking forward to seeing you.

Ticket is open. Come at your own convenience.

Hope to see you put on a fine performance...

Sincerely,

Lily Kobayashi
LEE'S TRAVEL SERVICE
for Ed Parker

EP/lk

enc: a/s

NOTE: Ticket is based on domestic excursion fare.
Travel is permitted between:

12 Noon/Monday - 12 Noon/Friday and
12:01AM/Saturday - 12 Noon/Sunday

cc: Mr. Ed Parker

Letter 24A

Description of Letter No. 24

Each of Bruce's letters or phone calls were very important to me and sincerely "humbled" me. His consistency of caring and brotherly love was unmatchable. After all these years, it still resonates to the highest degree with me and I strive to pass it over to my students as well.

Transcription

Taky, Sep 18 1964

I did not write because I was on tour ----- they flipped in Los Angeles and San Francisco after the performance.

Now I am debating whether I should go to New York with the group as my absence will influence the student rates ----- due to my long absence we have right-now 24 students. One thing though, they keep coming in steadily.

I am beginning to form a structure of my own principle using Wing Chun as foundation and my boundary lines as the skeleton ------ the method will be "freedom within boundary and beyond the boundary" I am going to invent these forms as the structure of my own school, the first will be concentrating on ELIMINATION --- to move within boundary; the second will be simplicity of attack / defense and finally the third, which will be the all in one and the one in all --- the grand harmony of sticking and non sticking. In other word, the third will be the training of freedom in which everything flow within and beyond the boundary using no limitation as limitation and no way as way. Wing Chun is very good but need to be transcribed --- to bring it out from the nutshell.

When I've completed this I'll teach them to you. Together with sticking hand, this method will form two halves of one whole and I can only say this ------- it will be most surging.

Linda is a very fine wife and I'm enjoying married life a lot. The kid (I hope it's a son) starts his side kick in the mother's stomach already. The doctor said it's a pretty big baby.

Taky, use your effort and thinking to keep the Jun Fan going in Seattle ---- do your very best to expand it. At the same time, work hard to and practice hard to back up the Way of Jun Fan. Do not let me down, I've placed my thought on you.

Write me often and keep me inform of situation up there.

Bruce

Sep 13 1964

Taky

I did not write because I was on a tour — They flipped in Los Angeles and San Francisco after the performance

Now I am debating whether I should go to New York with the group as my absence will influence the student rates — due to my long absence we have right now 24 student. One thing though, they keep coming in steadily.

I am beginning to form a structure of my own principle using Wing Chung as foundation and my boundary lines as the skeleton — the method will be "freedom within boundary and beyond the boundary" I am going to invent three forms as the structure of my own school, the first will be ~~the~~ concentrating on ELIMINATION — to move within boundary; the second will be simplicity of attack / defense and finally the third, which is all in one and the — the grand harmony and non sticking. In the third will be the training of Freedom in which everything flow within and beyond the boundary, ~~using~~ using no limitation as limitation and no way as way. Wing Chung is very good but need to be transcended — to bring it out from the nut shell.

When I've completed the I'll teach them to you. Together with sticking hand, this method will form two halves of one whole and I can only say this — it will be most swinging.

Linda is a very fine wife and I'm enjoying married life a lot. The kid (I hope it's a son) starts his side kick in the mother's stomach already. The doctor said it's a pretty big baby.

Taky, use your effort and thinking to keep the Jun

Letter 24B

Description of Letter No. 24

Each of Bruce's letters or phone calls were very important to me and sincerely "humbled" me. His consistency of caring and brotherly love was unmatchable. After all these years, it still resonates to the highest degree with me and I strive to pass it over to my students as well.

Transcription (continued)

(LINDA) Dear Taky,

Just thought I'd add a few lines to say hello. I suppose winter is already setting in on Seattle, but the sun is still shinning down here. It's quite a life – in fact it's 3:00 pm right now and we just finished breakfast. Hope you are not working too hard.

(BRUCE) (you know square Linda, she doesn't know what she's talking. I better shut her up right now!)

(LINDA) Sorry my letter is so uninteresting. Say hello to my mother if you see her.

Your square friend,

Linda

Bruce Lee in 1963, Hong Kong, at Yip Man's studio practicing with an acquaintance. While Bruce went back to HK in 1963 to visit his family, he was also investigating as many martial arts styles as he could, do to the fact that he wanted to bring that knowledge back to the United States.

Fan going in Seattle — do your very best to expand it. At the same time, work hard ~~to~~ and practice hard to back up the Way of Jun Fan. Do not let me down, I've placed my thought on you.

Write me often and keep me inform of the situation up there.

Bruce

Dear Taky,

Just thought I'd add a few lines to say hello. I suppose winter is already setting in on Seattle, but the sun is still shining down here. It's quite a life — in fact it's 3:00 pm right now and we just finished breakfast. Hope you are not working too hard

(You know Square Linda, she doesn't know what she's talking, I better shut her up right now!)

Sorry my letter is so uninteresting. Say hello to my mother if you see ~~you~~ her.

(SHE SHORE IS) → Your square friend,
Linda

Letter 25

Description of Letter No. 25

Bruce was getting dissatisfied with the many politics of doing the demonstrations. He felt how long could he keep that type of thing going without boring the audience within that repetitive act. Bruce was on a daily learning regime. He was constantly changing his view in how he would pursue his own destiny within the martial arts world. From the first demonstration he did which was mainly Gung Fu based, he came along way into what he wanted to share with the world, which was his development of Jeet Kune Do. I think it was not so much the struggle of the act of doing the demos, but more of he developing JKD on such a fast pace. What he would show in one demo one month, would be different the next month. Bruce also wanted to have more one on one sessions with me, because of the fact his JKD was taking over the basic teachings he gave me in the begining. So, it was in my best interest to know all he was doing on both sides of the table and when he introduced me to his Jeet Kune Do, it was like a light when off in my head and I said this is it. But for me, Bruce's Jun Fan Gung Fu and Jeet Kune Do compliment one another, you can't have one without the other, it is evolution...

Transcription

Taky,

Well, that Armstrong wired for apology----"do not understand mix-up accommodation", etc. etc. I told him I can't make it due to another commitment.

Really, I'm sick of demonstrations. I have established my position already in the world of martial arts. My name is known both East and West.

By now you might have received both the certification and editor I've sent. I've mailed them yesterday.

Since I'm not coming up this week. I'll be looking forward to your coming here in Nov. If you can stay more than the weekend, so much the better. As I've pointed out, this coming meeting will be the most beneficial to your cultivation in "Jeet Kune Do", no longer Wing Chun. It might be your enlightenment in the Way of combat.

I'm still working on my book. I hope to have it finished the end of the year.

Have you started on the "lesson plan" yet? I'm positive that it will bring result in the proposed time period.

Take Care my friend.

Bruce

Taky.

Well, that Armstrong wired for apology.... "do not understand mix-up accomodation", etc. etc. I told him I can't make it due to another commitment.

Really, I'm sick of demonstrations. I have established my position already in the world of martial arts. My name is known both east and west.

By now you might have received both the certificate and editor I've sent. I've mailed them yesterday.

Since I'm not coming up this week, I'll be looking forward to your coming here in Nov. If you can stay more than the weekend, so much the better. As I've pointed out, this coming meeting will be the most beneficial to your cultivation in "Jeet Kune Do", no longer Wing Chun. It might be your enlightenment in the Way of Combat.

I'm still working on my book. I hope to have it finished the end of this year.

Have you started on the "lesson plan" yet? I'm positive that it will bring result in the proposed time period.

Take Care my friend.

Bruce Lee at the Ed Parker Championships, demonstrating his speed and agility on a volunteer provided by Ed Parker. I can't help but say that anyone on the receiving end of Bruce's martial arts, would become a true believer afterwards.

Letter 26

Description of Letter No. 26

Bruce always updated me on his schedule. He always made time to work in Hollywood, but also make it to Seattle to make an appearance within the class, as well as teach me things that he developed as his martial arts progressed more into the "Jeet Kune Do" philosophy. He was very structured in what he was doing and he never forgot the other person or his obligations. He also expressed to me in how different projects were coming his way after "Green Hornet" wrapped up. Though he struggled at times after "Green Hornet", he always had many things to do on his plate and many wanted to work along side him too.

Linda's mother bragged about Bruce all the time to her friends in what he was doing martially as well as acting wise, so she asked Bruce to put on a demonstration for her and her friends. Bruce being very accommodating couldn't refuse. It was fun to do and Bruce always liked showing himself off.

Though this letter is in bad shape, I treasure it dearly. It was found after years and years in a box that suffered some water damaged, but when I had it in my hands, those memories came back two fold.

Transcription

Taky,

It looks like a 99% chance of my coming to Seattle on the 27th of this month. I'll come by way of New York, after my demonstration at the All American Open Karate Championship sponsored by Henry Cho.

The CBS. deal is pushed back to November and the one hr. fantasy they try to sell now as a one hr. special to Fox as a test like pilot to see reception (if it sells to Fox). This season They are very star conscious, they want big name, thus this turning into a special to see if my name can carry the show that is, the just test is if Fox is interested at all, since no one makes money on a special. All in all, the whole picture is as usual, one of waiting, waiting and waiting.

Did you find out about uniforms? Let me know on that.

I'll be leaving for Oakland just (probably this coming Monday nite) to bring my dog down to a vet (James student) to keep while I am away.

See you soon

(I'll stay three days this time)

Bruce
(OVER)

By the way, Linda's mother is planning on renting a hall to invite all her friends to come. So I can do a demonstration before them ~~~ she is carrying away ~~~ so I need your help if and when she does rent it. Linda is in Seattle right now, probably you can call her to find out more about it. Call her next week because by then I should know definite when I'm coming.

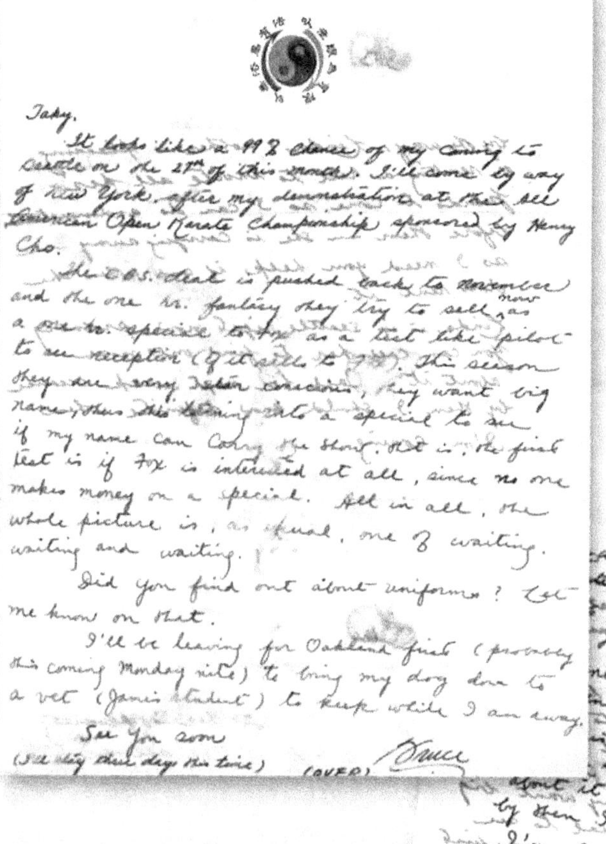

Taky,

It looks like a 99% chance of my coming to Seattle on the 27th of this month. I'll come by way of New York, after my demonstration at the All American Open Karate Championship sponsored by Henry Cho.

The CBS deal is pushed back to November and the one hr. fantasy they try to sell now as a one hr. special to Fox as a test like pilot to see reception (if it sells to Fox). This season they are very Nielsen conscious, they want big names, thus this turning into a special to see if my name can carry the show. That is, the first test is if Fox is interested at all, since no one makes money on a special. All in all, the whole picture is, as usual, one of waiting, waiting and waiting.

Did you find out about uniforms? Let me know on that.

I'll be leaving for Oakland first (probably this coming Monday nite) to bring my dog down to a vet (James' student) to keep while I am away.

See you soon
(I'll stay three days this time) (OVER) Bruce

... Linda & mother ...
... to Seattle all her ...
... to come so I can ...
them in she is carrying away.
need your help ...
... it.
... in Seattle ...
... her to find out ...
about it. Call her next week because by then I should know definite when I'm coming

Bruce Lee playing around in martial form with co-star Wendy Wagner on the 20th Century Fox studio lot.

Letter 27A

Description of Letter No. 27

This letter to say the least shows the success Bruce was accomplishing within in all aspects of his life. Everything seemed to be thriving for Bruce at that time and his celebrity client list was growing almost daily. Bruce's words to me were very consoling when he would tell me I was his most trusted friend. We both relied on one another completely and shared many private moments. Bruce is the one who brought me out of my shell so to speak after all the years I spent feeling less than human from my experience, being in the interment camps.

Transcription

Taky, *March 25 1966*

Received your registered letter. Thank you for your trouble.

It is always nice to hear from you. Taky, you are the senior student, my top student. You are the most trusted one and your loyalty is beyond compared with anyone here or in Hong Kong. I'm looking forward for the T.V. series of "Green Hornet" to come out so that Gung Fu will catch on. After that, you will be an important part of my institute plus being the Washington State representative of the Institute.

I'm still working on the private lesson ~~~~so far the prospective students are: - Steve McQueen, James Garner, Donald Gordon, Lloyd Thaxton, Paul Newman, ------- these suckers don't like to be pushed in to it. So I have to abide by the right time. Oh yes, Vic Damone is pretty sure of taking, and so is Carrol Shelby, the Industrialist of Ford racing car. The fees will be $25.00 an hour. strictly private lessons~~ Vic Damone is arranging a five men group for me in Las Vegas to teach (the first hour is $50.00 and hour). Vic is currently appearing in Sands and this sucker is yelling Gung Fu all over the place and Bill Jee to all his friends.

By the way, I've bought a Chevy 2 Nova 1966. Linda's mother helped us put the downpayment. she is really nice about the whole thing. As you know a car is indispensable, especially here in Los Angeles.

Currently, I'm taking acting lesson from a drama coach, a Mr. Jeff Cory. This man is credited to be the best in the movie industry. I believe 20th Century Fox is paying him like $70 an hour. I meet him for around three times a week. It's interesting because this cat is very Zen-ish.

I have my script with me ---- the "Green Hornet" and one scene is which Britt ("Green Hornet") turned to Kato and yelled "Gung Fu!!!" ---- of course Kato moves is and finishes the crooks.

Taky, march 25 1966

Received your registered letter. Thank you for your trouble.

It is always nice to hear from you. Taky, you *are* *the* senior student, my top student. You are the most trusted one and your loyalty is beyond compared with anyone here or in Hong Kong. I'm looking forward for the T.V. series of "Green Hornet" to come out so that Gung Fu will catch on. After that, you will be an important part of my Institute plus being the Washington state representative of the Institute.

I'm still working on the private lesson — so far the prospective students are:- Steve McQueen, James Gardner, Donald Gordon, Lloyd Thaxton, Paul Newman, ------- these suckers don't like to be pushed in to it, so I have to abide by the right time. Oh yes, Vic Damone is pretty sure of taking, and so is Carrol Shelby, the Industrialist of Ford racing Car. The fees will be $25.00 an hour, strictly private lessons— Vic Damone is arranging a five men group for me in Las Vegas to teach (the first hour is $50.00 an hour). Vic is currently appearing in Sands and this sucker is yelling Gung Fu all over the place and Bill Lee to all his friends.

By the way, I've bought a Chev II nova 1966. Linda's mother helped us put the downpayment. She is really nice about

As you know a car is indis-
lly here in Los Angeles.
I'm taking acting lesson
Coach, a mr. Jeff Cory. This
to be the best in the
I believe 20th Century Fox is
$70 an hour. I meet
three times a week. It's
this Cat is very Jewish.
my script with me — the
one scene in which
Hornet) turned to Kato
ng Fu !!!" ---- Of course
moves in and finishes the crooks.

The apartment needs to be cleaned up yet — of course there is the ironing --- and man like everything -----

I still remember the 8 mm. movie which I will shoot the first chance I have --- like the Tai Kik (Tai Chi); the techniques; and whatever you have in mind write me about it. I'm telling you! my old lady in Hong Kong is something else! I've just written her to rush her to rush the wooden dummy. The reason is one of the sister of my father died recently. Still, the dummy should be here long time ago! I mean like it was complete when I left Hong Kong and that was quite a time ago. Lucky you know me so well --- other person might think I didn't even order it.

(0164)

Letter 27B

Description of Letter No. 27

In his letter, Bruce always used to tell me what was happening in his life. When I look at this letter, I remember great moments of going out to eat with him and discussing the martial arts, as well as how his career was going. Bruce and I shared many moments like this.

Transcription (continued)

The apartment needs to be cleaned up yet ~~~ of course there is the ironing --- and man like everything-----

I still remember the 8mm. movie which I will shoot the first chance I have --- like the Tai kik (Tai Chi); the techniques; and whatever you have in mind write me about it. I'm telling you! My old lady in Hong Kong is something else! I've just written her to rush her to rush the wooden dummy. The reason is one of the sister of my father died recently. Still, the dummy should be here long time ago! I mean like it was complete when I left Hong Kong and that was quite a time ago. Lucky you know me so well ---- other person might think I didn't even order it.

(over)

At any rate, drop me a line more often and let me know how things are. If you have any question regarding Gung Fu – technical or administrational – feel free to ask.

Take good care of yourself.

Bruce

P.S. If Tosh, Chris or John likes to drop me a line, give them my address. When will Chris be coming down this way again?

At any rate, drop me a line more often and let me know how things are. If you have any question regarding Gung Fu — technical or adminstrational — feel free to ask.

Take good care of yourself.

Bruce

P.S. If Josh, Chris or John likes to drop me a line, give them my address. When will Chris be coming down this way again!

Stoic pose of Bruce Lee as Kato on set of The Green Hornet, *the "Praying Mantis" episode.*

Letter 28A

Description of Letter No. 28

Bruce was a very funny and witty guy. Here you can see his disappointment in having to keep waiting to get to work as Kato in the "Green Hornet". I think at this time he started to realize that Hollywood could be a little bit difficult to navigate in. He was really over the "Batman" show and felt it was really a nothing production, but he knew his place and waited it out. During down time in his quest to get recognition in Hollywood, Bruce would go to different places to be apart of karate / martial arts demonstrations and as mention in this letter, Bruce got a kick out of the mentioning that he was a legend. Fast-forward all these years and with no surprise, he is just that, a "LEGEND"!

Transcription

Taky,

The 20th Century Fox deal is further postponed to next year. They have to wait for rating of "Batman". As far as I'm concern the Batman got to go, but I heard the rating is good though, probably 99% from children and imbeciles.

At any rate William Dozier is willing to pay $1200 for the postponement (after all he is sincere) and that if the pilot is made for the "Green Hornet", I'll be Kato without further tests. Also, I receive a telegram from him that Life Magazine will contact me for action shots for advance publicity. So for I haven't heard from Life but I did write my agent (that good for nothing sucker) to request for $1800 for round trip tickets to Hong Kong for one year.

The following lists are books that when you have time you should read:

Fencing ---

(1) Fencing – by Maxwell R. $1.95) Garret (Athletic Institute series – 1961)

(2) Sports Illustrated Book of fencing ---- by editors of ($2.95) sport illustrated, 1962

(3) Fencing with the Foil --- By Roger Crosnier

Boxing --

(1) Boxing ---- by the U.S. Navy (u.w. use this as a text book for the boxing class – It's pretty thorough) written by Roy D. Simmons, IKE T. DEETER AND ANTHONY J. Rubino

(2) Boxing (The Barnes Sports Library) by Edwin L. Haisret

(3) Rocky Marciano's book of Boxing and Bodybuilding by Marciano & Goldman, Prentice-hall (1959)

I'm now waiting for (1) Dozier's money (2) Hong Kong visa and (3) Film Company reply from Hong Kong. Most likely I'm leaving on the early part of March.

Taky.

The 20th Century Fox deal is further postponed to next year. They have to wait for rating of "Batman". As far as I'm concerned the Batman got to go, but I heard the rating is good though, probably 99% from children and imbeciles.

At any rate William Dozier is willing to pay me $1200 for the postponement. (after all he is sincere) and that if the pilot is made for the Green Hornet, I'll be Kato without further tests. Also, I receive a telegram from him that Life magazine will contact me for action shots for advance publicity. So far I haven't heard from Life ~~and~~ but I did write my agent (that good for nothing sucker) to request for $1800 for round trip tickets to Hong Kong for one year.

The following ~~to~~ lists are books that when you have time you should read: —

Fencing —

① Fencing — by Maxwell R. Garret (Athletic Institute Series – 1961) ($1.95)

② Sports Illustrated Book of Fencing — by editors of Sports Illustrated 1962 ($2.95)

ncing with the Foil — By Roger Crosnier

xing — by the U.S. Navy (U.W. use this as textbook for the boxing class – it's pretty thorough) itten by Roy D. Simmons, Ike F. Deeter and Anthony J. Rubino.

XING (The Barnes Sports Library) by Edwin L. Haislet

③ Rocky Marciano's Book of Boxing and Bodybuilding by Marciano & Goldman Prentice-Hall (1957)

I'm now waiting for ① Dozier's money ② Hong Kong visa and ③ Film Company reply from Hong Kong. Most likely I'm leaving for the early part of March.

I'm asked for demonstration at two Karate World Tournament, one in San Jose Civic Auditorium on Feb. 20 and the other one in San Francisco Civic Auditorium on March 6. I haven't decided completely yet, but I think I probably make it. I have to, you know why, because one

Letter 28B

Description of Letter No. 28

Bruce would always update me in what he was reading martially and requested I would pick up the same books if he did not give them to me himself. Bruce was a dedicated reader and wanted to learn as much as he could, his library was stacked with vintage and up to date books. Just looking at his library, you would never think he could have read all those books, but he did.

Transcription

I'm asked for demonstration at Two Karate World Tournament, one in San Jose Civic Auditorium on Feb. 20 and the other one in San Francisco Civic Auditorium on March 6. I haven't decided completely yet, but I think I probably make it I have to, you know why, because one of the ad, on the Karate invitation printed my name on it and what is more they printed ---"Bruce Lee, if he is in the country at that time, will perform ----- he is a legend in his own time" well, I better train like hell to live up to the legend!

How are you coming along? I hope you have recovered completely. drop me a line and let me know how things are and is the meantime, take good care of yourself.

Bruce

Just sitting around doing nothing!

Bruce Lee posing in front of his library of books in his Barrington Plaza apartment office.

of the ad on the Karate invitation printed my name on it and what is more they printed --- "Bruce Lee, if he is in the Country at that time, will perform ----- he is a legend in his own time" Well, I better train like hell to live up to that legend!

How are you coming along? I hope you have recovered completely.

drop me a line and let me know how things are and in the meantime, take good care of yourself.

Bruce

Just sitting around doing nothing!

Letter 29

Description of Letter No. 29

Bruce went back to Hong Kong in 1965 with Linda and Brandon, initially to pay respects to his father who passed away at that time. This was the first time he took Linda to Hong Kong and she had a great time Bruce said. His family treated her like gold and Brandon was the focus of the huge family he had there. Bruce also was waiting to hear back from 20th Century Fox regarding his role as Kato in the "Green Hornet", so he was very anxious to get back to the States and proceed with that role if it were given to him. We all know now that the role was catered to Bruce as he made history as Kato worldwide.

From left to right are Linda Lee, Phoebe Lee Grace Lee Eva Tso holding little Brandon, Bruce Lee, Stephen Kwan (friend) Bruce's cousin Chan Tak Sung. Bottom left is Auntie number 8.

Transcription

Dear Taky,

Here I am writing once more from Hong Kong. Linda and I have been here for around three days now and she likes every bit of it, except the growing heat. She never had it so good ------ you know servants and what not.

I plan to stay here for around three months and as soon as 20th Century Fox writes me I have to go back to Hollywood Studios for either some more test or the pilot. As you've probably known

I've signed a contract with the agent, Belasco, who, by the way, is also agent for Nick Adam and many other.

Keep me inform on the club and if you send anything at all, do send it to my Hong Kong add. By the way, is there anything I can pick up for you in Hong Kong. Don't feel hesitate to ask.

I'll keep you inform of my trip.

Take care and have fun

Bruce

Dear Taky,

Here I am writing once more from Hong Kong. Linda and I have been here for around three days now and she likes every bit of it, except the growing heat. She never had it so good — you know servant and what not.

I plan to stay here for around three months and as soon as 20th Century Fox writes me I have to go back to the Hollywood studio for either some more test or the pilot. As you've probably known I've signed a contract with the agent. Belasco, who, by the way, is also agent for Nick Adam and many other.

Keep me inform on the club and if you send anything at all,

to my Hong Kong add

is there anything I can

for you in Hong Kong

hesitate to ask.

keep you inform

care and have fun

Bruce

AEROGRAMME

HONG KONG

Mr. Taky Kimura
908 - 8th Ave
Seattle 4,
Washington
U.S.A.

Sender's name and address: Bruce Lee
28 Nathan Rd. 1/F
Kowloon, Hong Kong

AN AIR LETTER SHOULD NOT CONTAIN ANY ENCLOSURE; IF IT DOES IT WILL BE SURCHARGED OR SENT BY ORDINARY MAIL.

Letter 30

Description of Letter No. 30

Bruce was in Hong Kong visiting family after his father passed away. Besides the sadness of returning there to morn, Bruce had a chance to really show Linda and even small Brandon where he came from and the many relatives who they never met. It was a bitter and sweet reunion.

Transcription

Taky, *May 28 1965*

I've been showing Linda around and that's why I've not written till now. Linda enjoys every bit of it – except the hot weather (not as bad as 1963) --- She has also bought quite a few tailor made clothes.

I'll be here till 20th Century Fox notifies me to return for the actual shooting, which will be another 2 more months I think. Although a contract has been proposed, the whole deal is not 100%, however, it is 70% that it will succeed. At least, that's what my agent told me.

In the meantime I've been teaching my brothers and some friends Gung Fu at my house. They are very enthused over the whole deal. I, too, am working on my transformation of simplicity to yet another more free flow movements of no limit limitation.

Oyama's book "This is Karate" is out and it is quite interesting as it contains quite a few of ancient Gung Fu method. As for actual application of techniques, it is still too far behind. He admits that Gung Fu's theory is more sound and practical.

Shock to hear of 2nd Clay- Liston fight. if it wasn't a fix, Liston must have timed in on the coming force of Clay's punch.By the way, if there is any dues I'll appreciate it if you can send them to me.

Also, do report on the class progress as well as yours and Charlie.

Bruce

Taky,

May 28 1965

I've been showing Linda around and that's why I've not written till now. Linda enjoys every bit of it — except the hot weather (not as bad as 1963) — She has also bought quite a few tailor made clothes.

I'll be here till 20th Century Fox notifies me to return for the actual shooting, which will be another 2 more months I think. Although a contract has been proposed, the whole deal is not 100%; however, it is 70% that it will succeed. At least, that's what my agent told me.

In the meantime I've been teaching my brothers and some friends Gung Fu at my house. They are very enthused over the whole deal. I, too, am working on my transformation of simplicity to yet another more free flow ~~m~~ movement of no limit ~~n~~ limitation.

Oyama's book "This is Karate" is out and it is quite interesting as it contains quite a few of ancient Gun

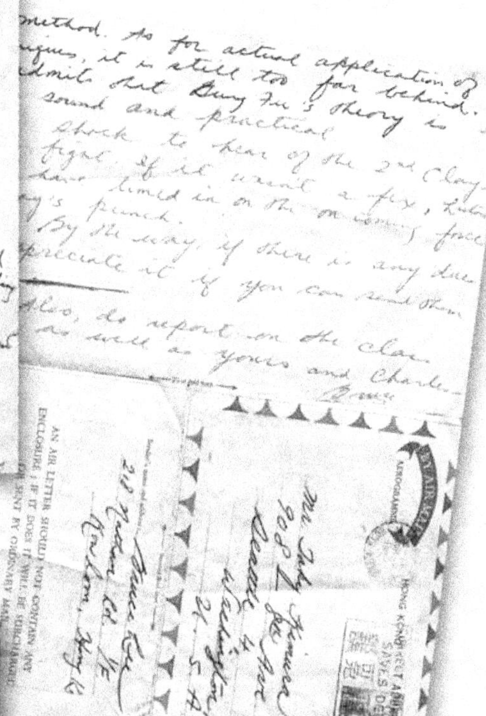

method. As for actual application of
...niques, it is still too far behind.
...dmits that Gung Fu's theory is
sound and practical.
Shock to hear of the 2nd Clay-
fight. If it wasn't a fix, ...
...y's punch.
By the way, if there is any dues
...preciate it if you can send them.
Also, do report on the class
as well as yours and Charles.
Bruce

Mr. Taky Kimura
908 ...
Seattle 4,
Washington
U.S.A.

Bruce Lee
218 Nathan Rd.
Kowloon, Hong Kong

AN AIR LETTER SHOULD NOT CONTAIN ANY ENCLOSURE; IF IT DOES IT WILL BE SURCHARGED OR SENT BY ORDINARY MAIL

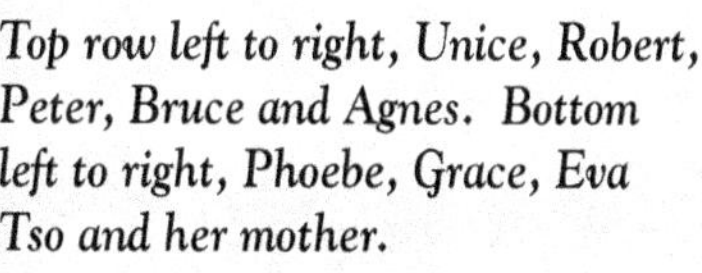

Top row left to right, Unice, Robert, Peter, Bruce and Agnes. Bottom left to right, Phoebe, Grace, Eva Tso and her mother.

Letter 31

Description of Letter No. 31

In this letter, Bruce talks about the "Batman", "Green Hornet" crossover episode that would introduce him to the world as Kato. Bruce was so funny, he couldn't stand the fact that he had to put up with Burt Ward's double, because he was so slow and he also hated the fact that the fight would come off 50/50, as he wanted to really cream Robin and show Kato's prowess. Later on, Bruce would also discover that Burt ward lived at the Barrington Plaza suite apartments like he did, that really threw him through a loop. I think at that time there was a lot of benign competition with them both in some ways. But we all now know that Kato came out on top!

Transcription

Taky,

Just got back from the sporting good store ---~ the special head-gear they have on sale are all sold out. However, I did find out about those gloves and you can send a check of $15 to Dan Inosanto and he will get it for you ~~ 212 Palos Verde Blvd. Redondo Beach, Cal. 90277 As for the headgear, buy a regular boxing head- gear (enclosed you will find some sample from Ring Magazine), it will be sufficient.

How's the class coming along? I'm sure everything will smooth out and shape up better and better.

I'm doing a "Batman" now ~~~~~ the "Green Hornet" and Kato will be the guest heros. I'm going to fight with Robin and we are supposed to come out 50/50 even and it's going to be a pain in the neck ~~~ that slow awkward double of his!

The Hornet series stopped shooting and will wait till April to find out whether or not we will be on for next year ~~~ as an hour.

Take Care my friend

Bruce

Bruce Lee fighting off Robin in the now famous cross over episode. Bruce hated the fact he had to be Robin's equal. He wanted to cream him good.

Taky,

Just got back from the sporting good store — the special headgear they have on sale are all sold out. However, I did find out about those gloves and you can send a check of $15 to Dan Inosanto and he will get it for you — 212 Palos Verdes Blvd. Redondo Beach, Cal. 90277 As for the headgear, buy a regular boxing headgear (enclosed you will find some sample from Ring magazine); it will be sufficient.

How's the class coming along? I'm sure everything will smooth out and shape up better and better.

I'm doing a Batman now — the Green Hornet and Kato will be the guest heros. I'm going to fight with Robin and we are supposed to come out 50/50 even and it's going to be a pain in the neck — that slow awkward double of his!

The Hornet series stopped shooting and will wait till April to find out whether or not we will be on for next year — as an hour.

Take Care my friend

Bruce

Letter 32A

Description of Letter No. 32

I receive this letter as one intimate brother to another. Bruce was explaining to me both the "positives" and the negatives. I was, and am, humbled that Bruce considered me as a true brother to him. I was privy to his most intimate feelings.

Transcription

Taky, 4/18/1966

It's nice to have received your letter. Everything is running smoothly here in L.A. If I didn't tell you, the date has set for the shooting (though as of now there isn't a "Green Hornet"); it will be on the 23rd of next month.

By the way, I'll be moving to another really "cool" apartment, the Barrington Plaza----a 27 stories high luxury tower living with doormen and attendant parking, laundry & dry cleaning valet service, olympic-sized pool, all-wool carpeting, all electric kitchen (dishwasher, built-in range and oven, etc.), electronic huge elevators.

I'll be living on the 23rd story (the higher the more expensive) and I'm telling you it's something else. However, do not think for a moment that I'll pay $300 a month for this apartment (that's how much it actually cost); you see the half owner of the apartment wishes to take Gung Fu from me and so I got a damn good deal on it. The present apartment I'm living in costs $120 (L.A. apartments cost more---especially in the western part) and get a load of this------for all those fancy deal (oh, there is a breakfast bar too) this apartment that I'm moving in now cost me $140 a month! All the services I've mentioned----like doormen, attendant parking, security guards, house services--------are all included in the deal. By the way, Batman and Robin also live there. So far tow hours on the private lesson for the owner, I only pay for half the rent. This Barrington Plaza is a famous spot here and you have to see it to appreciate it-----like a park inside with two gigantic 27 stories tower buildings surroundind it, with all kinds of stores and what not on the bottom level. They claim you can live a year inside the place with- out having to go out and buy anything!

So much for that. I'm glad to hear that the boys are loyal to the school. I think Chris should be promoted to 3rd. His loyalty certainly demands attention, but his laziness and drive is something else......well, I'll leave this matter in you

hand and you will have to judge and see what fits. You are the head instructor in charge and will decide on him----on the rest of the boys in fact. You have the authority to give out rank you know. By the way, you are the only one that can do so. So let me know what your decision is and if there is any membership card that needs to be stamped by my zeal just tell the student to send them to you and you mail them to me.

Let me tell you an incident that is a warning to us all. The Japan America Society of Southern California was presenting a demonstration of 'The Defensive Arts---Aikido, Judo, Kendo and Karate'. Hidetaka

4/18/1966

Taky,

It's nice to have recieved your letter. Everything is running smoothly here in L.A. If I didn't tell you, the date has set for the shooting (though as of now there isn't a Green Hornet) ; it will be on the 23rd of next month.

By the way, I'll be moving to another really "cool" apartment, the Barrington Plaza----a 27 stories high luxury tower living with doormen and attendant parking, laundry & dry cleaning valet service, olympic-sized pool, all-wool carpeting, all electric kitchen (dishwasher, built-in range and oven, ect.), electronic huge elevators............I'll be living on the 23rd story (the higher the more expensive) and I'm telling you it's something else. However, do not think for a moment that I'll pay $300 a month for this apartment(that's how much it actually cost); you see the half owner of the apartment wishes to take Gung Fu from me and so I got a damn good deal on it. The present apartment I'm living in costs $120(L.A.'s apartments cost more---especially in the western part) and get a load of this------for all those fancy deal (oh, there is a breakfast bar too) this apartment that I'm moving in now cost me $140 a month! All the services I've mentioned----like doormen, attendant parking, security guards, house services--------are all inclided in the deal. By the way, Batman and Robin also live there. So for two hours on the private lesson for the owner, I only pay for half the rent. This Barrington Plaza is a famous spot here and you have to see it to appreciate it-----like a park inside with two gigantic 27 stories tower buildings surroundind it, with all kinds of stores and what not on the bottom level. They claim you can live a year inside the place without having to go out and buy anything!

So much for that. I'm glad to hear that the boys are loyal to the school. I think Chris should be promoted to 3rd. His loyalty certainly demands attention, but his laziness and drive is something else......well, I'll leave this matter in your hand and you will have to judge and see what fits. You are the head instructor in charge and you will decide on him----on the rest of the boys in fact. You have the authority to give out rank you know. By the way, you are the only one that can do so. So let me know what your decision is and if there is any membership card that needs to be stamped by my zeal just tell the student to send them to you and you mail them to me.

Let me tell you an incident that is a warning to us all. The Japan America Society of Southern California was presenting a demonstration of 'The Defensive Arts---Aikido, Judo, Kendo, and Karate'. Hidetaka Nishiyama was heading the demonstration and I and the ex-publisher of Black Belt, Ed Jung was there. It was a dissappointment! The Nishyama of four years ago (in Washington) has slipped and

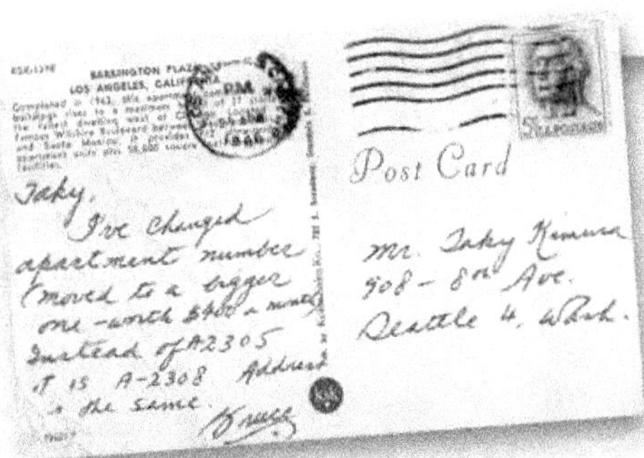
BARRINGTON PLAZA
LOS ANGELES, CALIFORNIA

Post Card

Taky,
I've changed apartment number
I moved to a bigger one—worth $400 a month
Instead of A2305
it is A-2308 Address is the same.
Bruce

Mr. Taky Kimura
908 - 8th Ave.
Seattle 4, Wash.

A postcard from Bruce Lee to Taky Kimura, telling him of his new found home.

Letter **32B**

Description of
Letter No. 32

Transcription (continued)

Nishiyama was heading the demonstration and I and the ex-publisher of "Black Belt", Ed Jung was there. It was a disappointment! The Nishyama of four years ago (in Washington) has slipped and what is now is an old man-like Nishyama who couldn't even snap decently nor can he show his techniques smartly----not even in a classical manner. It was a quick change from the last time I saw him. At least at that time he can classically demonstrate his techniques with precision and snap........So that goes to prove the old Chinese saying "song (singing) never leave the mouth, first never leave the hand". Do we have to work work, work--------the Aikido is something else! Completely out of reality. There might be a strong Aikido man, but his power is evidence only when he practice among his fellow partner who will dance with him and fool around with his flow of ki.

Taky, you have something over John Leong---that is not being classically inclined and the ability to express yourself explosively and economically. The more I observe the prevalent Karate men here the more I'm amazed at the public that ignorantly eat up such impractical mess and not to at least analyse Karate with their more alive and certainly more practical sport boxing! If you want to excel in Gung Fu, you have to throw away all classical junk and face combat in its suchness, which is simple and direct. Forms and classical techniques that John Leong teaches are "organized despair" that serve only to distort and cramp his students and distract them from actual reality of combat. Such means of practice(a form of paralysis) solidify and condition what was once free and fluid. Throw away mysticism and B.S., it is really nothing but a blind devotion to the systematic uselessness of practicing routines and stunts that leads to nowhere. Even a man that moves classically fast and snappy is really not too much to be praised----you see he is trying to set a rhythm not to adjust broken rhythm, which is the thing that will happen in actual combat. Then you have to take reactional speed ect. ect. into consideration. Most of the self-defense system are "dead" because the classical techniques are futile attempts to 'arrest' and 'fix' the ever changing movement in combat and to dissect and analyse them like a corpse. when you come down to it, real combat is not fixed and is definitely very much 'alive'.

I've been busy like hell with acting lessons and Gung Fu lessons (the same stuff I teach in the group class---nothing spectacular) and to-nite I'm invite to attend an academy award dinner party in Hollywood. Nick Adam (a black belt supposedly), Sal Mineo, etc., will be there.

what is now is an old man-like Nishyama who couldn't even snap decently nor can he show his techniques smartly----not even in a classical manner. It was a quick change from the last time I saw him. At least at that time he can classically demonstrate his techniques with precision and snap........So that goes to prove the old Chinese saying "song(singing) never leave the mouth, fist never leave the hand". So we have to work work, work,---------the Aikido is something else! Completely out of reality. There might be a strong Aikido man, but his power is evidence only when he practice among his fellow partner who will dance with him and fool around with his flow of ki.

Taky, you have something over John Leong---that is not being classically inclined and the ability to express yourself explosively and economically. The more I observe the prevalent Karate men here the more I'm amazed at the public that ignorantly eat up such impractical mess and not to at least analyse Karate with their more alive and certainly more practical sport boxing! If you want to excel in Gung Fu, you have to throw away all classical junk and face combat in its suchness, which is simple and direct. Forms and classical techniques that John Leong teaches are "organized despair" that steve only to distort and cramp his students and distract them from the actual reality of combat. Such means of practice(a form of paralysis) solidify and condition what was once free and fluid. Throw away mysticism and B.S., it is really nothing but a blind devotion to the systematic uselessness of practicing routines and stunts that leads to nowhere.

Even a man that moves classically fast and snappy is really not too much to be praised----you see he is trying to set a rhythm not to adjust broken rhythm, which is the thing that will happen in actdal combat. Then you have to take reactional speed ect. ect. into consideration. Most of the self-defence system are "dead" because the clasical techniques are futile attempts to 'arrest' and 'fix' the ever changing movement in combat and to dissect and analyse them like a corpse. When you come down to it, real combat is not fixed and is defintelly very much 'alive'.

I've been busy like hell with acting lessons and Gung Fu lesson(the same stuff I teach in the group class---nothing spectacular) and to-nite I'm invite to attend an academy award dinner party in Hollywood. Nick Adam (a black belt supposedly), Sal Mineo, ect., will be there.

I'll shoot the techniques and what not as soon as I can find time. I might fly to Vegas this week to meet Sinatra---nothing definite yet.

Good luck on the Japanese girls class. Use creativeness in the girl class and think in term of their liking without messing up the central theme. I'll mail smiling pointers when I find the time.

Take care my dear friend

Bruce

(ABOVE) Bruce, Linda and Brandon outside on the patio of their Barrington Plaza apartment.

(BELOW) Bruce, Linda and Brandon in their Barrington Plaza apartment posing for a publicity shot to promote Bruce's status as Kato.

Letter 32c

Description of Letter No. 32

Transcription (continued)

I'll shoot the techniques and what not as soon as I can find time. I might fly to Vegas this week to meet Sinatra---nothing definite yet.

Good luck on the Japanese girls class. Use creativeness in the girl class and think in term of their liking without messing up central theme. I'll mail saling pointers when I find the time.

Take care my dear friend
Bruce

My agent's address is: -
William Belasco
9000 Sunset Blvd.
L.A., Calif. 90069

My new address is:---
The Barrington Plaza
11740-Wilshire Blvd. Apt. A-2305
Los Angeles 25, California
Tel. 473-5219 (it's unlisted)

Father and son. Baby Brandon, provoking a battle with his father. As you can see, both were masters of weaponry.

My agent's address is :-

William Belasco
9000 Sunset Blvd.
L.A., Calif. 90069

My new address is:---

The Barrington Plaza
11740-Wilshire Blvd. Apt. R-2305
Los Angeles 25, California
Tel. 473-5219 (it's unlisted)

Letter 33

Description of Letter No. 33

I did not want to continue to "pester" Bruce, it was pleasantly confirming that his loyalty toward me was still in his mindset.

Transcription

Taky,

It has been quite a while since I last heard from you --------get on the ball man! And write me a letter to fill me in as to what on earth is happening.

20th Century Fox, as I have told you, has consented to fly us back, but instead of taking the plane, we are taking the slow boat to China. Linda's mother is coming down on the 14 of March to stay for a week. We are definitely leaving for Hong Kong on the 24th of March by the president lines.

The official rating of "Batman" is fantastically high and it looks like "Green Hornet" will be on even before this year is over, although the postponement is set for next Feb.

Will you find time to mail me the income tax statement as I have to complete it before leaving the country.

~~~~ and write and let me know how things are.

Bruce

Bruce in pose looking like James Bond in this publicity picture for the "Green Hornet".

Taky,

It has been quite a while since I last heard from you —— get on the ball man! And write me a letter to fill me in as to what on earth is happening.

20th Century FOX, as I have told you, has consented to fly us back, but instead of taking the plane, we are taking the slow boat to China. Linda's mother is coming down on the 14 of March to stay for a week. We are definitely leaving for Hong Kong on the 24th of March by the President Lines.

The Official rating of Batman is fantastically high and it looks like Green Hornet will be on even before this year is over, although the postponement is set for next Feb.

Will you find time to mail me the Income tax statement as I have to complete it before leaving the country. ~~~ and write and let me know how things are

Bruce

Letter 34A

Description of Letter No. 34

There are many things written in this letter, but most important is you can see Bruce in the beginning stages of developing his Jeet Kune Do. This is very important, because it shows the determination and will of Bruce in creating what will be the most prolific / important move in his life and in my opinion, martial arts history. I feel very fortunate that not only was Bruce Lee my best friend, but the fact in how he shared his most intimate self with me and what he was achieving privately and publicly. When I read this letter, it seems so simple to see his ideas on paper to see it now transpired, that's an amazing feeling indeed.

Transcription

Taky,

When I mail my letter to-day I've received your letter. Thank you for the income tax form and what not.

You know, if you were a Chinaman, I would think you are trying to be funny by ending the letter, your Si Hing. (Your senior,) Taky----Well, I guess I wouldn't be on Life magazine yet because they want to concentrate first on "Batman".

You better take damn good care of yourself and don't move too much yet and let Chris take care of the clan. You have to push pevonake (later on of course) to help push Gung Fu in Seattle.

John Leong is no sweat as he doesn't even understand what is rhythm (training) & distance, which is the core of all martial art. Of course, simplicity is the necessary component too when he does open the class. I do not think he will be a threat as I know you have better basic requirement, though he is "blown up" with so called muscle, not efficient one unfortunately.

My mother is something else! I'll see to it that the dummy will be on the way even if I'm to sent it myself.

I didn't give that demonstration on the 20th of this month because I am not in the mood for it -- --- I might keep Ralph Castro on his World Tournament this coming 6th of March.

I have stopped training for two weeks now and will resume again when I'm back in Hong Kong. On this trip I'll pick up more flowery forms and what not for the T.V. show ----------- the viewers like fancy stuff anyway.

The first chance I have I'll film the Wing Chun 3 forms and Tai Chi and whatever I feel that will be helpful and beneficial to you. It will be in 8mm.

My mind has made up to start a system of my own ~~~~~ I mean a system of totality, embracing all but yet guided with simplicity. It will concentrate on the root of things – rhythm, timing, distance ---- and embrace the five ways of attack. This is by

Taky,

When I mail my letter to-day, I've received your letter. Thank you for the income tax form and what not.

You know, if you were a Chinaman I would think you are trying to be funny by ending the letter, "your see Hing, (your senior,) Taky -----"

Well, I guess I wouldn't be on Life magazine *yet* because they want to concentrate first on Batman.

You better take damn good care of yourself and don't move too much yet and let Cris take care of the class. You have to push Pevonake (later on of course) to help push Guy Tu in Seattle.

John Leung is no sweat as he doesn't even understand what is rhythm (timing) & distance, which is the core of all martial art. Of course simplicity is the necessary component too

… on the class. I do not
… a threat as I know
… basic requirement,
… blown up" with so
… not efficient one unfortunately
… er is something else!
… hat the dummy will
… ven, I'll paint it myself.
… give that demonstration
on the 20th of the month because I am not in the mood for it ---) might help Ralph Castro on his World Tournament this coming 6th of March.

I have stopped training for two weeks now and will resume again when I'm back in Hong Kong. On this trip I'll pick up more *flowery* forms and what not for the T.V. show —— the viewers like fancy stuffs anyway.

The first chance I have I'll film the Wing Chun 3 forms and Tai Chi and whatever I feel

Letter 34B

Description of Letter No. 34

There are many things written in this letter, but most important is you can see Bruce in the beginning stages of developing his Jeet Kune Do. This is very important, because it shows the determination and will of Bruce in creating what will be the most prolific / important move in his life and in my opinion, martial arts history. I feel very fortunate that not only was Bruce Lee my best friend, but the fact in how he shared his most intimate self with me and what he was achieving privately and publicly. When I read this letter, it seems so simple to see his ideas on paper to see it now transpired, that's an amazing feeling indeed.

Transcription (continued)

far the most effective method I've ever encountered or will encounter. Anything beyond that has to be super fantastic. Wing Chun is the starting point, Chi Sao is the nucleus, and supplemented by FIVE WAYS. The whole system will concentrate on irregular rhythm and how to disturb and intercept the opponent's rhythm the fastest and most efficient way. Above all, this system is not confined to straight line or curved line but in content to stand in the middle of the circle without attachment. This way one can meet any lines without not being familiar with them. Wait till I assemble everything. Lately, I've been working on my book and is nearly finished except for more photos taking.

Enclosed find some pictures I happened to run into when I looked for my stuff. Old Charlie is in it.

Linda sends her regards. Brandon is growing and growing.

Take care and do not over-exercise yet.

Bruce

P.S. by the way, did you say you've lost your membership card?

Left to right, Daniel K. Pai, Bruce Lee, Jhoon Rhee and George Dillman, posing for a picture at a sponsored East Coast Karate Championship.

that will be helpful and beneficial
to you. It will be in 8mm.

My mind has made up to start
a system of my own — I mean a
system of totality, embracing all
but yet guided with simplicity. It
will concentrate on the root of things —
— rhythm, timing, distance — and
embrace the five ways of attack. This
is by far the most effective method
I've ever encountered or will encounter
Anything beyond that has to be super
fantastic. Wing Chun is the starting
point, Chi Sao is the nucleus, and
supplemented by the FIVE WAYS. The
whole system will concentrate on irregular
rhythm and how to disturb and intercept
the opponent's rhythm the fastest and
most efficient way. Above all, this
system is not confined to straight line
or curved line but is content to
stand in the middle of the circle
without attachment. This way one

without not being
wait till I assemble
been working on
nearly finished
photos taking.
Some picture
t, when I looked
Charlie is in

her regard.
Brandon is growing and growing

Take Care and do not
over-exercise yet.

Bruce

P.S. by the way, did you
say you've lost your
membership Card?

Letter 35

Description of Letter No. 35

Bruce Lee's ongoing sharing of his emotions, being very honest, telling me what was going on. Obviously, me being his closest friend I have to believe he maintained his "on going" mind set by letting his hair down and achieving a semblance of balance by sharing all with his true and respected buddy. Bruce would thrust the idea of "keep punching" with me, it was good for his "psyche" as well as mind. By keep punching he meant, keep fighting the good fight, "walk on" if you will.

Transcription

Taky,

A letter to let you know that the "Praying Mantis" episode will be on the 18th of Nov., which is 2 weeks from Friday (we're pre-empty because of a special). Also, a week after that "the Hunter & the Hunted", an episode in which I do Gung Fu without the mask.

The show is doing bad, rating wise. Dozier is trying to make it go by changing it into an hour show. Whether or not we can change it remains to be seen. For our sake, we better.

Next week I'm doing a pictorial layout of Gung Fu in color in the Doger Stadium for T.V. Guide.

You know, whether or not this show will go, the show will last at least till March. So Gung Fu will have enough exposure and so is Kato, Bruce Lee.

The schools will definitely go. I'll discuss with you in more detail. I'm preparing for it. Let's make use of this opportunity buddy.

Take care
Bruce

Bruce Lee as Kato in the episode "The Praying Mantis". Bruce knew that this episode was important to him, because he was able to show more of the Chinese culture in an intense way on martial arts level, on camera.

Twentieth Century-Fox Television, Inc.

Taky,

A letter to let you know that the "Preying Mantis" episode will be on the 18th of Nov., which is 2 weeks from this Friday (we're pre-empty because of a special). Also, a week after that "The Hunter & the Hunted", an episode in which I do Gung Fu without the mask.

The show is doing bad, rating wise. Dozier is trying to make it go by changing it into an hour show. Whether or not we can change it remains to be seen. For our …

Twentieth Century-Fox Television, Inc.

… I'm doing a … of Gung Fu in …er stadium for T.V. ~~Guide~~ Guide.

You know, whether or not this show will go, the show will last at least till March. So Gung Fu will have enough exposure and so is Kato, Bruce Lee.

The schools will definitely go. I'll discuss with you in more detail. I'm preparing for it. Let's make use of this opportunity buddy.

Take Care Bruce

Letter 36

Description of Letter No. 36

I can remember Bruce boasting about Brandon in how he was standing at such a young age. It really made him proud. It was always great to see Bruce and the family on the holidays. There was a closeness we all shared and that feeling has not gone away even to this day.

Bruce would always update me in how the "Green Hornet" was doing. He took that job very seriously and was concern with the ratings. But looking back after all these years, it is plain to see that the "Green Hornet" should have been called the "Kato" Show, because it was really all him.

Transcription

Taky,

Received telegram ~~~ thanks to you and the boys.

I'm coming up to Seattle to spend the Christmas. I'll have one week time and we'll get together and I'll train you in my method. Until then I'll tell you more about it. By the way, Linda, Brandon and I will come on the 24th, Saturday, in the afternoon. Linda's mother is coming to pick us up.

We've been shooting everyday and the show is doing 50/50.

Well, see you next month.

Bruce

Bruce Lee flying high in this 20th Century Fox promotional picture for the "Green Hornet".

Taky,
Received telegram — thanks to you and the boys.

I'm coming up to Seattle to spend the Christmas. I'll have one week time and we'll get together and I'll train you in my method. Until then I'll tell you more about it. By the way, Linda, Brandon and I will come on the 24th, Saturday, in the afternoon. Linda's mother is coming to pick us up.

We've been shooting everyday and the show is doing 50/50.

Well, see you next month.

Bruce

Letter 37

Description of Letter No. 37

Bruce would update me all the time through letters and phone calls in how the "Green Hornet" was doing and as you can see here, Bruce was very aware of the rating system that was in place in those days, in Hollywood. He knew the importance in how the ratings would dictate if the "Green Hornet" would survive it's run. Also in this letter, Bruce mentions for me to watch the GH episode called "The Praying Mantis"! This was a very important episode, because this was Bruce's chance to really show what he / Kato can do and I believe that it was this episode that made him a star among his fans. Daniel Inosanto is also in this episode doubling for Mako who played the bad guy in this particular show.

Bruce also always had time to update me with lesson plans he wanted me to teach to the Gung Fu class in Seattle.

Transcription

Taky,

Thank you very much for letter plus dues. The first national rating of "Green Hornet" was indeed not good; however, ABC and the Greenway Production are not too worry about it. The main reason of such low rating is due to the fact that Friday nites audiences are like half of the rest of the other days. Tuesday has the highest rate of viewers. When the national rating was set up, our low percentage of viewer was not considered. However, one thing is lousy; Tarzan beat us. Well, let's hope the 2nd rating will shape up.

By the way, the show you should be sure to watch is the "Praying Mantis" which will be on Nov. 18, an all out Gung Fu show. The one follow that "The Hunter and the Hunted" is also pretty good.

Well, back to Gung Fu. I believe that I should really start organizing the Jun Fan as the series is still on. This is one opportunity I should make use of.

I'm glad to hear that the class really shapes up. Put your mind to it as I have high hopes for Seattle. Disregard what will happen, Seattle will be a place to build up. Here is a cool routine program you should use.

PREPARATIONAL EXCERCISES: *- (non-stop) ~2 sets each*

1). alternate splits /3). run in place /5). jumping squat
2). shoulder rotation/ 4). waist twisting /6). shoulder circling
7). sit up /9). high kick 8). leg raises /10).

POWER TRAINING

1). Heavy bag ~~~ (a) right lead (b) left cross (c) left/right punching 2). Paper hanging ~~~ all punches (fight the paper various height) this can be a speed training~~~keep come in faster and faster 3). Kicking ~~~ (a) straight kick (b) side kick (c) back kick (d) knee & shin kick. I'll send you a 8mm. of a form that you can watch. copy and teach (to stretch the program). You have to get a 8mm. editor that will come in handy as the future film comes.

Pray that the series will really go, or at least stay. As I'm planning to come up to Seattle during Christmas. I hope by that time I can really train with you and give the Institute a plug.

Take care and write me whenever you have time.

Bruce

Taky,

Thank you very much for letter plus dues. The first national rating of "Green Hornet" was indeed not good; however, ABC and the Greenway Production are not too worry about it. The main reason of such low rating is due to the fact that Friday nite audience are like half of the rest of the other days. Tuesday has the highest rate of viewers. When the national rating was set up, our low percentage of viewers was not considered. However, one thing is lousy; Tarzan beat us. Well, let's hope the 2nd rating will shape u

By the way, the show you sure to watch is the "Preying M will be on Nov. 18, an all out show. The one follow that "The the Hunted" is also pretty good

Well, back to Gung Fu. that I should really start orga Jun Fan as the series is still one opportunity I should make

I'm glad to hear that the shapes up. Put your mind to have high hopes for Seattle. what will happen, Seattle will

place to build up. Here is a tol routine program you should use.

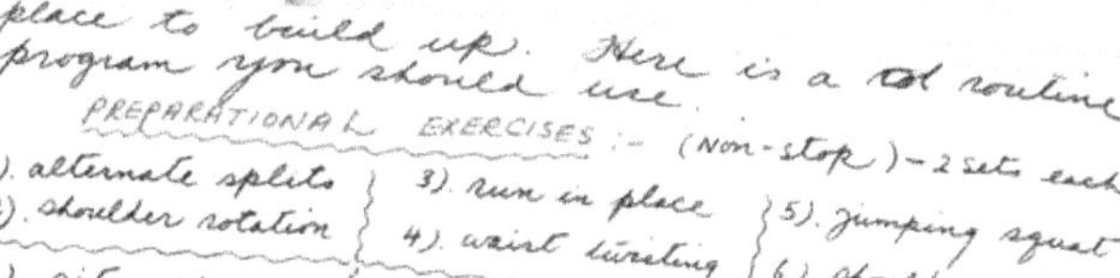

PREPARATIONAL EXERCISES:- (Non-stop)-2 sets each

1). alternate splits
2). shoulder rotation
3). run in place
4). waist twisting
5). jumping squat
6). shoulder circling
7). sit up
8). leg raises
9). high kick
10).

POWER TRAINING

1). Heavy bag — (a) right lead (b) left cross (c) left/right punching
2). Paper hanging — all punches [fight the paper at various height] THIS CAN BE A SPEED TRAINING — KEEP COME IN FASTER AND FASTER
3). Kicking — (a) straight kick (b) side kick (c) back kick (d) knee & shin kick

I'll send you a 8mm. of a form that you can watch. Copy and teach [to stretch the program]. You have to get a 8mm. editor that will come in handy as the future film comes.

Pray that the series will really go, or at least stay. As I'm planning to come up to Seattle during Christmas. I hope by that time I can really train with you and give the institute a plug.

Take care and write me whenever you have time.

Bruce

Bruce Lee in kicking form in this promotional picture meant for 20th Century Fox. Bruce told me that they wanted to see him not as Kato in some pictures, but as Bruce Lee the instructor. This helped 20th Century Fox promote him on another level.

Letter 38

Description of Letter No. 38

What comes to mind when I read this letter is, is the fact that Bruce had filmed himself doing kicking sets along with other type of training exercises and he sent the tapes over to me but to my dread, I somehow misplaced these treasures, or gave them to fellow students throughout the years. I am sure that this footage would be the holly grail in the Bruce Lee world if I could find them. I will keep on trying!

Transcription

Taky,

It has been raining and I just haven't the opportunity to shoot the kicking set. So on second thought, I think I'll drop by Seattle a couple of day to show you personally. You see, I'll be going to demonstrate in the Wash. D.C. tournament and on my way back I'll stop by Seattle and then go back to L.A. The one way back will be something like sixty and is deductable. The main thing now is time and as soon as I find out the schedule, I'll let you know. Chances are I'm coming probably on May 8 (Monday) and will leave most likely on May 9 (Tues.) So during these two days concentrate your time with me as it will be most beneficial to you as well as my only reason to come. ~~ will let you know in a week time. By the way, the shipment from Hong Kong is arriving on May 8. Also, the good new is that Dozier will probably pick up the option -----according to my agent ~~~~ and Fitzsimon, the vice president is working on a 1 hr. series for me.

Hope to see you soon

Bruce

Bruce Lee along side Hector Quinones in Washington D.C. 1967. Bruce was in Washington on tour promoting himself at a karate championship. I believe the "Green Hornet" was cancelled shortly after this.

Taky,

It has been raining and I just haven't the opportunity to shoot the kicking set. So on second thought, I think I'll drop by Seattle a couple of day to show you personally. You see, I'll be going to demonstrate in the Wash. D.C. tournament and on my way back I'll stop by Seattle and then go back to L.A. The one way back will be something like sixty and is deductable.

The main thing now is time and as soon as I find out the schedule, I'll let you know. Chances are I'm coming probably on May 8 (Monday) and will leave most likely on May 9 (Tues.). So during these two days concentrate your time with me as it will be most beneficial to you as well as my only reason to come. will let you know in a week time. By the way, the shipments from Hong Kong is arriving on May 8.

Also, the good new is that Dozier will probably pick up the option — according to my agents and Fitzsimons, the vice presidents is working on a 1 hr. series for me.

Hope to see you soon

Bruce

Letter 39

Description of Letter No. 39

This was all part of Bruce keeping me up to date and in the loop. His letters were always very timely and as I reflect when I read them, they were just what I needed to hear. Positive encouragement at the right time. Bruce also loved updating me in who his potential celebrity students were going to be. Bruce's popularity at that time as an instructor was growing on a daily basis, many were seeking him out for private instruction. His two most popular celebrity students were James Coburn and Steve McQueen. People also think that after the "Green Hornet" series was cancelled that no one had interest in him in Hollywood, but as you can see within this letter, there were many in the industry that wanted to work with him. He was very popular.
Bruce loved Bobo his Great Dane; they would run together all the time. He was very loyal to Bruce, but boy was he a scary looking dog.

Transcription

Dear Taky,

Enclosed you will find the new materials for the Jun Fan Gung Fu Inst. There are more coming for you to use in school ~~ enough for every student ~~~~ am waiting for shipment to come from Hong Kong. Also will print more copy. Understand James Lee has sent you some equipments ~~ have you mounted them up yet?

The school down in Chinatown has opened two weeks ~~ no signs outside, nothing ~~ we have close to 30 students now ~~ will reach 40 by the end of next month. Also started private lesson at $27.50 an hour. The students are coming in steady ~~ Stuart Whitman, Dino (Dean Martin's son) and the others are taking ~~ Paul Newman probably join in a week or two. Private lesson alone gross around a thousand a month. Things are shaping up.

A director called me to find out my commitment with Greenway. He has a starring role for me if "Green Hornet" doesn't pick up next year. Sounds great --- private eye type ~~ much better than the role of Kato.

Also just bought a great dane puppy she is expected to weigh around 170 (over) my best wishes for your plans and program. Take good care of yourself, and will send you all the stuffs as soon as I obtain them.

Best to you
Bruce

P.S. will you send me information of your date of rank promotion ~~ I need to have your record ~~~ also, send me your application card. Do you need stamping on your membership card? Any recommendation for promotion? Need any issuing of rank?

Dear Taky
Inclosed you will find the new material
for the Jun Fan Gung Fu Inst. There are more coming
for you to use in school — enough for every
student — am waiting for shipment to come
from Hong Kong. Also will print more copy

Understand James Lee has sent you some
equipments — have you mounted them up yet?

The school down in Chinatown has opened
two weeks — no signs outside, nothing — we have
close to 30 students now — will reach 40 by the
end of next month. Also started private lesson
at $27.50 an hour. The students are coming in
steady — Stuart Whitman, Dino (Dean Martin's son)
and the other are taking — Paul Newman probably
join in a week or two. Private lesson alone
goes around a thousand a month. Things
are shaping up.

A director called me to find out my
commitment with Greenway. He has a starring role
for me if Green Hornet doesn't pick up next
year. Sounds great ... private eye type —
much better than the role of Kato.

Also just bought a great dane puppy
she is expected to weigh around 170 (over)

...wishes for your plan and program.
...od care of yourself, and will send
...the stuffs as soon as I obtain

Best to you
Bruce

will you send me information of
your date of rank promotion —
I need to have your record
— also, send me your application
card. Do you need stamping on
your membership card? Any
recomendation for promotion? Need
any issuing of rank?

Bruce in his backyard in Los Angeles, taking care of a cropped ear Bobo. Bruce loved this dog and jogged with him on a daily basis.

Letter 40

Description of Letter No. 40

Bruce's continual uplifting persona influenced me greatly and I try to relay that to my students as well. Bruce was a very positive thinker and it paid off for him hugely.

Transcription

I'll send you a 8mm. of a form that you can watch. Copy and teach (to stretch the program). You have to get a 8mm. editor that will come in handy as the future film comes.

Pray that the series will really go, or at least stay. As I'm planning to come up to Seattle during Christmas. I hope by that time I can really train with you and give the institute a plug.

Take care and write me whenever you have time.

Bruce

Bruce at 20th Century Fox taking a break from filming the "Green Hornet", showing co-star Wendy Wagner how to do fight like Kato!

I'll send you a 8mm. of a form that you can watch, copy and teach [to stretch the program]. You have to get a 8mm. editor that will come in handy as the future film comes.

Pray that the series will really go, or at least stay. As I'm planning to come up to Seattle during Christmas. I hope by that time I can really train with you and give the institute a plug.

Take care and write me whenever you have time.

Bruce

Letter 41

Description of Letter No. 41

Bruce was still unrelenting in his quest to receive the uniforms from me. I had to explain to Bruce that when he was in Seattle his charm and good looks went a long way in getting things done from the numerous women who made such things as that, but when he left, the charm went with him and they ignored me.

Transcription

Taky,

Next week the advance copy of Black Belt will come out, I'll send it to you as soon as I obtain them.

I'm unpacking my stuffs in my new home and it's a hell of a job. At any rate, send all uniforms to this address

4114 Van Buren Place
Culver City, calif. 90230 l
Tele. 838-0241

As soon as I settle down I'll continue with the lesson plan. I can only have around 30 lessons, the rest is up to the instructor to drill and re-drill. however, from these 30 lessons, you can draw up a good program of teaching. I've analyzed John's program of teaching, too dissipated and drawn out~~~~I'll talk to you about it later on, but my idea is that from my private lessons. I've found out that a few simple techniques (or maybe an aim clearly seen), are better than a tangled mess or disorganized techniques.

Rush me those uniforms.

Bruce

Bruce doing a jumping front kick from a trampoline below him, for shoot that would be later used within the Fighting Method projects.

Taky,

Next week the advance copy of Black Belt will come out, I'll send it to you as soon as I obtain them.

I'm unpacking my stuffs in my new house and it's a hell of a job. At any rate, send all uniforms to this address

4114 Van Buren Place
Culver City, Calif. 90230
Tele. 838-0241

So soon as I settle down I'll continue with the lesson plan. I can only have around 30 lessons, the rest is up to the instructor to drill and re-drill. However, from these 30 lessons, you can draw up a good program of teaching. I've analyzed John's program of teaching, too dissipated and drawn out — I'll talk to you about it later on, but my idea is this from my private lessons. I've found out this a few simple techniques (or maybe an aim clearly seen), are better than a tangled mess or disorganized technique.

Rush me those uniforms. Bruce

Letter 42

Description of Letter No. 42

In this letter, Bruce talks about his cover as Kato for the Black Belt magazine publication. Bruce was very excited about this, because this was the first time he could be interviewed on a mass scale, so that the public could see and not just hear who he was through the grapevine. He did other type of interviews before, but the front cover was a huge deal in making him a household name.

Transcription

Taky,

A letter to ask you to hurry that Chinese guy for the uniform ~~~~~we want this matter to be settled as soon as possible.

Also, Ed Parker should contact you for plane ticket ~~~~~

In the Oct. issue (one after the next one) of Black Belt I will be on the front cover and there will be a three parts on me.

Write me and let me know how many days you can come out for that tournament. The day is on Sunday night. July 30th.

Let me know

Bruce

P.S. will you make a few of the emblems for samples I believe the first rank, a blank one should be cheaper

Little Brandon looks on as his father and Daniel Inosanto pose for pictures on a beach in Palos Verdes, California for what would be used in Bruce's Fighting Method project.

Taky,

A letter to ask you to hurry that Chinese guy for the uniforms —— we want this matter to be settled as soon as possible.

Also Ed Parker should contact you for plane ticket ——

In the Oct. issue (one after the next one) of Black Belt I will be on the front cover and there will be a three parter on me.

Write me and let me know how many days you can come out for that tournament. The day is on Sunday night July 30th

Let me know

Bruce

P.S. will you make a few of the emblems for samples I believe the first rank, a blank one should be cheaper

Letter 43

Description of Letter No. 43

This was certainly unexpected and humbling to me and Bruce being gone from those Seattle years we shared as friends since 1964 and to be the recipient of such high honor. It was the highest "testament" to a precious enduring friendship.

Transcription

Taky,

Your concluding statement in your last letter was well spoken ~"your faith in me is my faith in" ~~ rest assure that I do have faith in you, or else nothing as high as a fifth rank be granted to you.

You're right in the latest issue in Black Belt. I did help them ~~~to raise the sad level of the Chinese arts a little.

Did you also read the editorial?

Joe Lewis swallowed his pride and called for instruction ~~~ like Norris, Stone, I'll take him for a few lessons to establish the fact that he did come to me. All three of them are under me now.

Keep your newly promotion proudly, and let it be the reason for more training and further application.

I hope to see you somewhere in March. At that time, I'll get together with you for the most important— Jeet Kune Do sessions in your entire training.

Take care

Bruce

Bruce Lee congratulates Joe Lewis in winning the high honors as Champion at the Jhoon Rhee Karate Championships. Bruce trained Joe for a while and that helped him better his game, as well as helping him achieve the wins in other championships.

Taky.

Your concluding statement in your last letter was well spoken — "Your faith in me is my faith in" — rest assure that I do have faith in you, or else nothing as high as a fifth rank be granted to you.

You're right in the latest issue in Black Belt. I did help them — to raise the sad level of the Chinese arts a little. Did you also read the editorial?

Joe Lewis swallowed his pride and called for instruction — like Norris, Stone, I'll take him for a few lessons to establish the fact that he did come to me. All three of them are under me now.

Keep your newly promotion proudly, and let it be the reason for more training and further application.

I hope to see you somewhere in March. At that time, I'll get together with you for ~~the~~ the most important Jeet Kune Do session in your entire training.

Take Care.

Bruce

Letter 44

Description of Letter No. 44

This was added prestige to Jeet Kune Do and further showed the greatness of Bruce. Those guys were all in their primes at that time and for those guys to come to him for instruction was a great accomplishment. Through it all, Bruce was a very humble and positive person, giving those people the respect hey deserved.

Transcription

Taky,

The reaction of the articles in Black Belt is good. Of course, being a "different" and "unorthodox" approach, these are also a few controversial letters to the editors.

The Jan. issue of Black Belt will devote two pages "Bruce Lee Corner" for me to answer the incoming mails. Of course there will be some "cool" answers to those damn fools that write in ~~~~ one claimed that I down graded Karate! Now, this never occur in my mind----------------

Well, the latest news here in L.A. Mike Stone, the still recognized best Karate man here (people think he is better than Norris and of course Lewis) is now approaching me for lesson. In other word, he became my student. So is Mito Uyehara (publisher of BB) and possibly Hayward Nishioka, the once Grand Champion of Judo. Pretty soon Jeet Kune Do will be full of prestige ~~~ the professional of the professionals.

In closing I hope that you will rush those pants and also more new uniforms for me. I need around five large sizes now. Write and let me know about this plus what you think of the prices I discussed with you in the last letter.

Take Care my Friend
Bruce

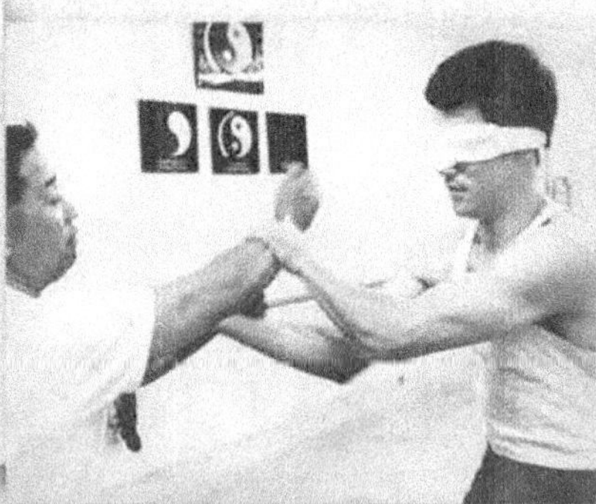

(LEFT) Bruce Lee and student Dan Lee giving demonstrations at the Los Angeles Chinatown school.

(RIGHT) Bruce Lee playing hands with student Dan Lee (chi sao) while blindfolded during an interview for Black Belt Magazine at the Los Angeles Chinatown school.

Taky

The reaction of the articles in Black Belt is good. Of course, being a "different" and "unorthodox" approach, there are also a few controversial letters to the editor.

The Jan issue of Black Belt will devote two pages "Bruce Lee corner" for me to answer the in coming mails. Of course there will be some "cool" answers to those damn fools that write in — one claimed that I down graded Karate! Now, the never occur in my mind ....

Well, the latest news here in L.A. Mike Stone, the still recognized best Karate man here (people think he is better than Norris and of course Lewis) is now approaching me for lesson. In other word, he become my student. So is Mito Uyehara (publisher of B.B.) and possibly Hayward Nishioka, the once Grand Champion of Judo. Pretty soon Jeet Kune Do will be full of prestige in the professional of the professionals.

In closing I hope that you will rush those pants and also more new uniforms for me. I need around five large size now. Write and let me know about this plus what you think of the price I discussed with you in the last letter.

Take Care my friend

Bruce

Bruce Lee at the head of the table giving a couple of the writers an interview at the Black Belt office.

Letter 45

Description of Letter No. 45

Sadly I have to admit, somehow the precious "film clips" Bruce had given me, fell through the cracks and I regret to this day the disappearance of all of them. Surely their value must be great and I hope to one day be reacquainted with them once again.

Transcription

Taky,

Enclosed find a operating instruction of the 8 mm. editor I sent to you.

The segment of "Ironside", "tagged for murder" will be on this coming Thursdya nite (Oct. 26) at 8:30 P.M. (I think, I'm not sure of the time). Check your local T.V. guide.

Are you going to the Karate tournament? Chuck Norris is going and I'll be seeing him this coming Friday before he leaves for the tournament. I don't think he will compete this one.

So my friend take good care of yourself as always ~~~~ looking forward to the uniform and hope that everyday is going well with you.

Looking forward to our gathering this coming November.

See you
Bruce

Bruce Lee along side friend and co-star Chuck Norris in Italy. Bruce welcomed Chuck upon his arrival to shoot his scenes in "Way of the Dragon".

Taky.

Enclosed find a operating instruction of the 8mm. editor I sent to you.

The segment of "Ironside", 'Tagged for murder' will be on this coming Thursday nite (Oct 26) at 8:30 P.M. (I think. I'm not too sure of the time) Check your local T.V. guide.

Are you going to the Karate tournament? Chuck Norris is going and I'll be seeing him this coming Friday before he leaves for the tournament. I don't think he will compete this one.

So my friend take good care of yourself as always —— looking forward to the uniform and hope that everything is going well with you.

Looking forward to our gathering this coming November.

See you

Bruce

Hayward Nishioka left, Bruce Lee center and Chuck Norris right, at the Black Belt Hall of Fame award event.

Letter 46

Description of Letter No. 46

I believe this was Bruce's way of sincerely consoling me during and after my brother's passing. My brother was a hero of mine and good man, and it is fitting that Bruce who was my closest friend sent me his words of encouragement to help me through that tough time in my life. Bruce had a gift, he always knew what people needed to get through the hard times.

Transcription

Taky,

See it as the inevitable and accept the cold fact and WALK ON. Walk on and flow with events that pass on for the next few days. Do not, Taky, isolate yourself from your every day life and add burden to your grief in lone thinking.

Taky, my thoughts are with you. Take very good care.

Will write you next week.

Bruce

This card was sent to me by Bruce and Linda, consoling me about my brother's passing.

Taky.

See it as the inevitable and accept the cold fact and WALK ON. walk on and flow with events that pass on for the next few days. Do not, Taky, isolate yourself from your everyday life and add burden to your grief in lone thinking.

Taky, my thoughts are with you. Take very good care.

Will write you next week.

Bruce

Letter 47

Description of Letter No. 47

The heart of this letter to me is the fact that Bruce was consoling me about the breakup of my marriage. We were like brothers, so this letter was very personal to me. Even though he had left Seattle, it was always an honor to have him writing me and giving me advice.

Transcription

Taky,

I am most happy to have received your letter. Did you receive the special plaque I have made for you? You did not mention in the letter.

Whatever you do is always okay to me. I think you have done the best thing, and that is to have the club still maintained by a handful of loyal member. After all the rent is not high and it is a historical place like for the Jun Fan Gung Fu Institute.

I think by now Gung Fu is pretty much part of your life and I'm sure as your burden lessened your feel for it will resume, especially when we will get together in the near future (your absence at our last meeting was regrettable on our part) and fill you up to the latest. In other word, when we meet again, your Gung Fu ability will from there reach toward the summit.

I thank you again for your constant support to my welfare and all that you have done. Do take good care of yourself under this unavoidable cycle of life and walk on as you would without deliberation and frozen thought. Remember everything lives by moving, and gain strength as they go. Workout a little bit when you're low, and remember that the whole Jun Fan Gung Fu Institute is always behind you. Always.

Bruce

Bruce Lee in battle with Taky Kimura and Charlie Woo as he blocks Charlie and delivers a straight kick to Taky's groin.

Taky. I am most happy to have received your letter. Did you receive the special plague I have made for you? You did not mention in the letter.

Whatever you do is always okay to me. I think you have done the best thing, and that is to have the club still maintained by a handful of loyal members. After all the rent is not high and it is a historical place like for the Jun Fan Gung Fu Institute.

I think by now Gung Fu is pretty much part of your life and I'm sure as your burden lessened your feel for it will resume, especially when we will get together in the near future (your absence at our last meeting wa regretable on our part) and fill you up to the latest. In other word, when we meet again, ~~as~~ your Gung Fu ability will from there reach toward the summit.

I thank you again for your constant support to my welfare and all that you have done. Do take good care of yourself under this unavoidable cycle of life and walk on as you would without deliberation and frozen thought. Remember everything lives by moving, and gain strength as they go. Work out a little bit when you're low, and remember that the whole Jun Fan Gung Fu Institute is always behind you. Always.

Bruce

Taky Kimura instructing the Seattle Gung Fu class in Chinatown. Among the many students Doug Palmer back right. Pak Sao was one of the main exercises the class worked on as seen in this picture.

Letter 48

Description of Letter No. 48

A very precious bit of psychology from a dear friend and teacher. Each time I read this, I am blessed of the precious friendship that Bruce and I shared. He was a true brother!

Transcription

Taky,

It was nice to hear your voice over the phone but as a friend I, too, feel this unfortunate break – up between you and Peggy.

Certainly, it would be dumb of me to offer you any consultation when I haven't even met Peggy. Therefore, I cannot advice you on something that you know best.

One thing though my friend --- remember my thought has always been with you because before I even start anything, I want you to know that I consider you as my best friend. So as a best friend I can only say this: in life, there are the pluses and the minuses, and it is time for you to concentrate on the pluses. It might be difficult but fortunately for us, as human being, we have self-will. Well, its time to employ it. Life is an ever-flowing process and somewhere along the path some unpleasant thing will pop up -------- it might leave a scar but then life is flowing on and like running water, when it stops, it grows stale. Go bravely on my friend because each experience teaches us a lesson and remember if there is anything at all I can be of help do let me know. Keep blasting because James Lee did and life is sometimes it is nice and sometimes it's not.

Take care and drop me a line, you are my number one friend and please keep me informed. Again take care.

My Warmest Personal Regards
Bruce

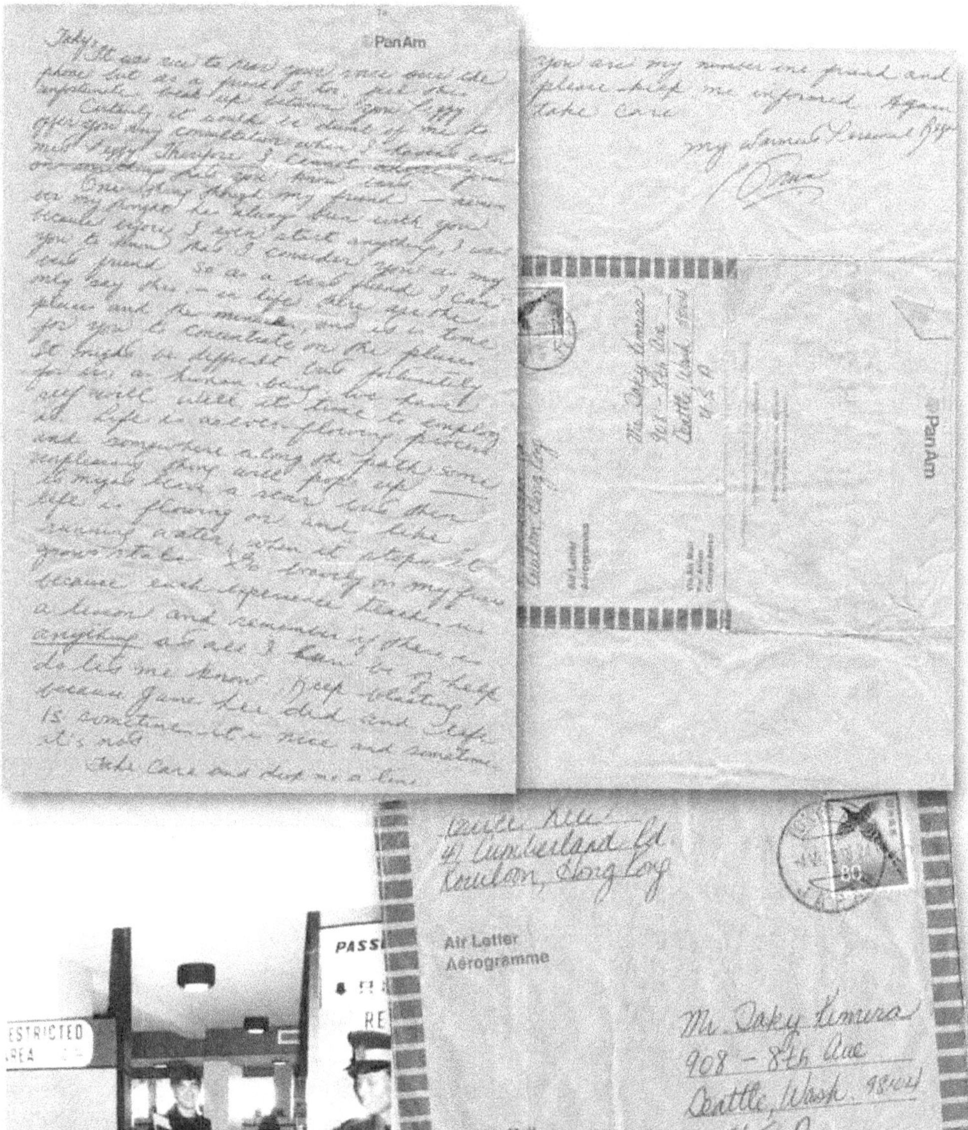

41 Cumberland Rd
Kowloon, Hong Kong

Air Letter
Aérogramme

Mr. Taky Kimura
908 - 8th Ave
Seattle, Wash. 98104
U.S.A.

Via Air Mail
Par Avion
Correo Aereo

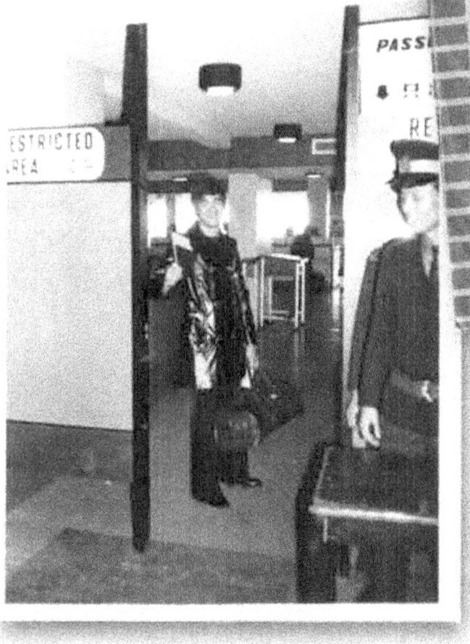

Bruce at Kai Tak airport in Hong Kong waving to the press.

Letter 49

Description of Letter No. 49

This was a very nice letter from Linda on her and Bruce's behalf in regards to the birth of my son Andy. Linda also would update me on things when Bruce was very busy and could not get back to me. Bruce and Linda worked like a team, he put his complete trust in her and they complimented one another completely.

Transcription

September 30 1971

Dear Taky and Peggy,

Congratulations! The birth of your baby sounds like it must have been a thrilling experience for both of you. It's amazing when you think of what a miracle two people can make. But like the song says, "You've only just begun." I hope little Andrew is a good baby – doesn't keep you up all night. But if he's a crier, you'll have consolation in knowing that he'll probably be very strong. Brandon was a screamer, but he's like a bear cub that doesn't know his own strength now. Reminds me of his father – terrible temper and hard as a rock.

Speaking of the rock, things have certainly been happening for him since the showing of the "Longstreet" episode two weeks ago. Both Paramount and Warner Bros. practically jumped on him to sign for a TV series. They both offer very attractive deals, but Bruce is being very careful in trying to choose the best project. You don't get too many chances in this business, so not only do you have to grab your chance, but you have to do it right. So it seems like everything is going so fast for Bruce and he has many things to take care of before leaving for Hong Kong. He has so many "believers" here that I'm sure this is only the beginning of a great career.

We are planning to leave for Hong Kong on Oct. 15. Bruce is really looking forward to the trip because he loves to make those movies back there. What makes him as happy is the creative powers he has is those films. And, since they're martial art movies, it's just what he loves most.

My mother is planning to come to Hong Kong during her vacation. It will really be a treat for her.

Take care

Bruce

MRS. BRUCE LEE
[illegible] Roscomare Road, Los Angeles, California 90024

September 20, 1971

Dear Toby and Peggy,

Congratulations! The birth of your baby sounds like it must have been a thrilling experience for both of you. It's amazing when you think of what a miracle two people can make. But like the song says: "You've only just begun" I hope little Andrew is a good baby - doesn't keep you up all night. But if he's a crier, you'll have consolation in knowing that he'll probably be very strong. Brandon was a screamer, but he's like a bear cub that doesn't kn[ow] his own strength now. Reminds me of his father - terrible temper and hard as a rock.

Speaking of the Rock, things have certainly been happening fo[r] him since the showing of the Longstreet episode three weeks ago. Both Paramount and Warner Bros. practically jumped on him to sign for a TV series. They both offer very attractive deals, but Bruce is being very careful in trying to choose the best project. You don't get too many chances in this business, so not only do you have to make your chance, but you have to do it right. So it seems like everything is going so fast for Bruce and he has so many things to take care of before leaving for Hong Kong. He has so many "believers" here that I'm sure this is only the beginning of a great career.

We are planning to leave for Hong Kong on Oct 15. Bruce is really looking forward to the trip because he loves to make those movies back there. What makes him so happy is the creative power he has in those films. And, since they're martial art movies, it's just what he loves most.

My mother is planning to come to Hong Kong during her vacation. It will really be a treat for her.

Bruce Lee and James Franciscus on set while filming "Longstreet".

Letter 50

Description of Letter No. 50

A very appreciative boost to my mind set from a very close friend and teacher.

Transcription

Taky,

I just got back from the East Coast when I received that happy announcement! Before I go on, I hate to say I will have to be back to the East Coast the same week-end of your wedding. I would not go except I have to meet with the president of Warner Bro. regarding the "Silent Flute," the film I'll be doing. So remember that my spirit will be with you and do give my best to your future wife, Peggy, and tell her I say she can't get a finer man than Taky Kimura.

I was in Hong Kong last month and my Jeet Kune Do rocked Hong Kong after two demonstrations on the two major networks. I was on the new (Lead lines mainly) everyday of the three weeks I was there. Before Hong Kong I was in Switzerland, London and the Dominican Republic. I'll be flying to Dominican Republic with my family for two weeks vacation then I'll be on teaching trips to Paris, London, Rome and possibly Switzerland again. by the way, I am teaching Internationally now and my fees are: - $250 per hr., $1000 for ten lessons, and $100 a week plus expenses for oversea instruction.

Also, the film is coming along and everything is going big fun.

I'll write again to let you know more of what's happening, Jeet Kune Do wise as well as film wise. In the meantime do drop me a line also to let me know how things are with you.

My best always
Bruce

Taky

I just got back from the East Coast when I received that happy announcement! Before I go on, I hate to say I will have to be back to the East Coast the same weekend of your wedding. I would not go except I have to meet with the president of Warner Bros regarding the "Silent Flute", the film I'll be doing. So remember that my spirit will be with you and do give my best to your future wife Peggy, and tell her I say she can't get a finer man than Taky Kimura.

I was in Hong Kong last month and my Jeet Kune Do rocked Hong Kong after two demonstration on the two major network. I was on the news (headlines mainly) everyday of the three weeks I was there. Before Hong Kong I was in Switzerland, London and the Dominican Republic. I'll be flying to Dominican Republic with my family for two weeks vacation then I'll be on ~~flying~~ teaching trips to Paris, London, Rome and possibly Switzerland again. By the way, I am

...n and my fees are :- $250 per hr,
...on, and $[illegible] a week plus expenses
...truction
...film is coming along and
...my big gun
...te again to let you know
...happening. Jeet Kune Do will
...[illegible]. In the meantime
...line also to let me know
...with you.

My best always

Bruce

Bruce being interviewed on Hong Kong TVB upon his arrival back to Hong Kong to seek international fame.

Letter 51

Description of Letter No. 51

Bruce always kept me in informed of his plans. We were always looking for better protective equipment as there were not many choices at that time. Much of what we used was improvised from other sports, or were made for him by George Lee, and James Lee. Also mentioned within this letter is his trip to India to scout locations for his "Silent Flute" project. Bruce was very excited to see this film come to light, but unfortunately it never came to be. Many of the silent flute ideas ended up within Bruce's game of death concept.

Transcription

Taky,

I've asked Linda to wrap four protective body guards to send to you. Sorry for the delay as I've been busy traveling. At any rate, I have yet find a protector up to standard. Among the four is an old brown one made of fiber glass, you might find that more functional. Or, you might try to wear two of them for maximum protection. You can use them for bridging the distance with forceful kicks.

I'm leaving for India on the 29th (next Friday) with Coburn & silliphant. This will be a pre-production survey trip. We are going by way of New York, London Moscow and finally to New Dahli. In India we will cover a lot of ground ---- Bombay, Kashmir, Bengal, etc. etc. Shooting will begin in September.

By the way, when I finished with my latest article, I'll send a copy to you, so you will hear of my latest feeling in martial art.

My regards to Peggy

Peace – Love – Brotherhood

Bruce

Bruce Lee in India, back toward the camera in philosophical pose, as Stirling Silliphant looks on. Bruce, Stirling and James Coburn went to India in search of locations for the film project "The Silent Flute" that unfortunately never came to be.

Taky

I've asked Linda to wrap four protective body guards to send to you. Sorry for the delay as I've been busy traveling. At any rate, I have yet find a protector up to standard. Among the four is an old brown one made of fibre glass. You might find that more functional. Or you might try to wear two of them for maximum protection. You can use them for bridging the distance with forceful kicks.

I'm leaving for India on the 29th (next Friday) with Coburn & Silliphant. This will be a pre-production survey trip. We are going by way of New York, London, Moscow and finally to New Dahli. In India we will cover a lot of ground — Bombay, Kashmir, Bengal etc. etc. Shooting will begin in September.

By the way, when I finished with my latest article I'll send a copy to you, so you will hear of my latest feeling in martial art.

my regards to Peggy

Peace-Love-Brotherhood

Bruce

Letter 52

Description of Letter No. 52

This letter was in regards to me playing the role of the "Praying Mantis" Master in the "The Game of Death". The first time I told him I couldn't do it. But he kept hammering me about it. This was when Linda wrote me and told me that if "Enter the Dragon" was a go they would shelf "Game of death" until after. Dan Inosanto and Kareem had already done their part. After "Enter the Dragon" was finished Bruce called me and told me he wanted me to come to Hong Kong and do my filming. In spite of my objections, he insisted that I be in it. So I agreed, but it never happened as he passed away just weeks after that.

Transcription

Dear Taky, *Oct. 2, 1972*

Just a short note to let you know what's happening here. It looks like your trip may even be later than when we talked on the phone. Warner Bros. representative has been here this week talking to Bruce about the film they are planning. In a couple of weeks we should know if the deal is going to go through and then Bruce can plan his time schedule. If everything goes as planned, he'll have to start filming the Warner thing around December, which means he will stop this film in the middle. He is coming to the States in about 3 weeks to finalize the details of that project.

So what it amounts to is this, if the Warner film goes ahead as planned, then your part in this film will be postponed until after the first of the year. If not, then about 4-5 weeks from now, although it is flexible to fit in with your schedule. I think the former is more likely. it's definitely still on though, as this film is already partly done.

Our regards to Peggy & Andrew

Sincerely,
Linda

Bruce Lee in his office at Golden Harvest in stealth posing for the camera, as he reads an article that highlights his filming of "Game of Death".

Oct. 2, 1972

Dear Taky,

Just a short note to let you know what's happening here. It's looks like your trip may even be later than when we talked on the phone. Warner Bros representative has been here this week talking to Bruce about the film they are planning. In a couple of weeks we should know if the deal is going to go through and then Bruce can plan his time schedule. If everything goes as planned, he'll have to start filming the Warner thing around December 1 which means he will stop this film in the middle. He is coming to the States in about 3 weeks to finalize the details of that project.

So what it amounts to is this, if the Warner film goes ahead as planned, then your part in this film will be postponed until after the first of the year. If not, then about 4-5 weeks from now, although it be flexible to fit in with your schedule. I think the former is more likely. It's definitely still on though, as this film is already partly done.

Our regards to Peggy & Andrew

Sincerely,
Linda

Linda Lee
41 Cumberland Rd
Kowloon Tong
Kowloon, Hong Kong

AN AIR LETTER SHOULD NOT BEAR ANY ATTACHMENT OTHER THAN POSTAGE STAMPS OR CONTAIN ANY ENCLOSURE; IF IT DOES IT WILL BE SURCHARGED OR SENT BY ORDINARY MAIL.

BY AIR MAIL
AIR LETTER
PAR AVION
AEROGRAMME

Mr Taky Kimura
908 8th Ave
Seattle, Wash. 98104
U.S.A.

Notes from the Master

When Bruce Lee passed away, the world was screaming for more. Behind the scenes there was also chaos within his martial arts teachings. It was very confusing at first, but as time went on, the ones closest to him would find the old letters, notes and drawings he passed on to us as learning guides for reminiscing. In fact, these notes have perfectly documented the way Bruce Lee trained and taught and was evolving up until he left us in 1973.

The way Bruce Lee taught in Seattle was different from Oakland and Los Angeles, but they all had Bruce's core influence he brought from Hong Kong and his experience there. Though I am schooled by Bruce Lee in the Jun Fan Method, he often taught me the JKD principles as well and the same went for James Lee in Oakland. Dan Inosanto learned both the Jun Fan Method as well as the JKD Method of doing things. I have always told my students, when I have finished teaching you all I can teach, then its time to look up Dan Inosanto to progress within their learning.

The notes within this section, document where Bruce Lee's mind-set was at on an instructional, creative and humanist level. To view these notes for the first time and see in how Bruce Lee conceived the Jun Fan Gung Fu Method and Jeet Kune Do Method is historic to say the very least.

To view these notes as being an outsider might not hit the point home so to speak, so when you are reading through this section, read carefully, investigate, contemplate and conclude as if you, the reader, were writing these important documents yourself and only then, will you understand the time, struggle and thought put into each note by Bruce Lee. Then, and only then, will you understand the journey and the man.

Note 1

Description of Note 1

This is my personal student record folder Bruce Lee made out to me. Every student and instructor had this folder to document name, birth, where they lived, experience in other martial arts and of course the level being obtained by the student. Bruce usually made two, one for the school and kept one in his possession at home for his personal records.

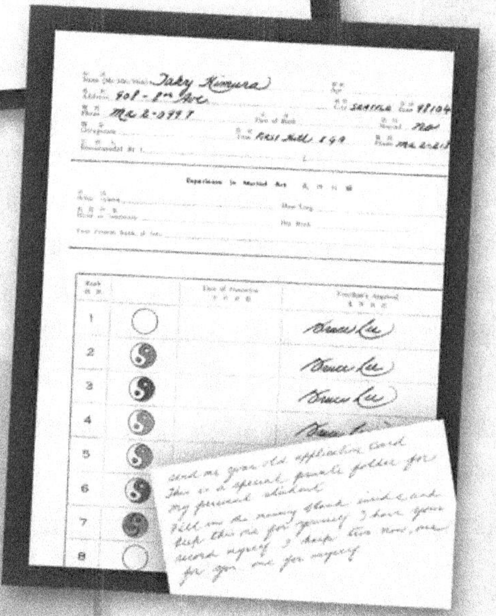

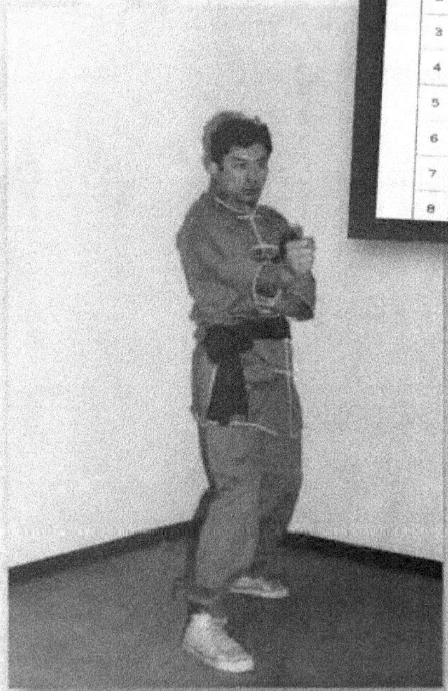

Taky Kimura posing for the camera at the Seattle Gung Fu Institute. This is one of a series of pictures taken for a book Bruce Lee was putting together on Gung Fu.

Note 2

Description of Note 2

Bruce Lee experimented in the design of the many Jun Fan Gung Fu Institute cards. The cards now known to the public are just a few that Bruce conceived and tried out until he decided on the ones that suited his cause well. These two cards were issued to me by SiFu Bruce, showing my 4th and 5th ranks as instructor, the highest rank given by Bruce. These cards were given out to all the students, documenting their growth within the Jun Fan discipline.

As Bruce Lee's martial arts grew, so did his vision in documenting and promoting his school through newer and more eye-catching material that highlighted the rank of his students. This also included his vision in promoting himself with various Bruce Lee business cards. Here you can see the blue and red striped Jun Fan Gung Fu Institute cards that documented the teacher and student rank. The differences in the color cards are only to show a seasonal change. Each season, the old and new students who joined would acquire that seasons color card. Bruce experimented in making numerous colors, but only decided on a certain few to use. These style type of cards were conceived when Bruce was in Los Angeles 1966-1967.

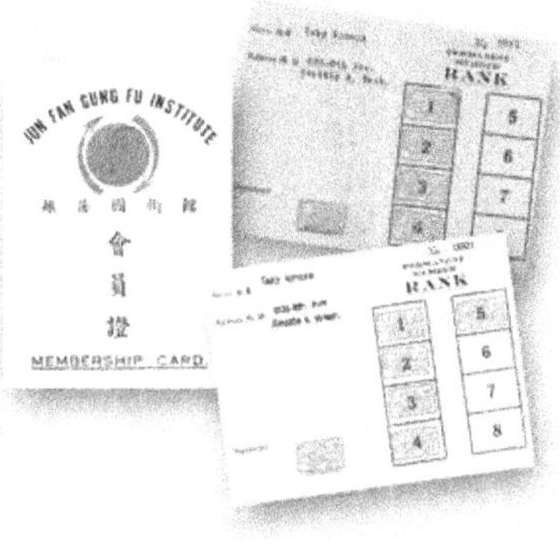

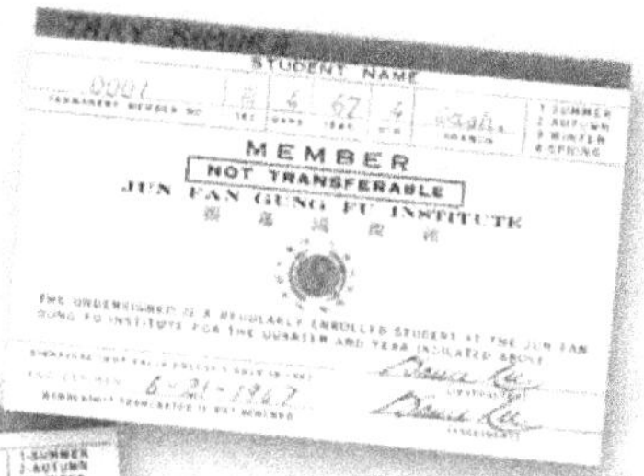

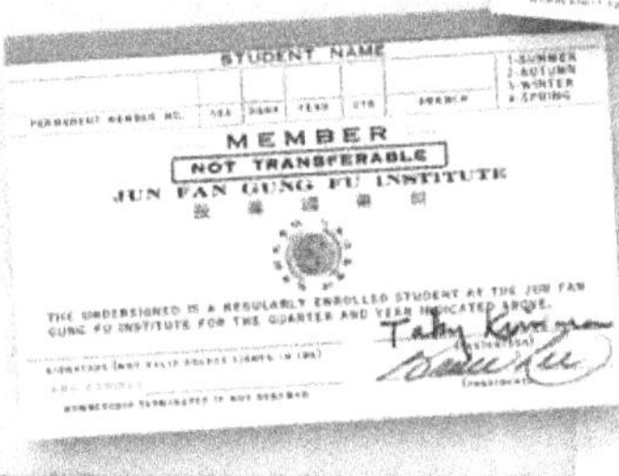

(ABOVE) Taky Kimura in traditional Gung Fu pose in this picture meant for one of Bruce Lee's Gung Fu book project.

(BELOW) Bruce Lee delivers a Bil Jee strike to Dan Inosanto's eye at a Los Angeles Chinatown demonstration.

Note **3**

Description of Note 3

I have kept this birthday card that was given to me by Bruce in1967. I cherish it. Bruce never forgot an occasion, good or bad, he was a true friend.

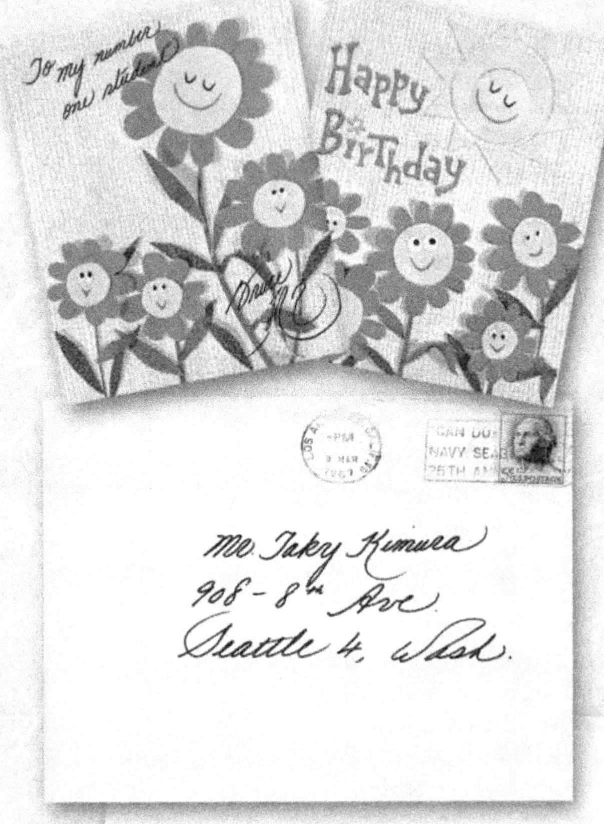

Bruce in fighting mode on the beach in sunny California, in a photo shoot that was to be a part of his Fighting Method book idea.

Note 4

Description of Note 4

This is one of many very detailed workout programs that Bruce Lee made up for himself. When it came to his physical being, he left nothing out. He systematically worked and trained every part of his body to perfection. He worked hard for those results.

Bruce coming in with a hook punch in this picture that was taken for his Fighting Method books he was working on.

Note 5

Description of Note 5

This note means a lot to me. Bruce wanted to make sure that I was taken care of legally by being his instructor in Seattle. He wanted to waive the 5% fee for instructor salary and give me 10% instead, as I was his close friend. I told Bruce then, and it still stays true to this day, I never would take a dime from him and have not profited all these years. He did so much for me that I feel that was payment enough.

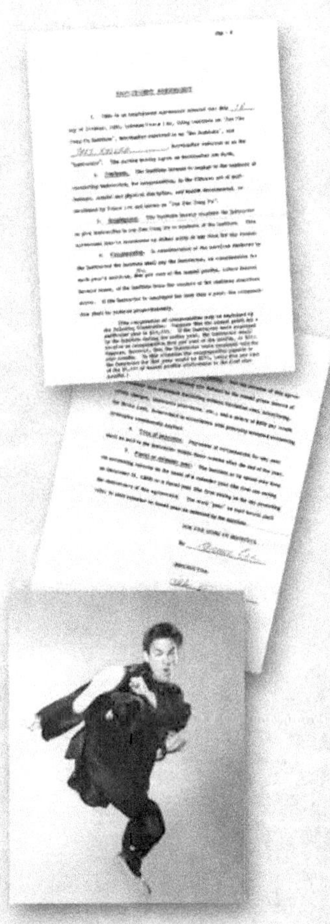

Bruce Lee flying high as he kicks at the camera in this rare picture taken as a promotional move for the "Green Hornet".

Transcription

EMPLOYMENT AGREEMENT

1. This is an employment agreement entered into this 18 day of October, 1963, between Bruce Lee, doing business as "Jun Fan Gung Fu Institute", hereinafter referred to as "the institute", and Taky Kimura, hereinafter referred to as the "Instructor". The parties hereby agree as hereinafter set forth.

2. Business. The Institute intends to engage in the business of conducting instruction, for compensation, in the Chinese art of self- defense, mental and physical discipline, and health development, as developed by Bruce Lee and known as "Jun Fan Gung Fu".

3. Employment. The Institute hereby employs the instructor to give instruction in Jun Fan Gung Fu to students of the Institute. This agreement may be terminated by either party at any time for any reason.

4. Compensation. In consideration of the services rendered by the Instructor the Institute shall pay the Instructor, as compensation for each years service, ten per cent of annual profits, before federal income taxes, of the Institute from the conduct of the business described above. If the Instructor is employed for less than a year, his compensation shall be reduced proportionately.

(The computation of compensation may be explained by the following illustration: Suppose that the annual profit for a particular year is $10,000. If the Instructor were employed by the Institute during the entire year, the Instructor would receive a compensation five per cent of the profits, or $300. Suppose, however, that the Instructor were employed only for nine months. In this situation the compensation payable to the Instructor for that year would be $375, being five per cent of the $7,500 of annual profits attributable to the first nine months.)

5. Computation of annual profits. For the purpose of this agreement, annual profits (or losses) are defined as the annual gross income of the business expenses (including without limitation rent, advertising, utility charges, insurance premiums, etc. and a salary of $300 per month for Bruce Lee), determined in accordance with generally accepted accounting principles consistently applied.

6. Time of payments. Payments of compensation for any year shall be paid to the Instructor within three months after the end of the year.

7. Fiscal or calendar year. The Institute at its option may keep its accounting records on the basis of a calendar year (the first one ending on December 31, 1963) or a fiscal year (the first ending on the day preceding the anniversary of this agreement). The word "year" as used herein shall refer to such calendar or fiscal year as selected by the Institute.

JUN FAN GUNG FU INSTITUTE

By Bruce Lee

INSTRUCTOR:

Taky Kimura

Note 6

Description of Note 6

This note gives you an insight to Bruce Lee's philosophical core. Not only did he visualize technique for the physical, but also everything he created martially had a deep philosophical or spiritual overtone. This drawing / note refers to the immovable elbow and its importance. Also, it has to do with the nucleus, or the core as being the center of power and motion.

Transcription

The immovable, the motionless center of vortices appears in manifestation as motion which incrreases velocity in the manner of a whirlpool or tornado (where epicenter is still) from nucleus is in reality, whereas the vortex is phenomenon in the form of multi-dimensional force-field – HOLD THE CORE!

Bruce Lee practicing the Iron Palm break moves on bricks. Bruce felt this type of thing was mostly for show, but then again, he also felt that practice in the focusing of your Chi on an object and then destroying that object, like this brick in the picture, was a workout for the internal as well as the mind. While in Seattle, Bruce came up with many interesting ways to challenge his physical and mental being.

Note 7

Description of Note 7

In my opinion, Bruce Lee was a philosophical genius. He studied the many philosophies from around the world and he realized that most of them had many things in common. He would discover ideas and make them his own ideals, by adding to them, or subtracting from them. He took from all he learned and made his own philosophical path.

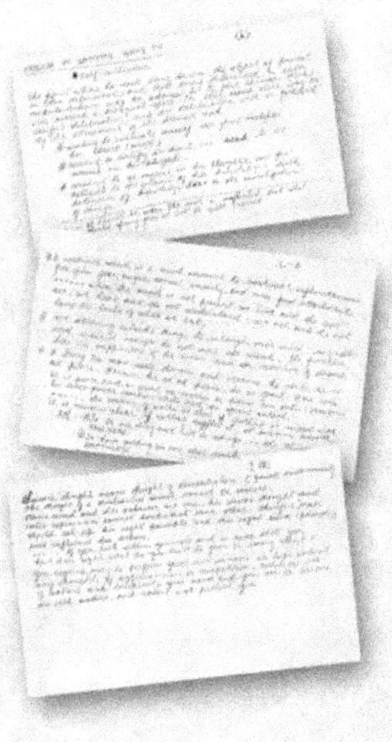

Transcription

PROCESS IN LEARNING GUNG FU (1)

self-cultivation

The point where to rest being known, the object of pursuit is then determined; and, that being determined, a calm Unperturbedness may be attained to. To that calmness there will succeed a tranquil repose. In that repose there may be careful deliberation, and that deliberation will be followed by the attainment of desire end.

 # wishing to cultivate oneself, one first rectifies his heart (mind)

 # wishing to rectify his heart, one seek to be sincere in his thoughts

 # wishing to be sincere in his thoughts, one first extends to the utmost of his knowledge such extension of knowledge lies in the investigation of things.

REMARK – *It cannot be, when the root is neglected, that what should spring from it will be well addressed'.*

 # A rectified mind is a mind immune to emotional influences ------ free from fear, anger, sorrow, anxiety, and even fond attachment. ------ when the mind is not present, we look and do not see; we hear and do not understand; we eat and do not know the taste of what we eat.

 # Not allowing outside things to entangle one's mind; in another word, outward changes do not move the mind. Its function lies in suppression of the senses and on reduction of desire

 # A Gung Fu man rests therein, and because he rests, he is at peace. Because he is at peace, he is quiet. One who is at peace and is quiet no sorrows or harm can enter; therefore his inner power remains whole and his spirit intact. the nature of water is that if nothing is mixed with it, it remains clear; if nothing ruffles it, it remains smooth.

Def. : - (1) To be one thing and not to change, is the climax of STILLNESS

(2) To have nothing in one that resists, is the climax of EMPTINESS

Sincere though means thought of concentration. (quiet awareness) the thought of a disturbed mind cannot be sincere. Man's mind and his behavior are one, his inner thought and outer expression cannot contradict each other. Therefore a man should set up his right principle and this right mind (principle) will influence his action. If you look within yourself and is sure that you have done right, what do you have to fear or worry about?

You require only to perform your own mission in life without any thoughts of aggressiveness or competition. Follow the will of nature and

Note 7

Transcription (continued)

coordinate your mind and your act to become one with nature, and nature will protect you.

(3) To remain detached from all outside things, is the climax of FINENESS.

(4) To have in oneself no contraries, is the climax of PURITY "NO MIND", "NO THOUGHT" discards all thoughts of reward, all hopes of praise and fears of blame, all awareness of one's bodily self, and finally closing the avenues of sense – perception and let the spirit acts as it will.

The highest skill operates almost on an unconscious level.

YIELDING

 # Yielding will overcome anything superior to itself; its strength is boundless.

 # The Yielding will has a reposeful ease, soft as downy feather ------ a quietude, a shrinking from action, an appearance of inability to do (the heart is humble, but the work is forceful).

Placidly free from anxiety, one acts in harmony with the opponents strength. One does not move ahead but responds to the fitting influence.

 # Nothing in the world is more yielding and softer than water; yet it penetrates the hardest. Insubstantial, it enters where no room is. It is so fine that it is impossible to grasp a handful of it; strike it, yet it does not suffer hurt; stab it, and it is not wounded.

** LAW OF NON – INTERFERING: - One should be in harmony with, and not rebellion against, the strength of the opponent. Such act will " preserve ourselves" by following the natural bends of things; consequently, we achieve immortality because we do not wear ourselves out. This theory is illustrated in Taoism about the perfect butcher whose carving knife remains perpetually sharp because it always goes between the bones and tissues and never meets any resistance.*

To rest in weakness is strength. "Alive, a man is supple, soft; In death, unbending, rigorous. All creatures, grass and trees, alive Are plastic but are pliant too. And death, all friable and dry".

Unbending rigor is the mate of death and yielding softness, company of life unbending solidness get no victories; the stiffest tree is readiest for the axe the strong and mighty belong to the bottom the soft and yielding rise above them all.

The strongest is he that makes use of his opponents strength – be the bamboo tree which bends toward the wind; and when the wind ceases, it springs back stronger thank before.

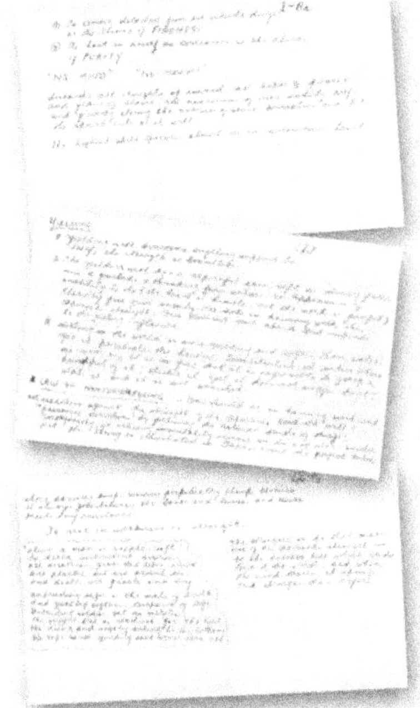

Bruce Lee in his Barrington Plaza apartment office striking a stoic and philosophical pose with his Japanese sword.

Note 8

Description of Note 8

This note is amazing on many fronts. Bruce wrote this note in Chinese to himself. A self-discovering enlightening note that in basic terms, described his make up as a human being and martial artist. Though to some, this may look like a simple note, this is actually a very complicated one. I have never seen another note that Bruce talked about Chi as he does here, it is almost like he is internally creating and describing himself as a martial artist from the ground up.

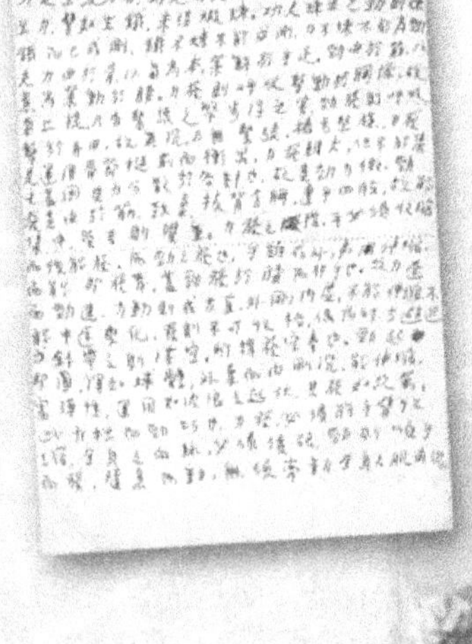

Transcription

Strength "Li" vs. Power "Jing"

Raw strength "Li" is a natural ability which people are born without training. Power "Jing" can be developed through training /Gung Fu. Raw strength is a form of untrained power, it is like a piece of raw iron, which has not been purified or strengthen. Power "Jing" is like steel, it has been cured and hardened. Raw iron cannot be steel without going through purifying and strengthening process of raw material, raw strength "Li" without proper training cannot become Power "Jing".

Raw strength "Li" uses Chi / Qi as its base, then translates into arm or feet movements. Power "Jing" would required tunneling through the waist area, using proper breathing technique in the chest area, bring "Qi / Chi" upward within the body, distribute through "Dan Tian" (center), along with a relaxed but strong and stable stance, power can then be discharged suddenly and quickly.

The effect of Strength "Li" is not dense but scattered. Power "Jing" does come from muscle strength. Sort of soft in a way, but by synchronizing your midsection makes the effect more damaging. "Li" might appear to be powerful initially, but it's actually soft and weak. Power "Jing" actually comes from the waist area but not from the limbs. Strength "Li" is slow and restricted, it is hard on the outside but soft on the inside, it's difficult to change and to contract movements quickly, the result is neither effective nor efficient.

The characteristic of Power "Jing" is like a bouncing ball, soft on the outside, but hard on the inside, one could quickly contract to change to the next movement. The movement is like a crashing wave, starts softly then gently crashes violently at the end. Power "Jing" generated from a powerful punch ideally should happen very naturally even without thinking, it should happen almost instinctively.

Bruce in bodybuilder pose! In actuality, he is channeling his Chi force and applying an isometric like movement to strengthen himself both internally and physically. Bruce always felt that it makes no sense in looking good on the outside if the inside does not feel as good.

Note 9

Description of Note 9

Not only did Bruce Lee investigate the martial arts and philosophies of the world, but also it was very important to him to understand the human condition. He felt that there were ways to treat one another respectfully, therefore getting better results in the lessons of humanity. Bruce was all very into the psychological games so to speak with treating others in a way so he could get what he needed as well, in a non-evasive way. Basically, Bruce knew what others needed and by doing that he prospered by their generosity as well.

Transcription

Characters of Social interaction

(1). We as human beings are not interacting based on pure logics. People in general all have emotions, have points of view, egos and self-esteem, therefore one should not selfishly and blindly criticizing others.

(2). The best way to speak to others, is to forget about oneself for a moment, one should always try to see from other people's perspectives. Eventually they will discover their many qualities, be sensitive to other people's emotion. Understanding people's feelings about you, do reflect on how you interact with them, best to speak less, and to listen more.

(3), People should be treated with respect and honesty, giving others compliments to their achievements, and to keep an opened mind, to be polite and always keep a smile.

(4), Traits of a well liked personality:

1, happiness 2, generosity 3, honesty 4, understanding 5, flexibility 6, stability 7, helpfulness, 8, humbleness 9, self-respect 10, sociability.

(5) People like to: Feel that they are important. Get along with others. Be acknowledged by others. Be trust worthy. Explore their interests. Have common sense with others. Help to give advice to others. Have others to open their heart to them. Have others to pay attention to them. Inspire others.

(6), Always respect the relationships with others, don't sweat the small stuff, be tolerant. If there are issues with others, don't suddenly lose your composure, but try to understand and to respect.

(7), Every person feels their opinions are the correct ones, but to interact and to accept, one must try to understand others, then others would be able to relate reciprocally.

(8), Converse with others to find out their interests, and study their body language then interact accordingly.

(9), When speaking to others, discuss topics based on that person's interests, keep your story short and brief. Don't make impolite gestures to others when attentions are needed. Go with the flow, don't be self-centered. If it involves with complex discussions, try to avoid conflicts, do not self promote. When speaking to others, always keep eye contact, be polite, and be truthful to others. Jealousy is the worst enemy, and try not to rain on other people's parade.

(10), To have others to agree or to relate to one's opinions, one must listen to others, try not to be overanxious, and not to dominate the discussion. One should always keep an open mind with honestly and listen to what others have to say. (Think more, Talk less).

Note: A reliable way to pay detailed attention to other's emotion is to study their gestures, reactions and the way they conduct themselves.

Bruce Lee in Hong Kong in 1963. Throughout his summer visit, he took many photo shoots at a local photography parlor, so that his family would have the pictures as reminder of the vacation they spent together when he went back to the States.

Note **10**

Description of Note 10

When Bruce had ideas about how he could better his martial arts capabilities, he would always draw or write notes about what was on his mind. When I use to have lunch or dinner with him, it was in the ordinary that he would always be writing something down at the table that highlighted his martial arts or philosophy. He was always investigating, adding or eliminating things, eventually creating his own fighting method.

Transcription

IRON SAND PALM

(1), Press Palm: Through center "Dan Tian" to generate power "Jing"

: Synchronized forearm power "Jing"

: Mental concentration

(2), Ridge hand strike: Unified

(3), Spear finger strike: Tight/dense fingers

Bruce Lee working on his Knife hand / Bil Jee / Iron Palm by thrusting his hand into sand / pellets. Bruce trained every part of his body to its maximum, but for striking, he trained with equipment that was extraordinary. He was a true innovator.

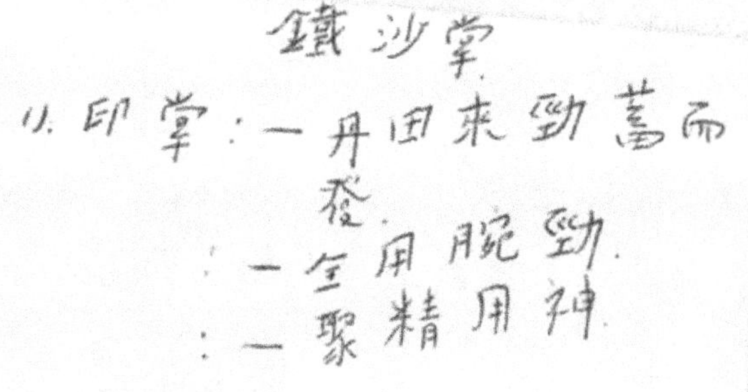

鐵沙掌

1. 印掌：—丹田來勁蓄而發.

：—全用腕勁.

：—聚精用神.

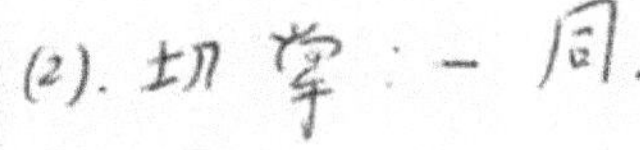

(2). 切掌：—同.

(3). 標指：—緊指.

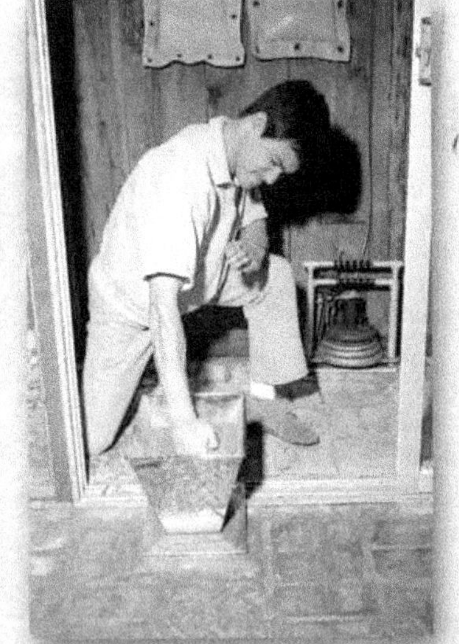

Note **11**

Description of Note 11

This drawing Bruce Lee made is a figure that is demonstrating the Immovable Elbow. A lot of people don't know this, but many times when he drew figures doing martial arts related techniques, he was drawing his own image. These notes were really started as for he to have somewhat of a self-reference guide for his ideas that would pop up almost on a daily basis. There were countless drawings and notes. Looking back now, it was obvious that he perfectly documented himself, without knowing that one-day all these treasure would document his life for all of us. Truly amazing.

Bruce in a pose that mirrors the drawing he created. This image is one of many that were taken for Bruce's Fighting Method books. Though he scrapped that idea, after he passed away, Linda released the books for the world to see to have some type of guide in what he was trying to accomplish within his teachings.

Note 12

Description of Note 12

During Bruce Lee's career and after, his role as Kato in the "Green Hornet" made him quite a celebrity and he would tour to different States and being a headliner guest at the many Karate / Martial Arts Championships his friends would put on annually. Bruce from time to time would put on great demonstrations that would blow people away. He converted many loyal practitioners of other martial arts to his teachings, which at times upset their instructors. Bruce trained many of the champions of that day like Joe Lewis and Mike Stone. They all came to him in interest to see what he had to offer. No one was ever disappointed in Bruce, he stayed true to his beliefs and people just wanted to follow him.

1967 National Karate Championship
D.C. Armory • 2001 East Capitol Street
Saturday, May 6, 1967—8:00 p.m.
Defender: JOE LEWIS, 1966 National Karate Champion
Special Guests: ROBERT CULP of "I Spy" and
BRUCE LEE, the KATO of Green Hornet
Sponsored by: Korean Cultural and Freedom Foundation
Presented by: Jhoon Rhee Institute of Tae Kwon Do, Inc.
For Information Call: DU 7-0800
or write: Jhoon Rhee Institute
1801 Connecticut Ave., N.W.
Washington, D. C. 20009
№ 1100
$5.00

Bruce Lee center, Jhoon Rhee picture left and Joe Lewis kneeling with championship flag after winning the highest honors at the Jhoon Rhee tournament in Washington D.C.

Note 13

Description of Note 13

This was an advertisement for Bruce Lee, promoting a demonstration he was to do while at the same time promote his appearance in the film "Marlowe" with James Garner.

Bruce Lee delivering a side kick to James Garner in the now famous film "Marlowe".

Note 14

Description of Note 14

This is the only proof needed to show how Bruce Lee was a self made man. He had a vision in who he was, and what he was going to accomplish. Though he passed away in 1973, in 1985 had he'd been here, his dreams would have been realized as it was written from pen to paper back in 1969. Bruce was not going to let anything stop him from achieving success and this note is proof of that.

Transcription

SECRET MY DEFINITE CHIEF AIM

I, Bruce Lee, will be the first highest paid Oriental super star in the United States. In return I will give the most exciting performances and render the best of quality in the capacity of an actor. Starting 1970 I will achieve world fame and from then onward till the end of 1985 I will have in my possession $10,000,000. I will live the way I please and achieve inner harmony and happiness.

Bruce Lee in stoic pose on the set of the film "Marlowe" about to shoot the most memorable scene in that film.

SECRET

MY DEFINITE CHIEF AIM

I, Bruce Lee, will be the first highest paid Oriental super star in the United States. In return I will give the most exciting performances and render the best of quality in the capacity of an actor. Starting 1970 I will achieve world fame and from then onward till the end of 1985 I will have in my possession $10,000,000. I will live the way I please and achieve inner harmony and happiness.

Bruce Lee

BRUCE LEE

(1/7/1969)

SECRET

Note 15

Description of Note 15

This is a note that Bruce Lee made shortly after arriving from his boat trip from Hong Kong to the United States. As you can see, he wrote down important dates and information he needed for his stay in America.

Transcription

Passport Number - 224821
Selective Service No. - 4, 36,40, 105
Social Security No. -564-58-5856
ASUW - 6150359

29, April 1959 (Wednesday), left Hong Kong 10 p.m.
17, May 1959 (Sunday), arrived in San Francisco.

Father's birthday:	*- Feb. 18th*
Mother's:	*- Nov. 8th (Chinese calendar)*
Eva auntie's:	*- Feb. 2nd (Chinese calendar)*
Pearl's:	*-14, August, '40 / July 11th*
Peter's:	*- Sep. 11th*
Agnes's:	*- Dec. 26th*
Howard's:	*- 23, July '44*
Robert's:	*- Nov. 16th*
Mary's m:	*- Mar. 1st (Chinese calendar)*
Sambo:	*- May 16, 1940*
	: - Mar. 21st
	: - Aug. 17th

Bruce Lee looking sharp in Seattle, just steps away from Ruby Chow's restaurant where he would live and work until he got on his feet.

Note 16

Description of Note 16

Much history was made when Bruce Lee began to teach some of the students from the University of Washington. For one, this is where he made his mark and people started to take notice of him and his skill. Secondly, and most important, this is where he met his future wife Linda. Those were great and memorable times.

Transcription

P.E. Department May Offer Gung Fu Class

Students taking P.E. next fall may have a chance to take a course in Gung Fu, an ancient Oriental system of hand-to-hand combat. Dr. Russell Cutler, executive officer of the men's P.E. Department became interested in Gung Fu some time ago, and had Bruce Lee, a University Sophomore, put on a demonstration in Meany hall to test student interest in Gung Fu.

About 200 people turned out for the demonstration. Consequently, the P.E. Department is seriously considering starting a class in Gung Fu.

Bruce Lee looking sharp on campus at the University of Washington. Bruce was so very proud to attend that college and his family was even more proud of him back in Hong Kong.

Bruce Lee relaxing next to Lake Washington on a Saturday afternoon, posing for the camera.

Note 17

Description of Note 17

It's amazing to see that Bruce documented his life in one way or another, his day-to-day life. Here is an example of he writing down a famous fight he had that staretd his liberation into finding a way to quicken the victory against his opponent. 13 seconds is fast, but Bruce never settled for fast, he wanted lightening.

Transcription

Against Karate black belt holder (Shodan) and 2nd degree black belt in Judo.

Place: - Downtown .Y M. C. A. (Seattle)
Date: - 1, Nov., 1960 (Tues.)

Result: - won. Knock him down
In 13 sec.; couldn't fight anymore.

Jun Fan stoically posing in a traditional Gung Fu uniform for the camera, taken at Ruby Chow's restaurant.

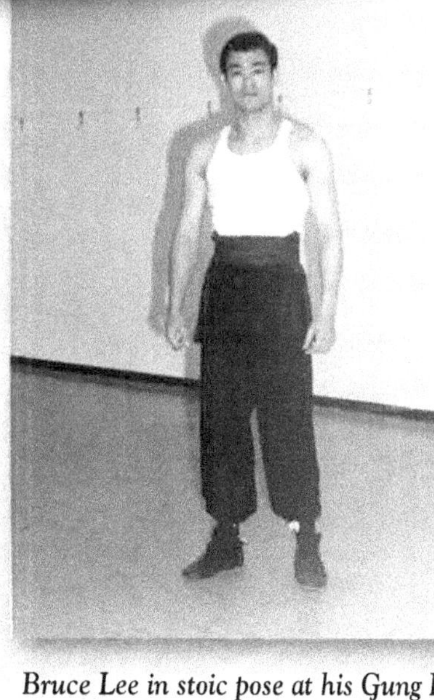

Bruce Lee in stoic pose at his Gung Fu School in Seattle.

Note 18

Description of Note 18

Bruce Lee was always in a state of self-investigation, as well as developing his martial arts for others to learn. At lunch or dinner, or just hanging out, he would always jot down his ideas on paper, holding on to them as a guide tool to what he wanted to achieve. Many times, Bruce would write notes down in regarding material that needed to be taught within his class, so he would write it down and then later on give it to me for me to apply it to the class.

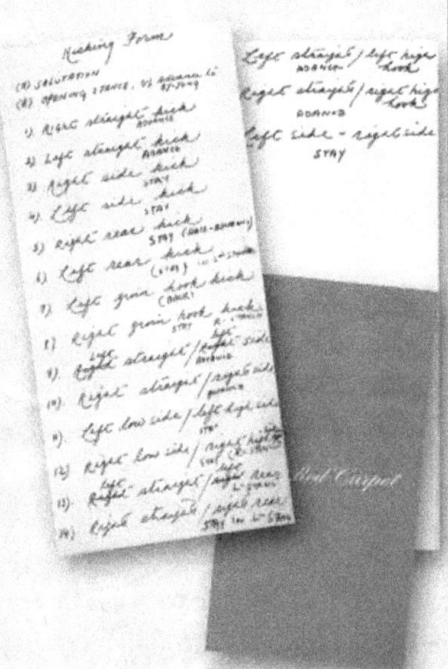

Transcription

Kicking Form

(A) SALUTATION

(B) OPENING STANCE, *b). Advance to* BY-JONG

1). Right straight kick ADVANCE

2). Left straight kick ADVANCE

3). Right side kick STAY

4). Left side kick STAY

5). Right rear kick STAY (HALF-ADVANCE)

6). Left rear kick (STAY) IN L-STANCE

7). Left groin hook kick (BACK)

8). Right groin hook kick STAY R-STANCE

9). Left straight / left side ADVANCE

10). Right straight / right side ADVANCE

11). Left low side / left high side STAY

12). Right low side / right high side STAY (R-STANCE

13). Left straight / left rear L-STANCE

14). Right straight / right rear STAY IN L-STANCE

15). Left straight / left high ADVANCE *hook*

16). Right straight / right high ADVANCE *hook*

17). Left side – right side STAY

Left to Right: Linda, Bruce and Dan Inosanto out to dinner in Los Angeles Chinatown with friends. Bruce loved going to lunches and dinners with family and friends. He loved the musings everyone shared. It reminded him of back in Hong Kong with his large family.

Note 19

Description of Note 19

These notes are just another example of Bruce Lee's incorporating martial arts skill with the base root of philosophy. To Bruce, saying a punch is just a punch meant nothing unless there was meaning behind it. It is only when you have perfected that punch, that the meaning leaves the mind freeing it, so the punch becomes an extension of your being, rather than an extension of your thoughts, it is automatic in other words. Bruce was amazing in his analogies when it came to teaching, but to experience what it was those teachings were like, well, that was a whole other world.

Transcription

First note upper left touches on direction of flowing energy and how the success of ones energy depends on the training becoming more intense. When one becomes familiar with the training, the growth happens and energy should be plentiful. Bottom of note shows a Gung Fu man holding a bar and it reads, "Be like an iron bar and you will be lifted!!" This meaning is more about the physiological / spiritual side of power and energy. If you can achieve the ultimate (the iron bar) then your mind and soul will be lifted from that burden and the act now becomes an extension of your being

Drawing note upper right describes water and how one should be like water in his or hers training. For Bruce, being like water was part of his everyday philosophy. He believed that water accommodates itself to everything. If a rock is thrown in a stream of water as depicted in this drawing top of note, then the water simply goes around the rock finding its flow and objective. And if the rock shall block the waters path, then the water shall penetrate the rock. Water is the most gentle, but yet destructive force in the world. Bruce shows in the drawing note bottom page in how water cannot be controlled and how it adapts to everything it touches. This is how a Gung Fu man should be he thought, adaptable and pliable to all, weak to none

Drawing note bottom left depicts a Gung Fu man holding a chain, suggesting one should be the chain, the flowing, snapping, reaching and adapting chain. The harder one trains, the more energy and strength the chain (Gung Fu man) becomes. When the training becomes part of the Gung Fu man's soul, then his movements will be like a chain that cannot be controlled.

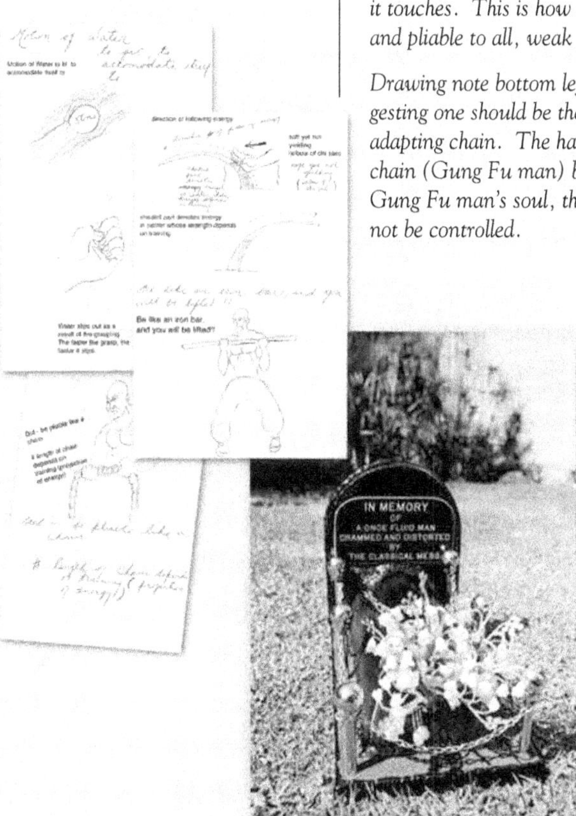

IN MEMORY OF A ONCE FLUID MAN CRAMED AND DISTORTED BY THE CLASSICAL MESS

This piece of equipment designed by George Lee has become famous in the Bruce Lee world. Bruce was always describing himself as a martial artist through the words of philosophy. Basically, the meaning on this tombstone means, a man free of attachments has succumbed to being caged by being infected by the grind and beliefs of others. One must free the mind to be fluid, therefore adapting to every situation life brings. Be fluid and strong, yet soft and yielding like water. Be water.

Note 20

Description of Note 20

Here is an example of Bruce's outlining a structure for his Gung Fu method. This was written and re-written until he was completely satisfied with the result. He found it important not only to have rules and guidelines, but behind all that, there had to be a philosophy to the demands / rules and WHY those rules must be applied.

The history of Chinese Gung Fu was to enlighten the students and the assistant instructors to the origins and meanings behind the Chinese way of fighting / pugilism. Bruce felt it necessary to explain in detail in where, why and how the history of Chinese fighting came to be. Without doing so, what he was teaching could have been perceived as an empty shell.

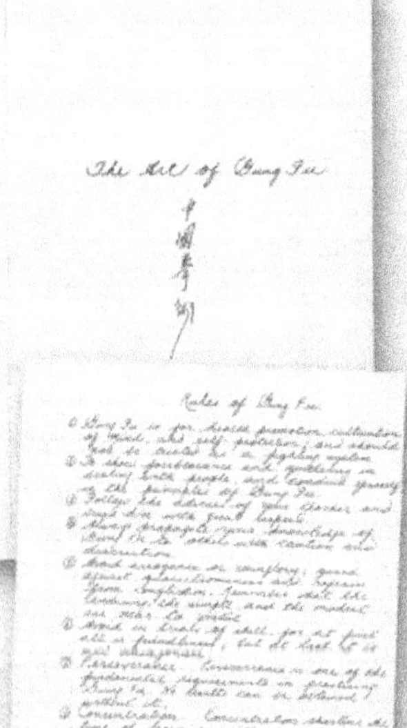
The Art of Gung Fu

中國拳術

Rules of Gung Fu

Transcription

The Art of Gung Fu

Chinese Fighting Techniques

Rules of Gung Fu

(1) Gung Fu is for health promotion, cultivation of mind, and self-protection; and should not be treated as a fighting system.

(2) To show forbearance and gentleness in dealing with people, and conduct yourself in the principles of Gung Fu.

(3) Follow the advices of your teacher and treat him with great respect.

(4) Always propagate your knowledge of Gung Fu to others with caution and discretion.

(5) Avoid arrogance or vainglory; guard against quarrelsomeness and refrain from confliction. Remember that the ending, the simple, and the modest are near to virtue

(6) Avoid in trials of skill, for at first all is friendliness; but at last it is all antagonism.

(7) Perseverance. Perseverance is one of the fundamental requirements in practicing Gung Fu. No results can be obtained without it.

(8) Concentration. Concentration shortens the time of learning. With concentrated attention one may master the art quickly and thoroughly.

(9) Gradualiness. One should practise according to the order specified, and avoid trying any movement before the preceding one is completely mastered. Non-observance of this rule will result in total failure.

Brief Introduction to Gung Fu
Chinese Fighting Methods (Chinese Pugilism)

Gung Fu (Chinese art of Pugilism), the oldest of all hand to hand combat, is practiced for health promotion, cultivation of mind, and self-protection. Because it has been shrouded under a veil of utmost secrecy, Gung Fu is almost unknown to the outside world. Its history covers 5000 years. At first, in the mists of antiquity, Gung Fu was simply no-hold-barred fighting, but as the centuries went by, countless generations of its practitioners gradually perfected it, smoothing out the rough spots, polishing the techniques, until it began to emerge as something definitely superior. Since to a great extent, Gung Fu was used by Chinese monks and Taoist priests, they also saw, and taught, the connection between

Note 29

Description of Note 29

Another example of Bruce Lee creating the curriculum for his Jun Fan Gung Fu. He left no rock unturned. For such a young age at that time, his actions were of a much older and mature Master. Bruce was one of a kind.

Transcription

COPY DOWN
REGULATIONS OF GUNG FU

1). Gung Fu is for health promotion, cultivation of mind, and self-protection. It should not be treated as a fighting system.

2). Follow the advice of your teacher and treat him with great respect.

3). Conduct yourself in the principle of Gung Fu by showing forbearance and gentleness in dealing with people.

4). Always propagate your knowledge of Gung Fu to others with caution and discretion.

5). Avoid arrogance and guard against quarrelsomeness. Remember that the enduing, the simple, and the modest are near to the principles of Gung Fu.

6). Avoid in trials of skill, for at first all is friendliness; but at last it is all antagonism.

Announcements

From now on the rules and etiquette of Chinese Gung Fu will be enforced. The students are required to follow them at all time. Here are but some of the rules that will be given in more detail in the very near future.

rule 1: During and after practice students should salute to the Sea Fu (instructor). This rule also applies to practice among students.

rule 2: Students must be punctual to come for practice. When a student arrives late. And the practice has already begun, he is required to salute to the instructor.

rule 3: When the word "Ju Jee" is given, all students must be in the position of attention (illustrate).

rule 4: Any assignments given for any specific day must be completed on that given date without any delay.

rule 5: Be attentive during lectures as concentration shorten the time of one's learning. Absent-mindness during instruction is treated as disrespectful to the instructor.

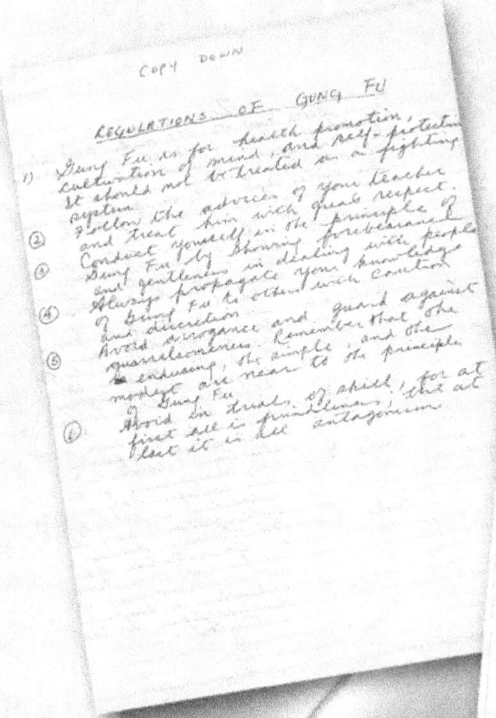

COPY DOWN

REGULATIONS OF GUNG FU

1) Gung Fu is for health promotion, cultivation of mind, and self-protection. It should not be treated as a fighting system.

(2) Follow the advices of your teacher and treat him with great respect.

(3) Conduct yourself in the principle of Gung Fu by showing forbearance and gentleness in dealing with people.

(4) Always propagate your knowledge of Gung Fu to others with caution and discretion.

(5) Avoid arrogance and guard against quarrelsomeness. Remember that the enduring, the simple, and the modest are near to the principle of Gung Fu.

(6) Avoid in trials of skill, for at first all is friendliness; but at last it is all antagonism.

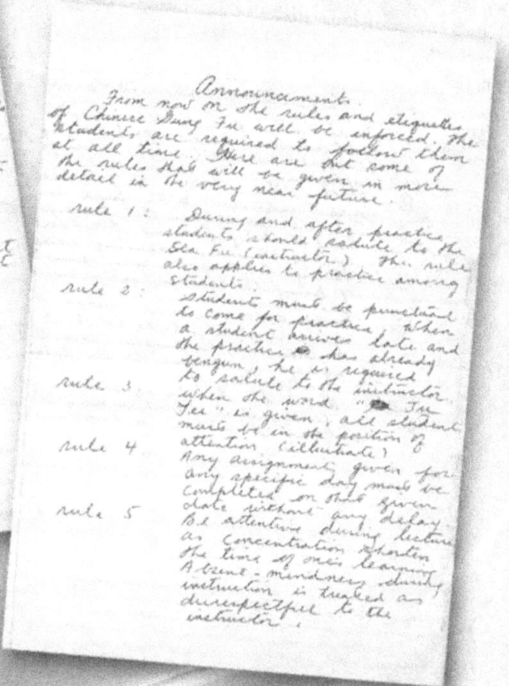

Announcement.

From now on the rules and etiquettes of Chinese Gung Fu will be enforced. The students are required to follow them at all time. Here are but some of the rules that will be given in more detail in the very near future.

rule 1: During and after practice students should salute to the Sia Fu (instructor). This rule also applies to practice among students.

rule 2: Students must be punctual to come for practice. When a student arrives late and the practice has already begun, he is required to salute to the instructor.

rule 3: When the word "Tai Yee" is given, all students must be in the position of attention (illustrate).

rule 4: Any assignment given for any specific day must be completed on that given date without any delay.

rule 5: Be attentive during lecture as concentration shortens the time of one's learning. Absent-mindedness during instruction is treated as disrespectful to the instructor.

Bruce Lee teaching class at the Seattle Gung Fu Institute.

Note **30**

Description of Note 30

Though Bruce was not in Seattle anymore, he still contacted me to make sure all procedures were followed. He left nothing unturned. If there were an absence on my behalf in relaying information to the class, Bruce would contact me by phone or mail to let me know in an underline and diplomatic way to get things done. He knew I had a lot on my plate, so when he asked things from me, they were not demands, but structured in kind of like lesson plans. For example, his psychology was like this. If I had to teach the class a certain technique and was delinquent in doing so, Bruce would suggest that I work and better myself with the technique and afterwards, show the class, instead of demanding it from me angrily. He had a way of uplifting others around him to get the job done.

Transcription

From now on have two folders made of each student. One is to send to me so I can record his rank, quarterly card, letters, etc. etc. without having to have you constantly sending me informations.

We have a lot of application cards. If you need any, let me know. So send me students' folders when you have them ready. Check the old one in file box, send me those if students are still. Taking yours too

Thank you.

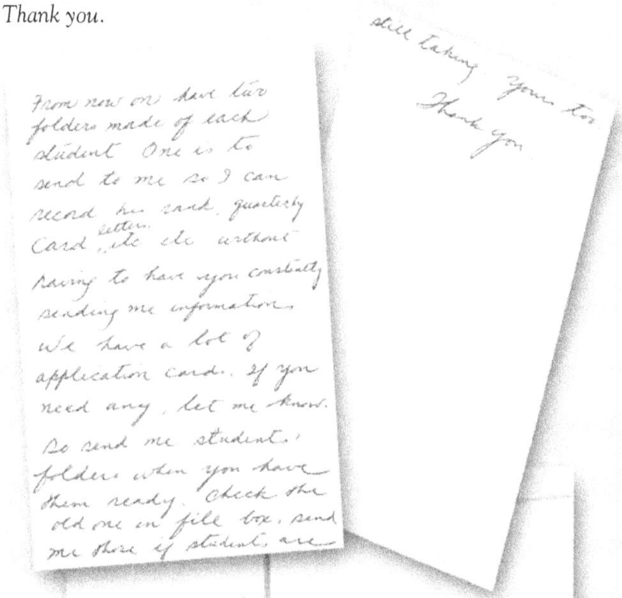

From now on have two folders made of each student One is to send to me so I can record his rank, quarterly Card, letters, etc etc without having to have you constantly sending me informations. We have a lot of application cards. If you need any, let me know. So send me students' folders when you have them ready. Check the old one in file box, send me those if students are

still taking Yours too
Thank you

Bruce Lee in Wing Chun Gung Fu pose for the camera in Seattle 1962.

Note 31

Description of Note 31

Another example of a basic structured Gung Fu Program that Bruce wanted me to share with the class. Bruce was constantly changing the program and structure of his teachings, as he got deeper and deeper into the Jeet Kune Do way of things. He kept true to his Jun Fan Gung Fu as the base, but his mindset went far beyond what he had learned in Hong Kong. He took what he learned and made it better by adding and subtracting from it.

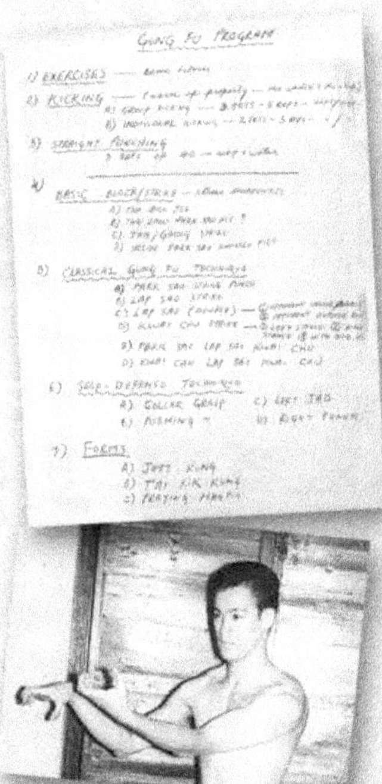

Bruce Lee in Gung Fu pose in 1963, in Hong Kong, back for a visit with family and friends at his house, 218 Nathon Road while his younger brother Robert takes the photo.

Transcription

GUNG FU PROGRAM

1). EXCERSISES ~~~~ Basic Fitness

2). KICKING ~~~~ (warm up properly ~~ the water & the whip)

A). GROUP KICKING ~~ 2 SETS – 5 REPS – LEFT / RIGHT
B). INDIVIDUAL KICKING ~~ 2 SETS – 5 REPS – " / "

3). STRAIGHT PUNCHING

3 SETS OF 40 ---- whip & water

4). BASIC BLOCK / STRIKE --- stress AWARENESS

A). THE BILL JEE
B). THE LOW PARK SAO HIT?
C). TAN / GAONG STRIKE
D). INSIDE PARK SAO KNUCKLE FIST

5). CLASSICAL GUNG FU TECHNIQUE

A). PARK SAO STRIKE PUNCH
B). LAP SAO STRIKE
C). LAP SAO (DOUBLE)
(1) OPONENT INSIDE BLOCK
(2) OPPONENT OUTSIDE BLOCK

D). KWAI CHU STRIKE
(1) LEFT STANCE
(2) RIGHT STANCE
(3) WITH SIDE KICK

E). PARK SAO LAP SAO KWAI CHU
D). KWAI CHU LAP SAO KWAI CHU

6). SELF-DEFENSE TECHNIQUE

A). COLLAR GRASP C). LEFT JAB
B). PUSHING? D). RIGHT PUNCH

7). FORMS

A). JEET KUNG
B). T'AI KIK KUNG
C). PRAYING MANTIS

Note 32

Description of Note 32

Bruce made this training program for me to help me better my flexibility and agility, along side my speed and strength. Bruce analyzed me and what I needed work on and gave me this guide to follow as his top instructor of the Seattle Institute. He was able to customize any workout program for any individual, knowing at the end, the program he made would fully excel the student's abilities.

TAKY KIMURA

FUNCTIONAL FITNESS — 1) FORWARD BEND ------- 3 SETS
2) SIT UP TWIST ----- 3 SETS OF 15
3) LEG RAISES ------- " " "

AGILITY TRAINING ---- 1). Jumping squat ---- 3 sets
2). alternate splits --- 3 sets
3) Jumping press-ups ---- " "
4) Cross-sticks jump ---- " "
5). side jump over rope ---- " "
6). Double & cyclone kicks --- " "
7). Form practice ---- " "

PUNCHING POWER --- 1). GLOVE PUNCHING

GUNG FU TRAINING --- 1). STICKING HAND ---- 3 RDS. of 2 min.

SPEED TRAING --- 1). ENTERING TRAINING.

Taky Kimura in kicking form for the camera in Gung Fu pose, at the Seattle Jun Fan Gung Fu Institute.

Note 33

Description of Note 33

As Bruce was developing the structure for the Seattle Gung Fu Institute, he was also developing my training programs for me as his student, as well as other programs for me to teach as an instructor. This wonderful note was one of the first guidelines / training programs that he wanted me to follow to better my Gung Fu, and then as I became proficient with his instructions, I then added some of the program to the class structure.

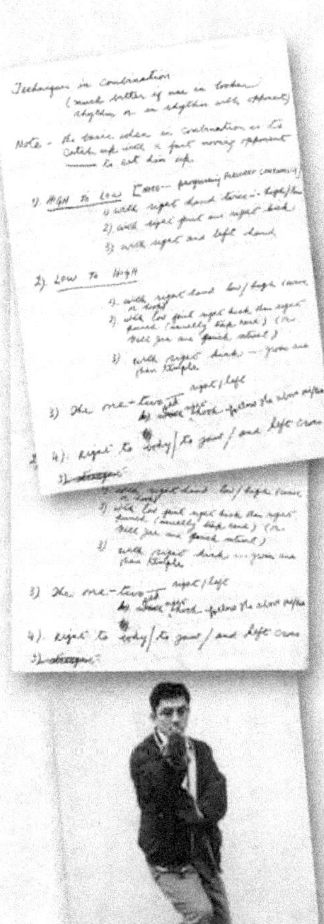

Transcription

Taky Kimura

*1). Practice of footwork ------*MOBILITY *Note – use breaking & gaining ground in all Technique whenever possible* PRACTICE DISTANCE!)

2). The practice of kicking FROM ALL POSSIBLE ANGLES *with speed, directness, and quick returning to guard or containing the attacking (well covered!)*

3). The practice of the leading right punch & kick (especially the shin & knee kick) ~~~because 90% of all hitting & kicking are done with the leading right hand and foot, it is important to be proficient to whip (forcefully) the right (hand and / or foot) to head or body, with singly or in combination.

4). Practice all movement directly FROM YOUR READY STANCE *(whether straight, hook or curve) So that added surprise will be on your Side ----* not to mention added speed.

5). Cultivate AWARENESS *---- this quality will slow the opponents speed at least 40% ~~ It is also this quality (plus distance) that you can slip or grasp the opponents hand or leg.*

Techniques in combination (much better if use in broken rhythm or in rhythm with opponent)

Note – the basic idea in combination is to Catch up with a fast moving opponent _________ to set him up.

1). HIGH TO LOW (NOTE *--- programming* FORWARD CONTINOUSLY)

1). With right hand twice – high / low
2). With right feint and right kick
3). With right and left hand

2). LOW TO HIGH

1). With right hand low / high (curve or hook)
2). With low feint right kick then right punch (usually trap hand) (or Bill Jee and quick retreat)

2). With right kick --- groin and then temple
3). The one – two right / left
a). Add right hook follow the above one/two
b).

4). Right to body / to jaw / and left cross

Sifu Taky Kimura in a traditional Wing Chun Gung Fu pose that would make Master Yip Man proud, outside the Seattle Gung Fu Institute.

Best Wishes
Bruce Lee

Captured Moments

A picture is worth a thousand words they say and in Bruce Lee's case; there are no numbers to define the countless photographs that have documented his life. You do not have to have the knowledge of the English language to understand the stories told behind the cameras that have captured the most influential martial artist of all times.

The passing of Bruce Lee at the age of 32 was sudden and unexpected. Put into the fact that he was an on going evolving man who was constantly changing his philosophy on the way he saw the world and the martial arts, then you would understand that his vision would have been lost to us all if it were not for his writings and pictures to document his journey.

In this section, you will find many rare and unseen pictures taken of Bruce Lee from the first time he set foot in the States in 1959, up until his passing in 1973. It was my vision to pick what I felt were the most rare and influential images from my collection in how I saw and remember the man I called my best friend.

I hope that you, the reader, will feel that you were there as well when these memorable photos were taken and that we can all share the experience together. For Bruce Lee's legacy will be remembered and preserved by us all through the pictures taken of him in his short, but revolutionary life.

Bruce and Taky Practicing the Jun Fan Method at Beacon Hill Park

Description

Every weekend Bruce and I would find a variety of places to train. We would find gymnasiums, parking lots, empty back apartment lots and parks. We would usually choose the less inhabited place at the time so we could concentrate in what we were doing. Sometimes it would be a few of us practicing and other times just Bruce and me. The images in the sections show Bruce and I practicing martial arts at Beacon Hill Park. We usually started training around noon and ended 3:00PM give or take. Wherever we trained it would bring on many onlookers who had not really seen the martial arts before, so the interest in what we were doing was very obvious. In these images you can see Bruce and I practicing Gung Fu techniques in which I was always on the receiving end. Those days bring back wonderful memories of my sifu teaching me and enlightening me as well with his philosophy.

The Seattle Jun Fan Gung Fu Institute

Description

Bruce was always documenting through picture shoots the development of his martial arts. Be it for a book, magazine, or just for self-discovery and reference, they're seemed to always have been a camera around to document what was going on within the progression of what he was doing. Bruce felt it important to express himself to the world through pictures; this was a goal of his and what better way to do this and reach out to others who could not be there to witness his prowess first hand. These series of images were taken at the University Way Jun Fan Gung Fu Institute. These pictures were taken for a few reasons, a book, magazine coverage and personal reference for Bruce. As you can see, Bruce Lee is defended against an attacker, (me) and doing what he did best, taking me out with flawless technique and speed.

(A) Bruce Lee facing us and teaching us a traditional Wing Chun move at the Institute. The Jun Fan Gung Fu class practicing some traditional Wing Chun moves. (B) Linda far right practicing with a fellow student. (C) Linda performing a Bil Jee move on me as Bruce far right looks on with the class.

Jun Fan Gung Fu Photo Shoot with Bruce and Taky

Bruce Lee and Taky Kimura demonstrate at the Ed Parker Internationals

Description

Numerous times I performed with Bruce Lee at different demonstrations throughout our early friendship and student teacher relationship. The most enjoyable times were when Bruce and I would perform at the Ed Parker Internationals. Bruce would usually come out after being announced and explain his style of martial arts, followed by him doing one finger pushups, or one inch punch, all these to show strength and technique. After all of this, Bruce would wave me in and he would demonstrate techniques on me in front of a packed house in Long Beach, California. In the beginning, it was hard for me to give Bruce the reactions he wanted to express to the audience, so on one occasion at the hotel before we went over to the arena, Bruce told me he wanted me to be more aggressive so it looked more realistic to the onlookers. I told Bruce I just did not have that in me and that is when Bruce slapped me across the face very hard. I got so angry I rushed him and by

Description (continued)

mistake he tripped over a stool that was in back of him. When Bruce got up from the floor you could see the red in his eyes, I thought I was going to be killed. Then all of the sudden the anger from his face turned into a smile with laughter and he said to me "That's it! Do it just like that when we are on stage". Bruce always knew what to do to get the right reaction from you, he was brilliant. I miss those times dearly. Through 1964-1967 I was at Bruce's call for many demonstrations.

Bruce Lee in San Francisco

Description of Photos

When Bruce arrived in San Francisco in 1959, he only had a couple hundred dollars to his name, but he was full of vigor and excitement in coming back to where he was born. He felt that America was full of great opportunities and he was going to take advantage of all the good things it had to offer. He loved the water and had frequented the pier on many occasions.

(Top Left) Bruce posing along side his friend Jerry at the pier in San Francisco 1959.

(Top Right) A young and fresh off the boat Bruce Lee in San Francisco visiting the pier in 1959 upon his arrival to the States.

(Above) Just moments into San Francisco harbor Bruce poses with two fellow passengers in celebration of the conclusion of their long journey from Hong Kong.

(Left) Bruce Lee and his friend Jerry walk the streets of San Francisco taking in the sights on Saturday evening. Jerry was a distant friend of Bruce's who had interests in the martial arts who lived locally in SF. Jerry showed Bruce around when he arrived from Hong Kong.

Bruce & Peter Lee

Bruce and Peter Lee in 1961, brothers together again, taking a picture with one another in a photo booth located in downtown Seattle.

Bruce Plays Cowboy

Description of Photo

Bruce Lee playing cowboy while posing with rifle and gun, visiting Skip Ellsworth's cabin.

Bruce in his room at Ruby Chow's

Description of Photo

Bruce Lee looking sharp before hitting the Seattle town, posing for a picture in his room above the Ruby Chow restaurant.

Bruce Training the Iron Palm

Description of Photos

Bruce Lee demonstrating the finer points of brick breaking. Actually, Bruce really did not care for stunts like this, because he felt it was strictly a show, a magician's trick. Strength and power play a role, but really, it's the way the technique is executed that results in the breakage of the bricks.

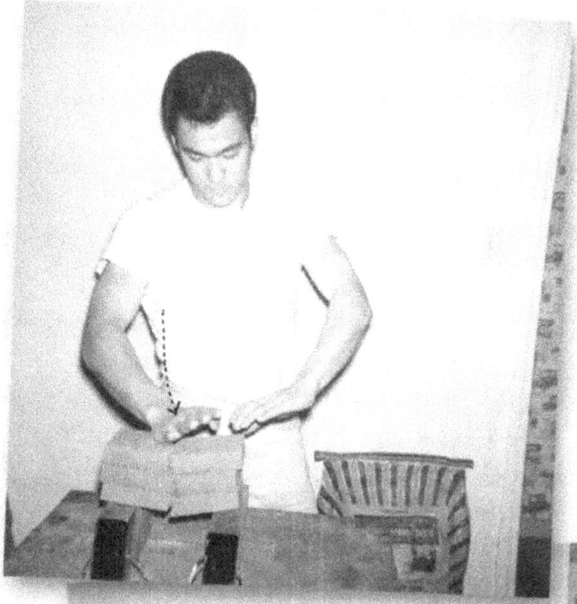

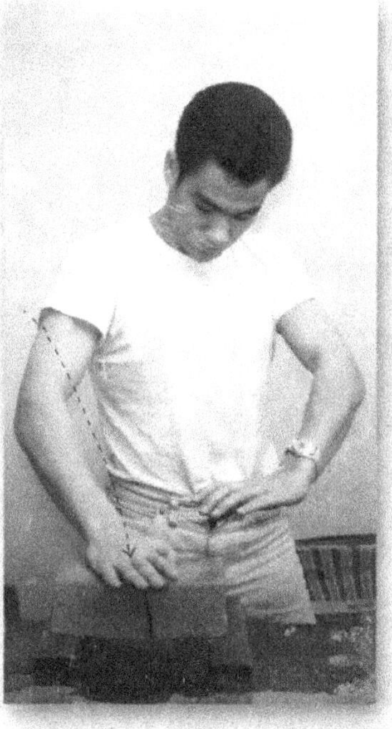

Bruce at the University of Washington

Description of Photos

Bruce on campus at the University of Washington posing with his distant cousin.

Bruce looking sharp while posing for the camera on campus at the University of Washington.

These are some of the school papers that highlight Bruce Lee's school career while in Seattle Washington. In 1959, Bruce Lee was accepted into the Edison Technical School in where he prepared himself for his stay at the University of Washington. While at the University, Bruce excelled at many things including, Philosophy, theatre and Wrestling.

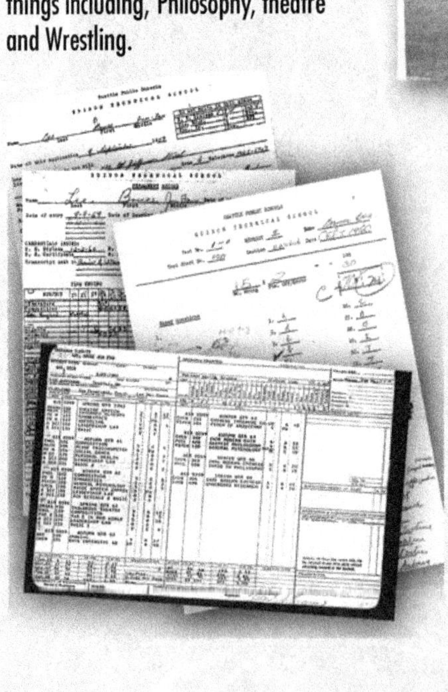
SEATTLE PUBLIC SCHOOLS

EDISON TECHNICAL SCHOOL

Bruce and Judo

Description of Photos

Though Bruce Lee was known for his prowess in Kung Fu and the customized methods he made like Jun Fan Gung Fu and Jeet Kune Do, he always had a deep interest in other martial arts from the diverse cultures worldwide. He was always seeking out different styles to study and dissect. Bruce never hated any martial art; he was just trying to make the prefect one by learning all he could by highlighting the pros and cons of each one.

One of the martial arts he liked was Judo and he researched the art as much as he could. Bruce even joined a Judo class at the University of Washington that was taught by a great Judo master by the name of Shuzo Kato. Bruce loved those classes ad respected Kato for his expertise. Bruce also trained with another Judo man named Fred Sato who was an incredible Judo practitioner as well. Bruce loved exchanging ideas and ideals with other martial artists and he felt that the more you knew about other martial arts, the more you would grow as a martial artist.

Bruce Lee was the best because he studied the best and he added and subtracted to his method many times until he came up with the perfect way, and even then, he was in a constant state of change always bettering himself physically and philosophically.

A stoic Jun Fan stands proudly in his Judo Gi showing off his honorary black belt given to him by Fred Sato.

• *Fred Sato showing Bruce Lee the art of Judo throwing in Seattle 1960.*

• *Bruce Lee doing a Judo throw on friend Fred Sato in Seattle 1960.*

• *Bruce Lee stands center, proudly next to Fred Sato, picture left as he and Fred Sato's Judo class pose for a picture in Ruby Chow's restaurant, Seattle 1960.*

Bruce in the R.O.T.C.

Description of Photos

Bruce was born In America, so part of his civic duty while attending the University of Washington was to be a part of the ROTC program, not only protecting the grounds of the University, but the mindset was also one of showing national pride in protecting America. Bruce disliked it very much and thought it was really much to do about nothing. He often laughed and thought how could a kid from Hong Kong be appointed the ROTC savior of the world. Bruce did his duty but was much pleased to deviate from that type of thing in the end.

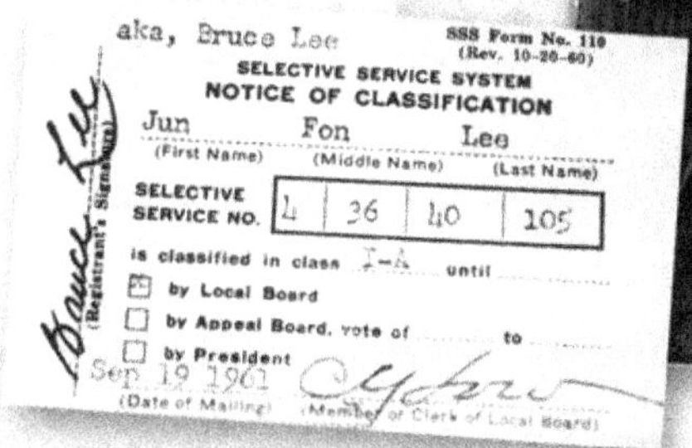

aka, Bruce Lee
SSS Form No. 110 (Rev. 10-20-60)
SELECTIVE SERVICE SYSTEM
NOTICE OF CLASSIFICATION
Jun (First Name) Fon (Middle Name) Lee (Last Name)
SELECTIVE SERVICE NO. 4 | 36 | 40 | 105
is classified in class I-A until
☒ by Local Board
☐ by Appeal Board, vote of ... to ...
☐ by President
Sep 19 1961 (Date of Mailing) (Member or Clerk of Local Board)
Bruce Lee (Registrant's Signature)

• Bruce in theatrics and making fun of his ROTC duty for the University of Washington, wearing his uniform with much pride.

• This was Bruce's selective service card he carried with him when he was performing his ROTC duties.

• Bruce standing proudly beside his car in his military / ROTC uniform. Bruce thought it was all a joke, but knew he looked good just the same.

Bruce at the Jun Fan Institute

Description of Photo

Bruce coming back from a long day at school, posing in front of the Jun Fan Gung Fu Institute on University Way.

Bruce was always well-dressed

Description of Photo

It was very important for Bruce to look his best at all times. He felt that first impressions were the lasting ones. No matter if it were he teaching class, in school or out on the town, he always looked his best. He was very fashionable and head of the curve as far as trends. He would always try to get me and others to dress as he did, as he wanted to groom us into the 20th century. He was quite the guy.

Bruce Lee looking very colligate in his letterman jacket in Seattle just steps away from Ruby Chow's restaurant.

Bruce goes out for the day

Description of Photos

Bruce Lee standing in front of the car park where we practiced our Gung Fu early on. This location was central to Ruby Chow's restaurant where it was convenient for Bruce to teach us all. We also practiced in the parking lot of Ruby Chow's as well.

Bruce Looking Sharp

Description of Photo

Bruce Lee suited up and posing for the camera just steps away from Ruby Chow's restaurant on a hot July afternoon.

Love Birds: Bruce & Linda at University Way

Description of Photos

When Bruce Lee met Linda Emery at the University of Washington. It was safe to say it was love at first sight for Bruce. He loved the fact that Linda was a sweet but tough girl who could handle herself as she proved many times in his Gung Fu class. I think for Bruce, Linda embodied everything he loved, strength, honesty, purity and loyalty. Bruce knew that Linda was his backbone even in the early days. Before Linda, Bruce had many girlfriends; he was a young and attractive man with great fashion sense. I was witnessed to many women swoon over him, but for sure, it was Linda who made him realize that he was here to do a lot more on this earth than simply be another run of the mill Joe and for that, Bruce loved her dearly.

Bruce and Linda at 4750 University Way enjoying the day in a rare sunny Seattle.

Bruce and Linda on the streets of Seattle enjoying their time together.

Bruce Visits Lake Washington

Description of Photos

Bruce loved Lake Washington; it reminded him a bit of home in Hong Kong, near the harbor. Bruce told me when he was young, his father would take him and the rest of the family fishing and the lake reminded him of those times. Bruce felt at peace near the water and at times would meditate, as the breeze would rush by. We would sometimes go there to relax and clear our minds. Those were memorable times.

Bruce Lee posing for the camera on a lovely weekend afternoon at Lake Washington.

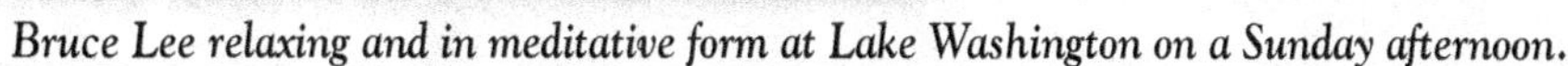

Bruce Lee relaxing and in meditative form at Lake Washington on a Sunday afternoon.

Bruce Lee looking sharp and posing for the camera at one of his visits to Lake Washington in Seattle.

Bruce, Linda & Taky at Beacon Hill

Description of Photos

It was not uncommon for Bruce Lee to be the focus of many staged pictures that were taken for many reasons. Mostly, Bruce wanted to document what he was doing martially on every level. Many images were taken for the purpose of future books Bruce had envisioned, or for the purpose of training examples for his students. He was changing his view on martial arts so quickly; many images were never used do to his evolving vision on things. This is no to say that he felt everything he was doing was absolute when he discovered other ways of doing things, he was simply a work in progress, striving for perfection in himself and what he wanted to express to the world.

(Top) Bruce Lee and Taky Kimura at Jefferson Park on Beacon Hill, posing for pictures to document the Jun Fan Gung Fu Method.

(Bottom) Bruce Lee center, displaying the Three Sectional Staff and how it can defend against long range weaponry like the traditional Chinese spear Taky Kimura is attacking with. Linda looks on as Bruce and Taky pose for the camera at Jefferson Park on Beacon Hill.

Bruce, Taky & Sue Ann Kay

Description of Photos

- *Bruce Lee, Taky Kimura and Sue Ann Kay at the park on Beacon Hill.*
- *Bruce Lee with assistant instructor Taky Kimura and high-level student Sue Ann Kay enjoying the day and sightseeing around Seattle.*

- *Left to Right: Taky Kimura, Bruce Lee and Charlie Woo posing for a picture after class and outside the Jun Fan Gung Fu Institute.*

Bruce Driving in Seattle

Description of Photos

It was important to Bruce, to show his family back in Hong Kong how he was coming along as a success in the States, especially his father. Before Bruce landed in the States in 1959, he was a rebellious youth in Hong Kong, sometimes getting into trouble with various individuals. His family thought he was going nowhere with that type of existence, so they thought it best for he to visit the land that he was born in. At every opportunity, Bruce would take pictures of himself in stoic and intellectual poses to show his family he meant business and that he was becoming someone special. In retrospect, the best thing Bruce's parents did for the world, was to send their son to the USA to become famous.

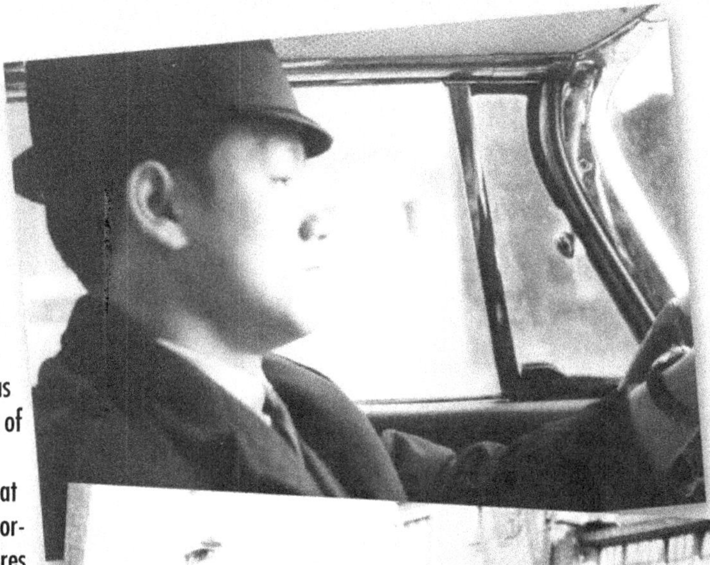

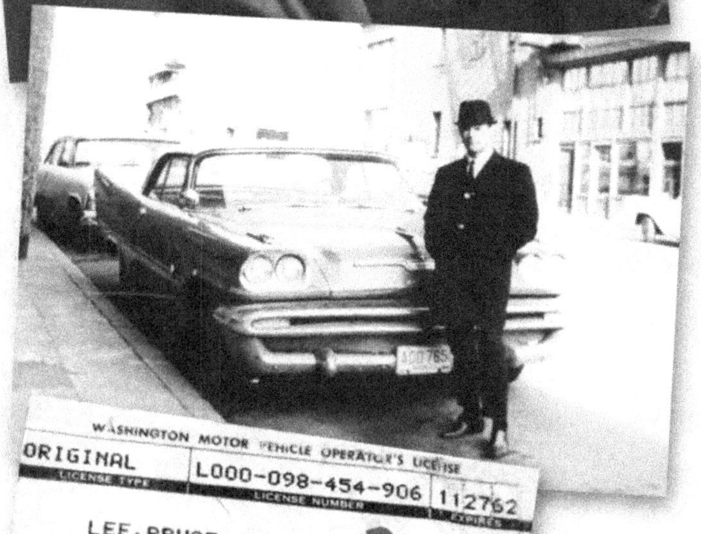

(Top) Bruce looking sharp while taking a drive through the Seattle downtown area.

(Middle) Bruce posing for the camera looking like a professional business man standing next to his car in what would be a picture that would be sent back to Hong Kong to show his family how well he was doing in the States.

WASHINGTON MOTOR VEHICLE OPERATOR'S LICENSE

ORIGINAL — LICENSE TYPE
L000-098-454-906 — LICENSE NUMBER
112762 — EXPIRES

LEE, BRUCE JUN FAN
1122 JEFFERSON ST
SEATTLE WASH

MINOR

x Bruce Lee — SIGNATURE OF OPERATOR

SEX	HAIR	EYES	WEIGHT	HEIGHT	BIRTH DATE	RESTR
M	BLK	BRN	143	5O8.0	112740	0

NOTE RESTRICTION CODE ON REVERSE

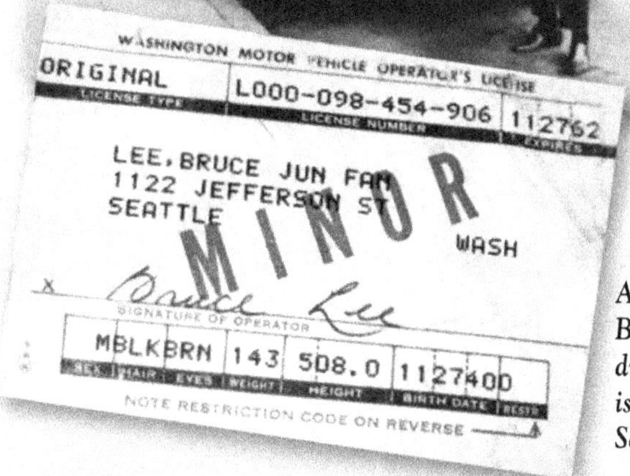

A rare look at Bruce Lee's driver license, issued to him in Seattle.

Bruce & Master Yip Man

Description of Photos

Bruce would make it a point to include Master Yip Man in all aspects in what he was teaching me and the others in Seattle. He wanted us to know that his foundation (our foundation) originated from Yip Man. Bruce told me that Master Yip Man was fast and very technical, strong as well. Bruce also told me that he would sometimes wait in front of the school an hour early, turning away the other students, telling them Master Yip Man was sick, so the others students would turn away and that Bruce could have quote on quote, private lessons from his SiFu. This caught on and Yip Man put a stop to it.

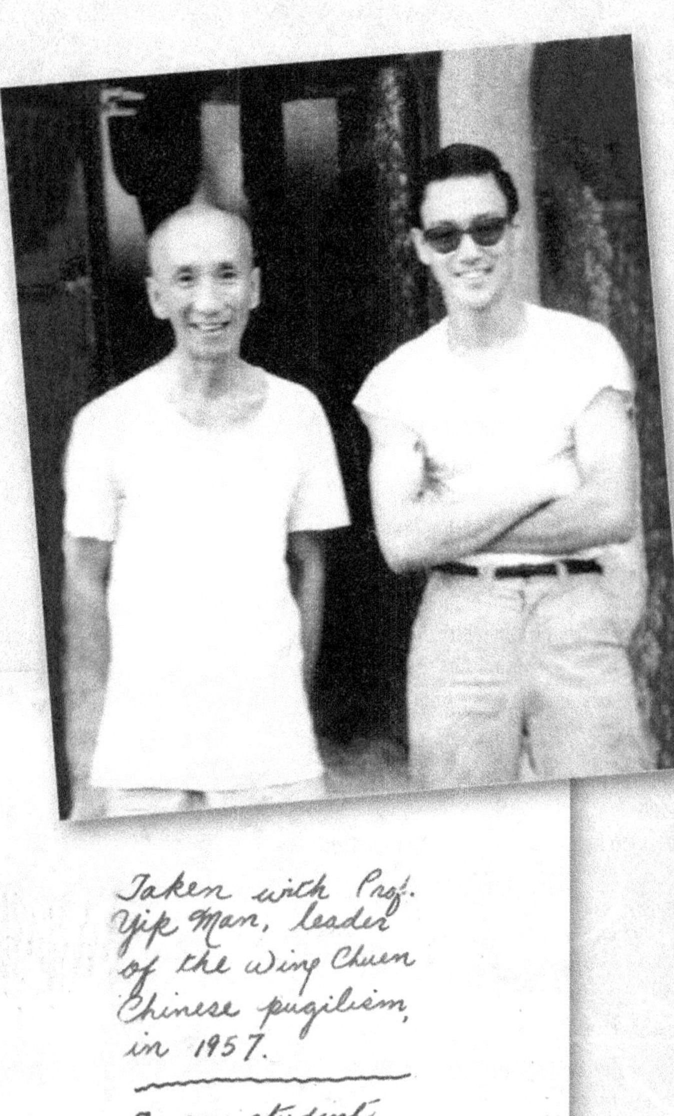

Bruce Lee at the age of 17 standing next to his SiFu, Master Yip Man, in Hong Kong, outside Yip Man's flat / studio.

Back of picture reads:

Taken with Prof. Yip Man, leader of the Wing Chun Chinese Pugilism, in 1957.

~~~~~~~~~~~~~~~

To my student

Taky from Bruce

In Chinese characters it reads: Sifu

To My Student Taky

Description of Photo

Bruce was a deep human being and many times he would give me pictures of himself with philosophical messages about life's journey written on them, showing me how to better myself as a human being / find my own path so to speak. To this day, I am amazed that such a young man at that time could communicate so eloquently with not only his peers, but friends that were many years older than he was. Bruce had this thing where he knew what each individual needed as far as emotional content and he was ever so good at getting us to express ourselves physically and emotionally through his verbal teachings. Bruce was a true teacher in every sense of the word and the gift he handed down to me and others who knew him well, has now been past down by us to our students, family and friends.

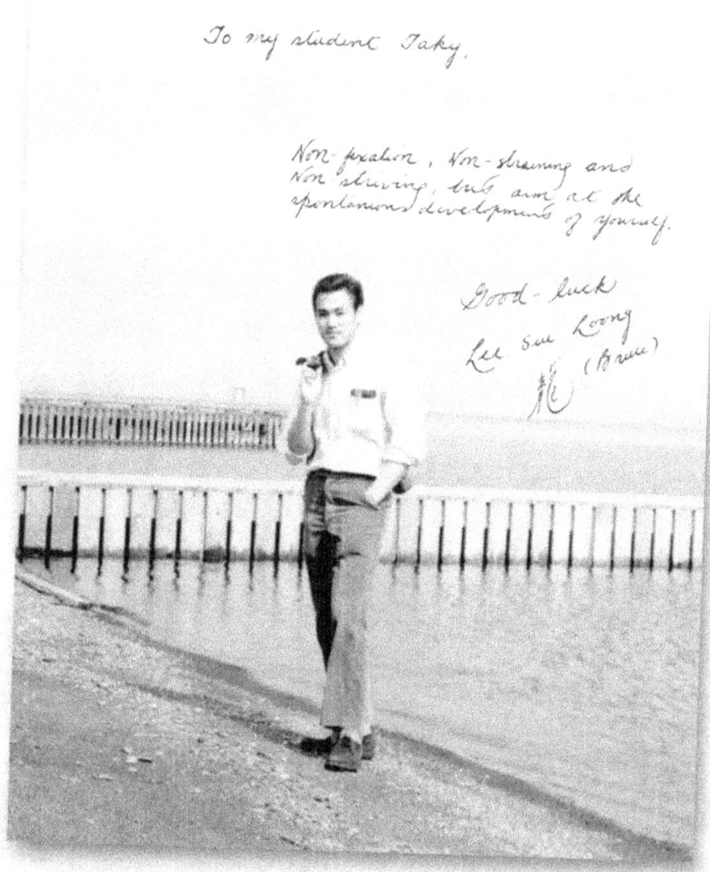

Bruce Lee posing for the camera at Lake Washington where he found peace and relaxation during his many outings there. Inscription reads,

To my student Taky,

Non-fixation, Non-sharing and

Non-striving, but aim at the

Spontaneous development of yourself.

Good – luck

Lee Sui Loong

(Bruce)

Bruce's First School

Description of Photos

Besides working out with Bruce at parks and car park structures, there were three schools that were opened by Bruce that housed his students and assistant instructors. Bruce's first school was at 609 South Weller St. in Chinatown. The second school was at 420-1/2 8 Ave South, in Chinatown. The third school was the most popular and well known; it was located at 4750 University Way. I can remember the excitement on Bruce's face as he walked through the doors of his first school, it was like he was a self made man on his way to greatness. There were great memories everywhere we trained and I can honestly say without being cliché, that the blood, sweat and tears we all put in made us all better human beings.

Bruce Lee standing outside the new Jun Fan Gung Fu Institute school at 609 South Weller St. in Chinatown.

(Top) Bruce Lee at 609 South Weller St. in Chinatown, just steps away from his very first Institute.

(Middle) Bruce Lee standing outside the new Jun Fan Gung Fu Institute school at 609 South Weller St. in Chinatown.

Seattle Demonstrations

Description of Photos

For Bruce, doing demonstrations at first was an enjoyable thing to do. He liked the fact that he could show to the world what he could do martially. He also wanted to show the beauty to the crowds at large the Chinese way so to speak. When Bruce put on demos, they were not just from the physical standpoint; there were also philosophical lessons to be learned as well from what he was demonstrating. For the most part, the many who came to see the demonstrations were more interested in seeing a Chinese cultural display, but what they walked away with was a lesson and day they would never forget. Bruce would amaze the audience with his prowess and by doing so; he not only gained new students, but fans as well. As the years went on, Bruce felt he had enough with being a part of demonstrations, as it was becoming more of a task and not a labor of love. I would say around 1967 he had enough as he felt who needed to know him, already knew what he was all about and at that time, he was concentrating more on his acting and had less time to share himself with the masses.

• Bruce Lee demonstrating the Jun Fan Gung Fu Method on student Jesse Glover at the Trade Fair in Seattle in 1961.

Bruce Lee during demonstration at the Trade Fair (1961)

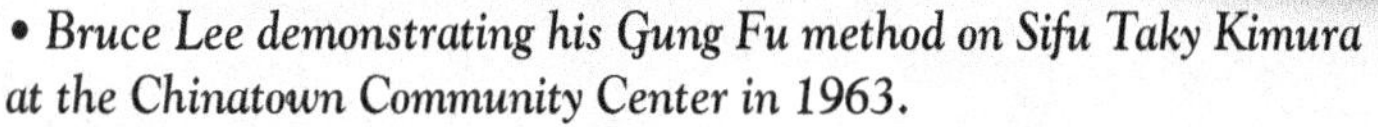

• Bruce Lee demonstrating his Gung Fu method on Sifu Taky Kimura at the Chinatown Community Center in 1963.

Bruce's Chinese Gung Fu

Description of Photo

Bruce Lee's Chinese Gung Fu book was a huge growing point for him, it put him on the map so to speak and a respected authoritative figure of the Eastern martial arts / philosophy. After this book came out, students at the Seattle Gung Fu Institute grew from a set few, to many. At this time, Bruce was asked to be a part of many interviews and demonstrations and a few on T.V., as well. These were great times for Bruce and all of us as well who supported him in Seattle.

Here is an example of the creation process that it took to make Bruce Lee's Chinese Gung Fu book. Back in the old days, there was a lot of cutting and gluing and then printing on a press. Bruce was in every way part of the conception, creating and printing process.

11-C

11-A, B A intends to throw B as shown in picture A & B. (There are, by the way, 36 throwing techniques and 72 joint locks in the art of Gung Fu.)

11-C Turning his waist, B grasps A's left hand and at the same time turns his shoulder out and downward against A's shoulder.

59

Visiting Ralph Castro

Description of Photos

Ed Parker is really responsible for giving Bruce Lee the opportunity to show off his martial arts prowess. In 1964, Bruce Lee was invited by Ed Parker to come to Los Angeles / Long Beach, California to showboat what he could do in front of countless onlookers who attended the Ed Parker's Internationals. Bruce Lee was a hit and was invited back numerous times as a special guest, especially during the Green Hornet era. Bruce and James Lee met up with Ed Parker and Ralph Castro in San Francisco at Ralph Castro's Karate school to exchange ideas and to feel one another out. The meeting was a hit and Ed Parker and Bruce Lee became friends.

• *Bruce Lee, Ed Parker, James Lee and Ralph Castro.*

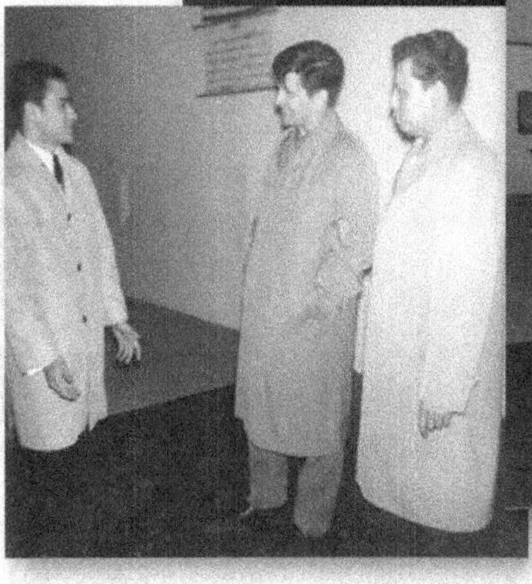

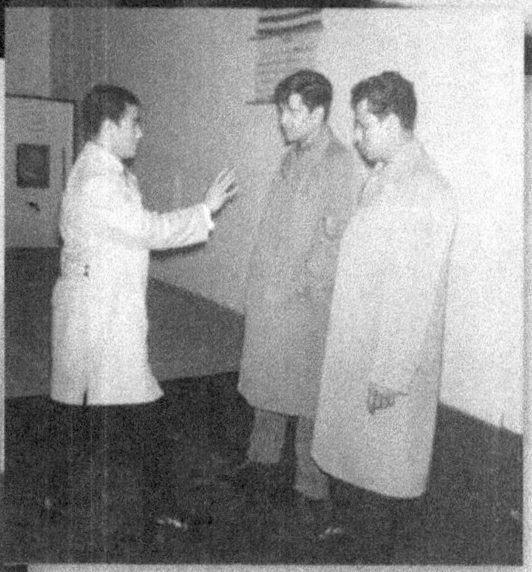

• *Bruce Lee arriving at Ralph Castro's school to exchange ideas and ideals within the martial arts world. Ed Parker and Ralph Castro stand opposite of Bruce.*

• *Bruce Lee explaining his philosophies of Gung Fu to Ed Parker and Ralph Castro.*

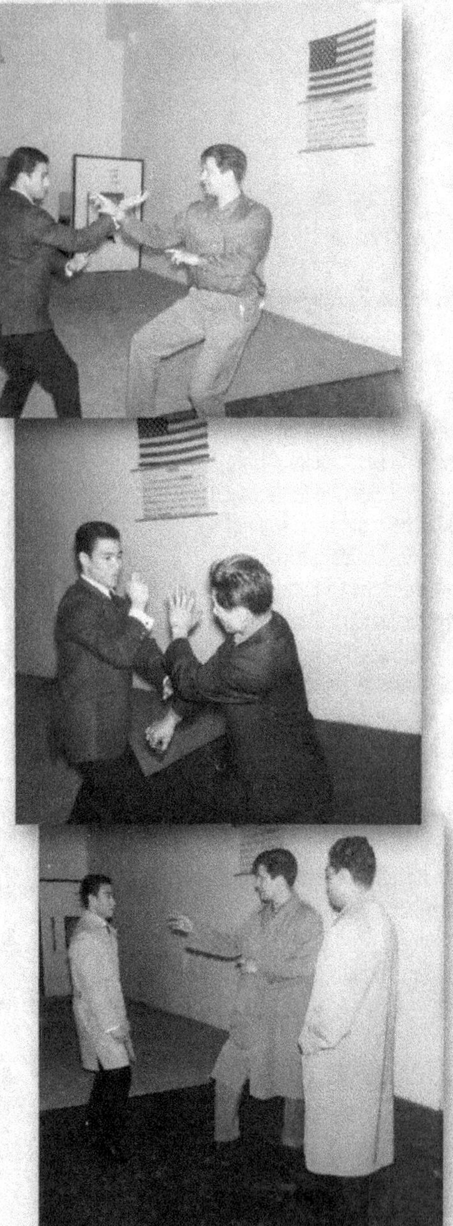

• Bruce Lee demonstrates the Bill Jee technique from Wing Chun as Ed Parker looks on.

• Bruce Lee and Ed Parker take a break from exchanging martial arts stories at Ralph Castro's Karate school in San Francisco.

• Bruce Lee demonstrates a classic Gung Fu move on Ed Parker while James Lee looks on.

• Bruce Lee and Ed Parker in martial arts standoff pose for the camera at Ralph Castro's Karate studio.

• Bruce Lee and close friend and student James Lee play hands as the camera snaps the picture.

• Parker shows Bruce the Kenpo stance.

Bruce Returns Home to Hong Kong, 1963

Description of Photos

In 1963, Bruce went back to Hong Kong to visit his family and friends. His family was so excited to see in how the young Bruce they remembered four years previously, changed into a young dashing man who was becoming a success. While Bruce was there, he would send me postcards and letters, expressing to me what was going on within that long hot summer he spent there. Doug Palmer met Bruce in Hong Kong and they both had a fantastic time. When Bruce came back to the States, he was relieved in many ways that he could show his family how he was achieving his dreams. In retrospect, Bruce was happy that his father got to see in how he changed for the good, because his father passed away in 1965 while Bruce was in the States, so seeing his father 2 years earlier was a heavy weight lifted off his head.

(Top) Bruce posing for the camera at his family home as his younger brother Robert takes the picture upon his return to Hong Kong to visit in 1963.

(Middle) Bruce Lee and his cousin Frank doing Chi Sao in Hong Kong 1963 on a family vacation in Shatin upon his return home to visit his family.

Bruce playing sticky hands, (Chi Sao) with family friend Stephen Kwan in Hong Kong 1963, while vacationing in Shatin.

Los Angeles

Description of Photos

When Bruce Lee moved to Los Angeles he kept in contact with me in some form a few times a month. He would touch on everything from his Jeet Kune Do, to his family and acting career. Los Angeles was a busy time for Bruce, he was truly finding himself physically, philosophically and spiritually. The "Green Hornet" was both a godsend and disappointment to Bruce. On one hand, he was working in Hollywood and gaining many fans, but on the other hand, he wanted more and not just to play the traditional "chop socky" servant roles. He was excited to get many of the top Hollywood actors as students. He knew that this would help him in many ways get acclaim through the lips of those students. Los Angeles groomed Bruce for the overnight success in what he would encounter in Hong Kong.

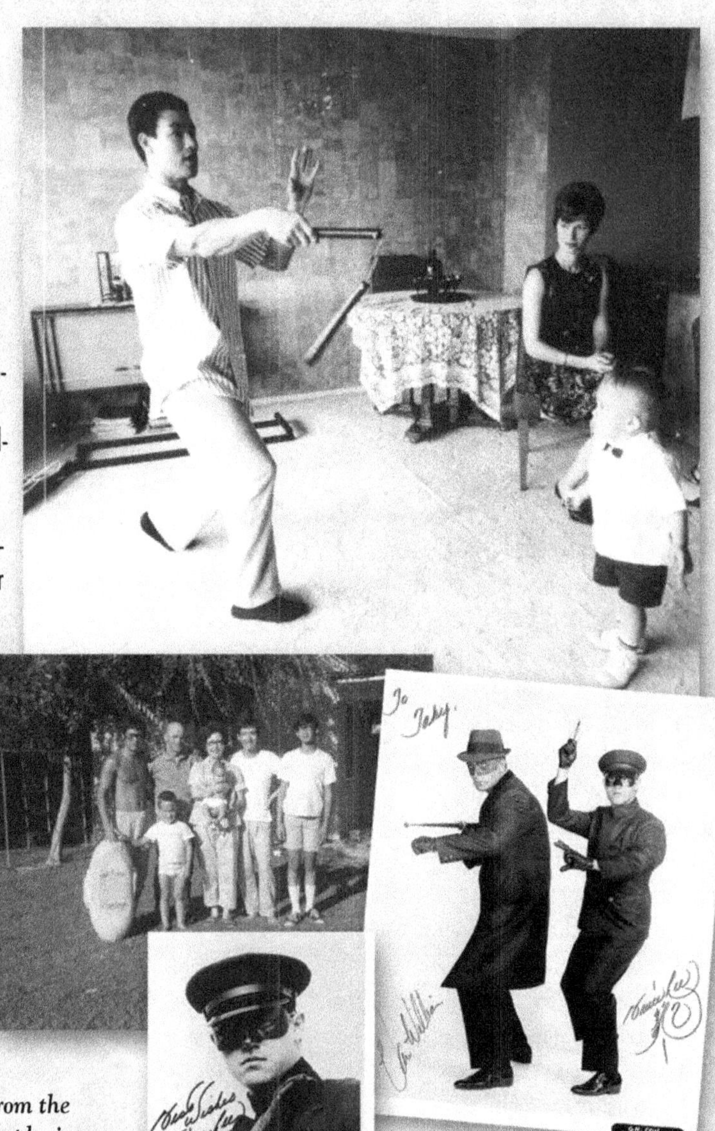

• *A large promotional still from the "Green Hornet" with autograph signatures to Taky Kimura from Bruce Lee and Van Williams.*

• *Bruce Lee left, Herb Jackson, Grace Lee Robert Lee, family friend Randy Mah and a young Brandon and Shannon in Los Angeles in the backyard of Bruce's Roscomare home in Bel Air as wife Linda takes the picture, 1969.*

• *Bruce Lee posing for a promotional picture for the "Green Hornet" with his nunchakus, in his Barrington Plaza apartment as wife Linda and son Brandon look on.*

• *Autograph picture of Bruce Lee as Kato in the "Green Hornet" given to Taky Kimura in 1966.*

Game of Death

Description of Photos

These "The Game of Death" stills were sent to me by Bruce to show me what he had been filming up to that time, before I was supposed to go over to Hong Kong and shoot my scenes. Bruce had an on set photographer commissioned by Golden Harvest to take pictures for continuity as well as pictures for promotional use when it came time to endorse the film to the masses. Bruce sent many of these images to me, to enlighten me, excite me and get me committed to doing my part for the film. I was hesitant, but Bruce talked me into it. I still can remember his words; "Taky, you and I are going to take on the world with this film and do many things afterwards!" Needless to say I was very excited and nervous at the same time. I just did not want to embarrass Bruce and I told him that I had two left feet and would make the film look bad. Bruce told me that he would make me look like a pro, so I took his word and prepared for my trip. Unfortunately, I never did get a chance to go, Bruce passed away shortly after "Enter the Dragon", before he went back to complete "The Game of Death".
The following pictures are from the lot Bruce sent me from Hong Kong.

• Bruce Lee, Kareem Abdul Jabbar and James Tien pose for a promotional shot for "The Game of Death".

• A promotional picture welcoming Kareem Abdul Jabbar to Hong Kong for the filming of his scenes in "The Game of Death".

• A promotional picture of Bruce and Kareem shaking hands as their battle scenes for "The Game of Death" wrap up.

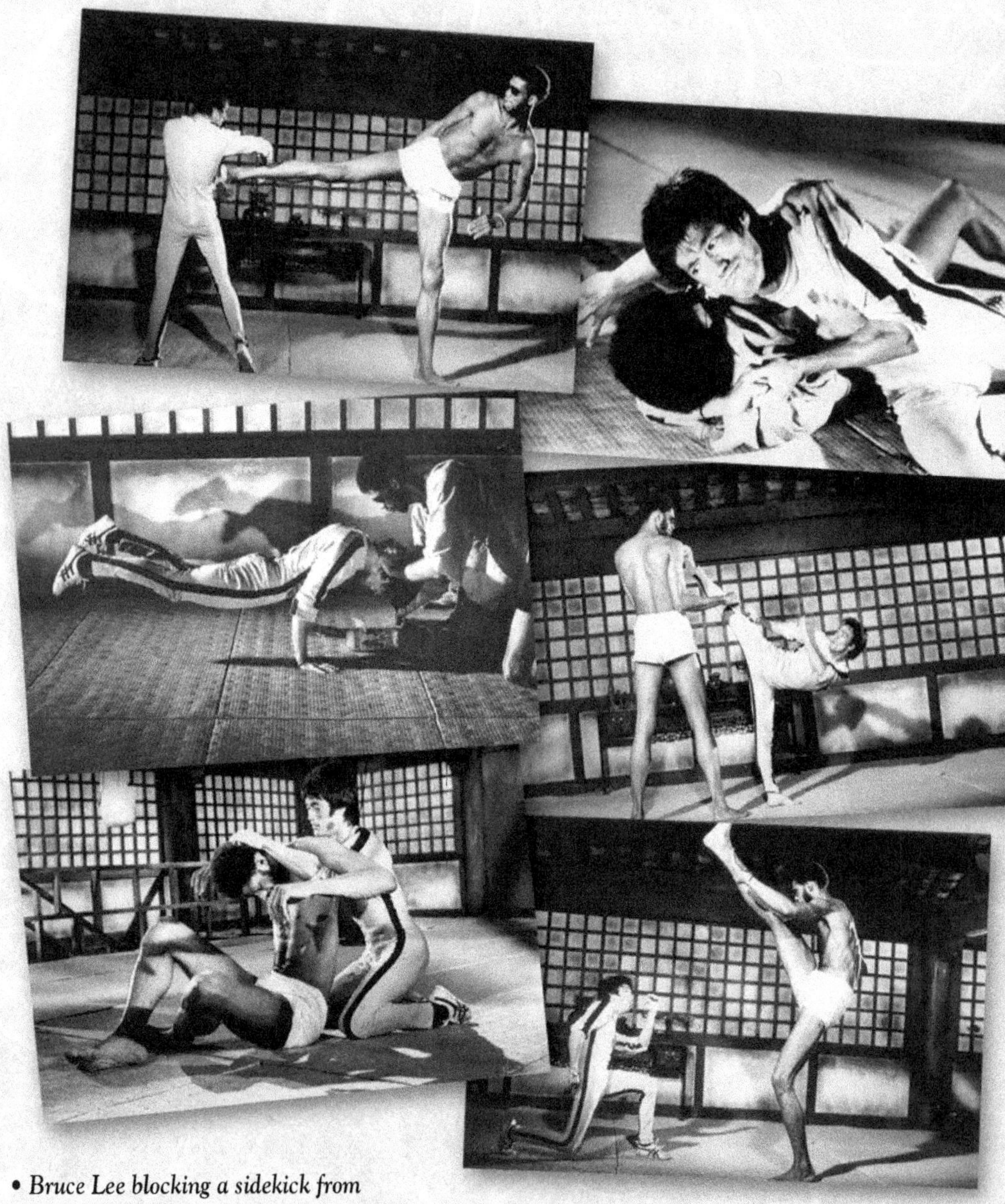

• *Bruce Lee blocking a sidekick from Kareem Abdul Jabbar in a publicity shot to promote the film "The Game of Death".*

• *Bruce Lee showing an amazing feat of strength by elevating his body off the floor while filming a scene in "The Game of Death" with Kareem Abdul Jabbar.*

• *Bruce and Kareem take time out from their grueling film schedule to stretch it out on set of "The Game of Death".*

• *Bruce Lee chokes out Kareem Abdul Jabbar in "The Game of Death".*

• *Bruce smiling as he sends kick to Kareem's head in this promotional picture meant for the promotion of "The Game of Death".*

• *Bruce Lee ducks down as Kareem Abdul Jabbar sends a kick to his head in this promotional picture taken on the set of "The Game of Death".*

The Game of Death

(Top) Bruce Lee in battle form with his nunchaku, posing for the camera in the New Territories in Hong Kong while filming sequences for "The Game of Death".

(Bottom) An exhausted Bruce Lee takes time out to be a daddy for his children Shannon and Brandon on the set of "The Game of Death".

Bruce Lee in mid battle with Ji Han Jae on the set of "The Game of Death".

Bruce Lee with Dan Inosanto on the set of "The Game of Death".

Bruce & Ping Chow in Seattle

Description of Photo

In his letter, Bruce always used to tell me what was happening in his life. When I look at this letter, I remember great moments of going out to eat with him and discussing the martial arts, as well as how his career was going. Bruce and I shared many moments like this.

Bruce and Ping Chow
in Seattle, Washington

Ving Tsun Athletic Association honors Taky Kimura

Description of Photos

I was very honored to except these certificates of membership into the Kushu Federation of the Republic of China. The federation is a great entity that unites martial artists from around the world to exchange ideas with one another under one roof. I feel it is important to exchange ideas and ideals with others from around the world so you can have another perspective in the way other martial artists train, both mentally and physically.

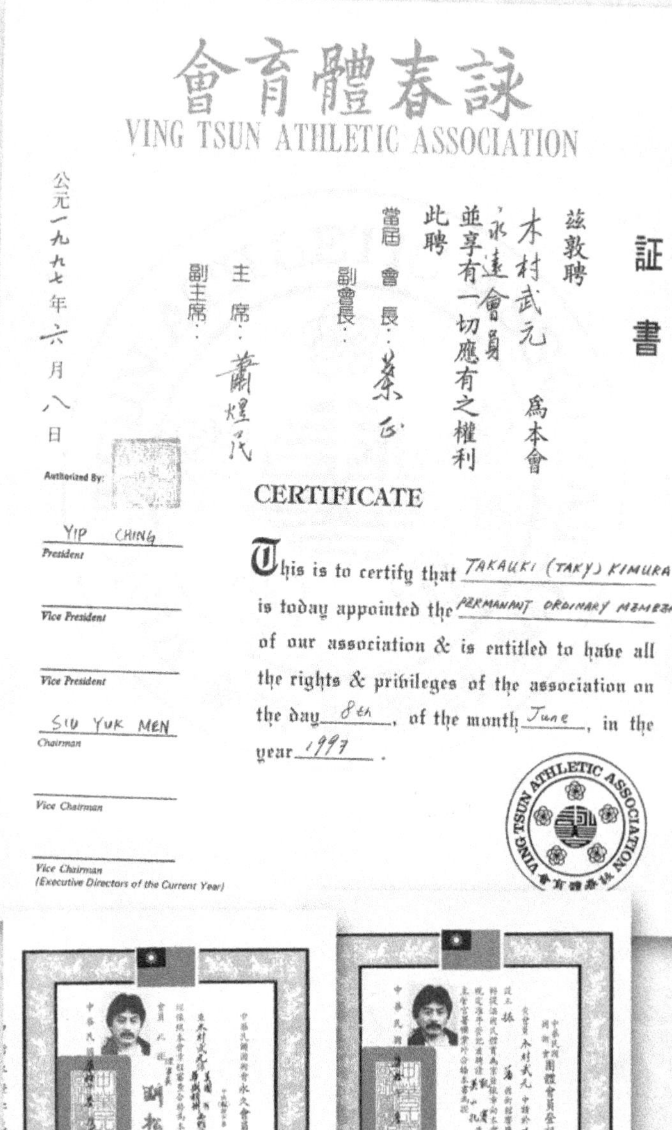

詠春體育會
VING TSUN ATHLETIC ASSOCIATION

証書

茲敦聘
木村武元 為本會
永遠會員
並享有一切應有之權利
此聘
當屆 會長：
副會長：
主席：
副主席：
公元一九九七年六月八日

Authorized By:
YIP CHING
President
Vice President
Vice President
SIU YUK MEN
Chairman
Vice Chairman
Vice Chairman
(Executive Directors of the Current Year)

CERTIFICATE

This is to certify that TAKAUKI (TAKY) KIMURA is today appointed the PERMANANT ORDINARY MEMBER of our association & is entitled to have all the rights & privileges of the association on the day 8th, of the month June, in the year 1997.

Permanent Membership Certificate
Kuoshu Federation
of
The Republic of China

This certificate was given to me by Yip Ching, the son of the legendary Yip Man who taught Bruce Lee the art of Wing Chun. The VING TSUN ATHLETIC ASSOCIATION is a prestigious group who stay true to the traditional teachings of Master Yip Man. I was honored to receive this certificate of membership as it is a very difficult journey to be accepted into their association.

Making of "Chinese Gung Fu"

Description of Photos

The time surrounding the making of the Chinese Gung Fu book was not only exciting for Bruce, but all us who helped with it as well. It was an exciting time for all of us, knowing that we all would be in print, helping our Sifu Bruce Lee share his vision to the world. When I look at this book today, I think of not only the learning that can be gained from it, but also the legacy it has left worldwide. Because of Bruce Lee's popularity, this small yellow book will always be consider a great work of art as well as a great learning guide. I remember clearly the days we worked along side Bruce, posing for the camera, and to see our work in print after all these years would do Bruce proud.

This book was an important venture for Bruce Lee as it marked the success of many great things to come for him. Bruce was only in his early 20's at that time, but he was already a self made man. It was an honor for me as well as the others to watch him work his way to greatness.

(TOP) Taky Kimura left and Charlie Woo right, help Bruce illustrate this technique that would be included in Bruce's Chinese Gung Fu book. Bruce Lee demonstrating for camera defensive moves against multiple attackers.

(BOTTOM) A stoic Jun Fan Lee posing for the camera and showing off his martial arts prowess for pictures that would be included in his Chinese Gung Fu book, published in 1963. These pictures and many within that book were taken in the parking lot of Ruby Chow's restaurant.

Bruce Lee and Taky Kimura side by side demonstrating the Jun Fan Method for Bruce Lee's Chinese Gung Fu book. Over the course of two months the book was planned out in how Bruce wanted to shoot each sequence. Many pictures were taken but only a few were used for the publication.

Bruce's First White Christmas

Description of Photos

Bruce Lee's first Christmas in Seattle in 1960 was a blast for him; he was amazed at how everything was covered white with snow. He loved it! Though he was a mature young man, the snow brought out the young kid in him. He never played in the snow before. Ping Chow, Ruby's husband was a very kind man and loved playing with Bruce as if he were his father. From tropical to frigid, it was hard for Bruce to adapt at first, but soon enough, he was a Seattle man who could handle the Seattle weather.

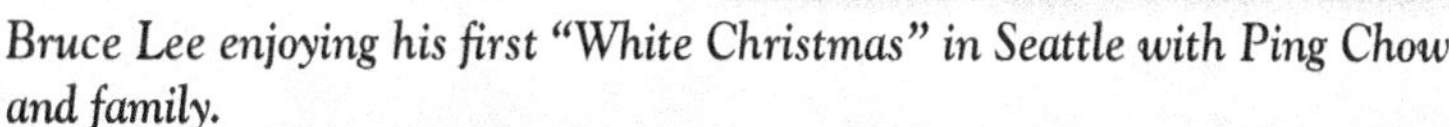

Bruce Lee enjoying his first "White Christmas" in Seattle with Ping Chow and family.

Bruce's First White Christmas

Description of Photos

Bruce Lee posing solo and enjoying his first winter in Seattle, Washington as he poses in front and around his first place of residence, Ruby Chow's restaurant in 1960.

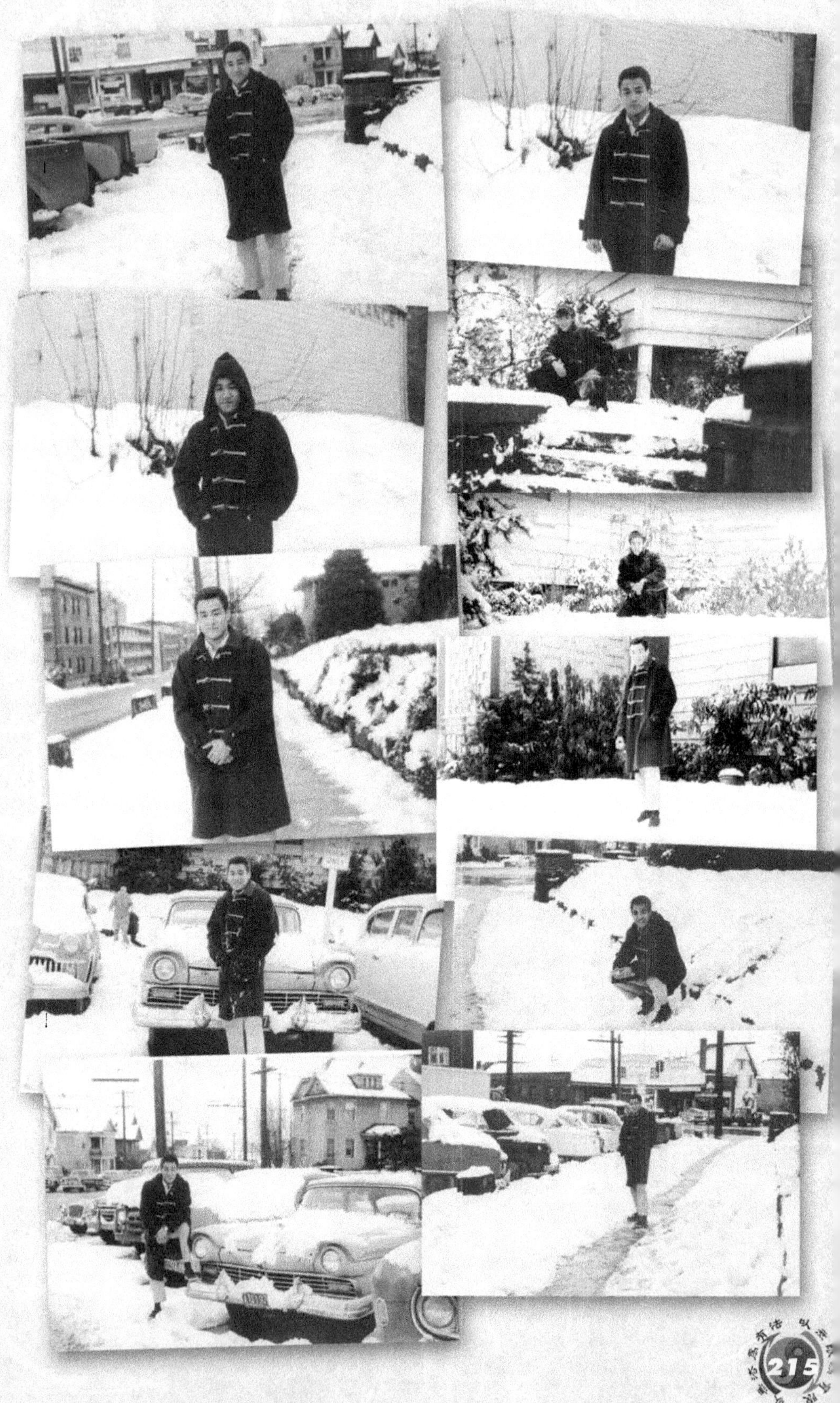

Like Father, Like Son

Description of Photos

Taky's relationship with his son Andy has always been a close one and in fact, Andy has always viewed his father as his hero. Taky with much love, raised his son Andy into a fine man, sacrificing many things in his life to make sure that Andy would never go without. Taky took Andy under his wing from a very young age, teaching him what Bruce Lee taught him, handing down all his knowledge so that one day, he would be able to take over where he leaves off. The legacy of Bruce Lee has been enriched even more by the hands and heart of Sifu Taky Kimura and when people speak of Bruce Lee for generations to come, they will also speak of Taky Kimura as well.

Father and son 4 year old Andy battling it out in the basement of their grocery store that also doubles for their Gung Fu Institute in Seattle, Washington.

In daddy's arms at the young age of 4 years old. Andy Kimura protected by his hero, Taky Kimura.

Bruce & James Lee in Oakland

Description of Photo

After Bruce met James Lee, they hit it off right away, Bruce liked James' street fighting mentality. Bruce would travel from Seattle to Oakland to visit James, eventually appointing him the head of the Oakland Jun Fan Gung Fu Institute. Bruce eventually moved to Oakland for a while with Linda and lived with James for some time before moving to Los Angeles in where he would live before going back to Hong Kong to seek international fame.

Bruce Lee and James Lee practicing the art of Gung Fu in Oakland in James Lee's garage. Pictures like this were taken to be included in future book projects Bruce was working on.

Residing at Ruby Chow's

Description of Photos

At first, Bruce found comfort in having a place to live when he arrived in Seattle, but after a while, he realized he needed his complete freedom to go and stay as he pleased. He felt confined and stopped working for the Chow's and found another place to live about six months after being there. It was a good experience for Bruce while he was there, but there were greater things ahead for him and so he moved on.

For over 60 years, Ruby and Ping Chow have contributed immeasurably to the local community and Puget Sound society. Together, this dynamic duo threw themselves into supporting charitable projects, de-mystified Chinese cuisine and culture for Greater Seattle, and changed forever the face of local politics.

Their remarkable partnership began in the early '40s when Hong Kong opera star Ping Chow, stranded in New York City after the outbreak of WWII, joined the army. He met waitress Ruby Mar, an ardent Cantonese opera fan and armed services volunteer.

They married, moved to Seattle and started their family and the legendary Ruby Chow's restaurant. After the restaurant closed at 2 a.m., head chef Ping continued performing in Cantonese operas through his operatic connections, turned Seattle into a Cantonese opera capital. As author Frank Chin has pointed out, the sleepy backwater of Seattle, with its tiny Chinese population, drew the superstars of the Chinese operatic world. Ruby and Ping

Bruce walking up to his bedroom apartment at Ruby Chow's restaurant.

Bruce entering the back of Ruby Chows after a hard day at school.

took care of them. Because of their selfless volunteer work, one troupe donated its gross receipts from a Seattle Opera House performance for the purchase of property to enlarge the playfield behind Chong Wa.

Ruby Chow's became the must go to restaurant for Seattle's elite, visiting Hollywood celebrities and jazz greats. Using the restaurant and Chinese community as a base, they embarked on a public relations campaign to engender understanding of Chinese cuisine and culture in the general public. With other community leaders, they brought Chinese New Year celebrations into public consciousness, and through their work with the March of Dimes, The Seattle Times charity, the P-I Christmas Fund, and Seafair, brought into prominence a small Chinese community. Along the way, they published the first Chinese cookbook, hosted the first Chinese cooking show and started the first Chinese frozen food business. They formally started the Seattle Chinatown Dragon Team and the Chinese Community Girls Drill Team, which have benefited thousands of youths of Asian descent.

In a break with tradition, progressive Chong Wa Benevolent Association members, dubbed "Young Turks" by a Seattle daily, campaigned for and elected Ruby Chow president, the first woman president of any Chong Wa worldwide. Seven other women joined her on the board.

Under Ruby and Ping's leadership, the Chinese community began the annual Governor's Chinese New Year Dinner in 1964, the annual Elders' Banquet to honor the community's senior citizens, and Chinatown beautification

Description of Photos

When Bruce arrived in Seattle he was so proud to be on American soil. Whenever the chance arose, he had pictures taken of himself at many different locations, one being Ruby Chow's restaurant. He would send the pictures back to Hong Kong signed and dedicated to his family and friends. On many occasions, Bruce would dedicate the signed photos to his second mother, Eva Tso. Eva Tso and her husband were very close friends to Bruce's family and Bruce had also dated Eva's daughter Pearl. It was always Eva Tso's wish that one day Bruce would marry Pearl, but Bruce fell in love with Linda and the rest is history.

A dashing Bruce Lee standing outside Ruby Chow's before work, posing for the camera 1960.

Bruce Lee standing outside in front of Ruby Chow's before work 1960.

projects, such as the public Chinatown bulletin board in 1965, and the hanging of 119 red lanterns across King Street.

They donated meals for volunteers and fund raisers for the Wing Luke Memorial Museum in its early, lean years. Many other projects benefited from their generosity.

At the request of then Mayor Wes Uhlman, Ruby Chow arranged with the federal housing director to locate the first two low-income apartments in Chinatown and Japantown. She established the first language bank at Harborview Hospital, had a volunteer translate the city's health manual into Chinese so that the many restaurant workers could better prepare for the food service permit exam. And she had the first health clinic serving Asians moved from Pioneer Square into Chinatown proper.

In 1974, she and other members of Chong Wa called on Seattle schools Superintendent Troxel to start a transitional bilingual program for immigrants whereby the children would receive assistance in their native languages until they could function in an all English environment. She persuaded the county to hire the first court interpreters.

Politically, Ruby and Ping's relentless public relations campaign kick started the state's Asian political renaissance by first creating a favorable climate for Asian candidates.

And when Chong Wa, a non-profit, had to turn down Wing Luke's request for help in his bid for a seat on the Seattle city council, he turned to Ruby Chow, who rallied community support behind him. She had Chinese restaurants give out fortune cookies with "Wing Luke says ...." in them. She and Ping backed other successful candidates,

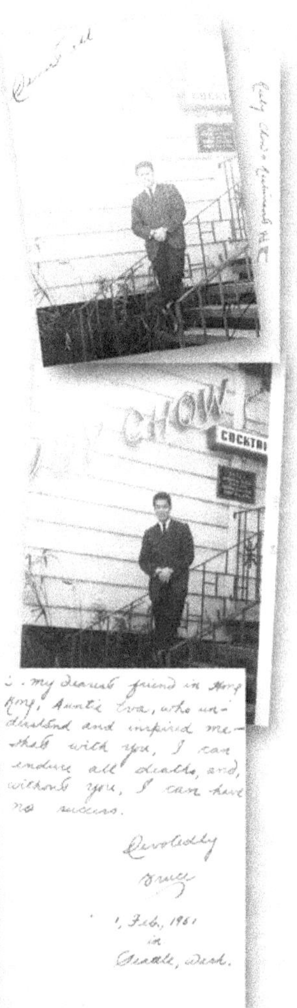

Two pictures of Bruce Lee in front of Ruby Chow's 1960. Inscription on back of picture left reads; To my dearest friend in Hong Kong, Auntie Eva, who understand and inspired me – that with you, I can endure all deaths, and, without you, I can have no success. Devotedly Bruce 1, Feb, 1961 in Seattle, Wash. Picture right is inscribed on front; Dearest all, Bruce and back of picture right is inscribed; Ruby Chow's Restaurant. In Chinese characters its says FRONT DOOR.

and in time, Ruby Chow won a seat on the King County Council, the only Asian American to do so. Legislative aide Doug Eglington, said of her three terms, "She brought a personal touch to the council by bringing constituent issues to the fore, from the first airport noise abatement study to helping an immigrant Lebanese family to locating bus shelters in low-income neighborhoods." Grateful constituents named a Georgetown park after her.

In the '90s, Washington State had so many Asian elected officials, far out of proportion to their population, that officials in the other Washington took note. Journalist Terry McDermott ascribed this phenomenon to Ruby Chow, noting that Gary Locke, the first Asian American governor of a mainland state, would not be governor were it not for her early efforts. She and Ping had created a climate favorable to Asians. Former Gov. Locke, in his first Lunar New Year Governor's Dinner speech in 1997 remarked, "The fact that I am here today goes back to the long time work of Ruby and Ping Chow."

They prevented use of the INS building as a jail and later, as a federal prison. Through "roast duck diplomacy," County Councilwoman Chow flew to Washington, D.C. with a Chinese roast duck, expertly prepared by Ping, for a meeting with the late Sen. Warren Magnuson. To stop the proposed prison, they collected thousands of community, resident and property owner signatures on a petition and presented it to federal officials.

Ping and Ruby Chow helped virtually anyone who asked—from those seeking political office to appointments to high level positions. They have done so quietly and without fanfare. In so doing, they have improved the quality of life for thousands and left an indelible mark on local history.

Description of Photos

Bruce was nineteen in 1960 and traveling to the Untied States was exciting for him, but there was also an urgency for him to establish himself with a place to stay and a job to secure financial stability. Ruby and Ping Chow took Bruce in as a favor to Bruce's parents who were long time friends of the Chows relating back to the opera days that Li Hoi Chuen (Bruce's father) shared with Ping Chow. At times it was tough for Bruce living with Ruby Chow, as she was very domineering. Her philosophy was, she would treat Bruce as she does her own children as a favor to Bruce's parents and sometimes that did not work so well.

In the summer of 1960, Peter Lee arrived from Hong Kong to visit Bruce for part of the summer. These were good times for Bruce as he did miss his family and having Peter there if only for a short time, really grounded him.

INTERVIEW WITH CHERYL CHOW

RFTD: How did Bruce Lee come to live and work with you?

CC: Bruce was starting to get roles in Hong Kong movies and indicated to his dad that he was going to quit school so he could do more movies. His father called my parents because they knew each other via Chinese Opera circles and my mom helped set up a foundation to help aging actors.

Bruce's father asked if he could send his son to live with our family and get an American education.

RFTD: How was your family first introduced to the Lee's?

CC: My parents had met Bruce on their trips to Hong Kong.

RFTD: What year did Bruce come to live and work at your restaurant?

CC: Look up what year he graduated from Garfield High and go back a couple of years---I am guessing about 1960 or 61.

RFTD: What were Bruce's responsibilities there?

CC: He was like another older brother to me and lived in a bedroom on the 3rd floor with my two other older brothers. He worked as a bus boy/waiter like the rest of our family.

RFTD: Was he a good worker?

CC: I remember him having a sense of humor, very flirtatious with the girls and charming with the customers. He was like any teenage boy working at our restaurant - he worked hard when he saw my mom coming around the corner.

RFTD: What did your mother and father think of Bruce's martial arts prowess?

CC: They were aware and fine with it - he set up his wooden dummy in our back yard and he had a Judo friend give us lessons Sunday morning in the back of the restaurant.

RFTD: Did Bruce give demonstrations of his Gung Fu at the restaurant?

CC: Some of my older brothers' friends came over to see him do his routines, but he did not do anything for a public or restaurant folks.

RFTD: There are rumors about the heated relationship between your mother and Bruce. Can you tell us about this?

CC: It was a typical "mother and son" type of relationship. His father told my parents to treat his son like their son and have him do what she would expect her son to do......this is where it became a very typical mother-son situation - my mom expected ALL of us to do certain chores around the household and restaurant, do our homework, come home at designated times and behave and talk in respectful manner.

When and if any of my brothers misbehaved and/or showed attitude she would call them on it - this included Bruce and he was not use to it and did not like it! There was an incident where Bruce was wearing clothing that was not familiar and my mom asked about it - not sure about all the details, but it was basically "found" items and he did not want to return them - so he and my mom bumped heads about that and trust was lost.

RFTD: As Bruce became more popular in Seattle with his Gung Fu, did that attract any customers to the restaurant?

CC: I do not believe it attracted customers to the restaurant because the clientele at that time was mostly middle aged Caucasian adults and their young families.

RFTD: Was Bruce ever challenged at the restaurant?

CC: I remember one time there was a bunch of guys his age in the backyard and so I went back to see what all the noise was about. Bruce said he could beat anyone with his eyes closed. So this one guy he was sparring ducked and came behind him and hit him in the back of his head - Bruce got mad and opened his eyes and his hands went so fast and hit this guy up on the garage wall - it was almost like watching a cartoon because the guy sort of slid down the wall like a shadow - then Bruce started yelling at him for "cheating" and coming from behind. The guy got up, jumped over our 4' gate and took off in his car. That is the only time I know it happened at our place.

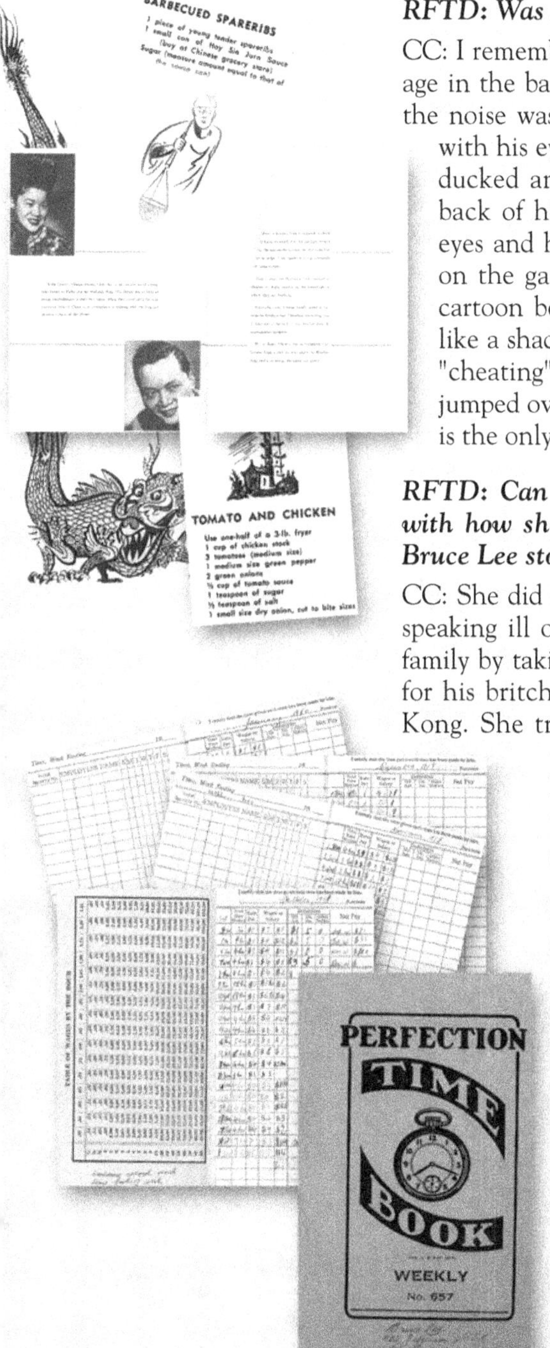

RFTD: Can you tell us if your mother was pleased with how she was portrayed in the film Dragon the Bruce Lee story?

CC: She did not see the movie and I do not recall her speaking ill of him. She was just doing a favor for his family by taking him in when he was getting too cocky for his britches and for his dad to deal with in Hong Kong. She treated him like a son and disciplined or talked with him when it was needed. Remember, he was a teenage boy at the time - who wanted to stay in Hong Kong and just do movies.

RFTD: What are your fondest memories of Bruce Lee?

CC: He was like a big brother that I never had an argument with! He came over as the Hong Kong Cha Cha Champion, so he taught me and my group of girlfriends how to Cha Cha. I was very proud and pleased he asked me to be in a Cha Cha demonstration for a class he took at Central Community College. I also remember when he came to my speech class at Franklin High School as part of my presentation of Gung Fu and he demonstrated for the class.

The other fun memory was when he scared my cousin and girlfriends with this Halloween mask he had - like a scary old guy from horror movies

RFTD: *What were your impressions of his prowess within his films?*

CC: It was great to see a Chinese hero on TV and the theater.

RFTD: *After Bruce left the restaurant, did he ever return to visit or keep in touch with your family.*

CC: Not sure since I was up at Western in Bellingham, but saw him in Hong Kong on one of my visits.

RFTD: *I have many pictures with Bruce and your father Ping, what was their relationship like?*

CC: My dad and he got along - especially because my dad was able to communicate in Cantonese - besides my dad is NOT the disciplinarian so he was seen as the "good cop while my mom did the hard work of disciplining role or bad cop". My dad always spoiled all of us, so that really put my mom in a hard place with a group of teenagers whose job in life is to test and push adults to the brink!

RFTD: *There are some wonderful pictures of Bruce in winter time in front of the restaurant with your family and having fun. Can you tell us about those times?*

CC: My mom and dad always worked hard to give us all opportunities to enjoy life - once again Bruce was like family so yes we had lots of good times thanks to both of my parents.

RFTD: *We all know about Bruce Lee the legend, but in closing, can you tell about Lee Jun Fan the man?*

CC: I really only have knowledge of his late teenage and early 20's. Per my comments above, he came to Seattle to live with our family because his dad was not happy with his behavior and attitude towards education and life in general. He was very confident as a teenage guy because of his accomplishments in Hong Kong movies, Gung Fu skills, HK Cha Cha Champion - and he knew he was good looking. I am sorry his life was cut so short, because I believe he would have matured into a great role model for our Asian boys and girls.

Taky, Then & Now

Not much has change with the Seattle Gung Fu Institute; I keep to Bruce Lee's true vision in what he taught me back in the early 60's. The faces have come and gone over the years, but the ideals and ideas of Bruce Lee still unite us all to this day. My journey as appointed head instructor of the Seattle branch has been a long and fruitful one and from then to now, I would not change a thing.

In this section, I hope that you, the readers, will feel that you were on the journey with me captured by the camera. Behind these many photographs taken of me, there is blood, sweat and tears within. When I look at these images now, I see a man who has grown a lot from the philosophies handed down by Bruce Lee, but has kept true to the teachings his SiFu left him.

Sifu Taky Kimura

Description of Photos

After Bruce passed away, it was hard for a while to keep the school in running order; it felt hollow without Bruce behind the scenes of it all. I later discovered that keeping Bruce's memory alive through his teachings was the best way for not only me to heal the loss of my best friend, but also celebrate his martial arts achievements with the world, by keeping the school going. While training myself throughout the years, I always had Bruce by my side, I could feel him there.

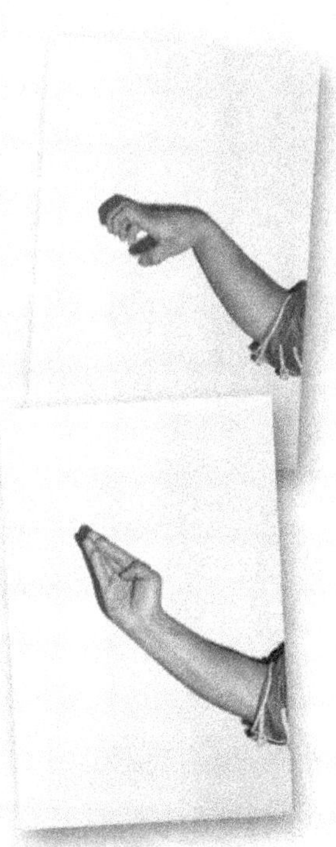

Taky practicing his martial arts legacy, handed down to him by Bruce Lee. To be at peace with oneself and to honestly express yourself is the true goal that Taky Kimura lives by.

Taky Kimura Today

Description of Photos

Taky Kimura's dedication in upholding his Sifu's legacy can be seen in the techniques and philosophies taught to him by Bruce Lee. There is no better honor than to live your life with truth and honesty through the teachings of your mentor. For Taky Kimura, everyday is an expression of what he learned from "The Little Dragon".

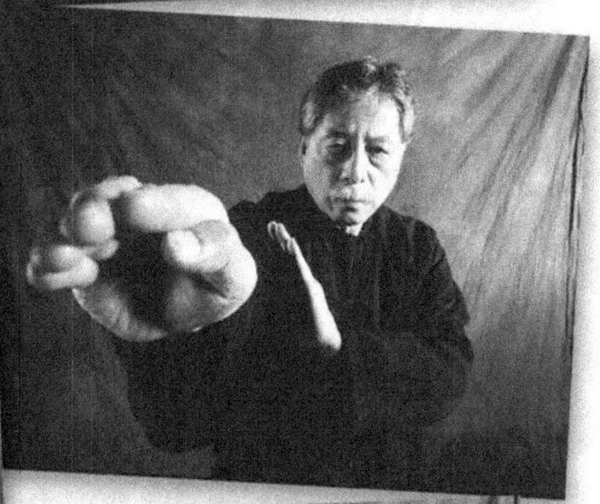

Taky Kimura posing for the camera in traditional Jun Fan Gung Fu form. The precision and form Taky Kimura acquired while training with Bruce Lee in those early years are evident in his flawless execution within his technique.

The Bruce Lee Legacy Continues

Description of Photos

(Top row) SiGung Dan Inosanto, SiFu Jeff Imada and SiGung Taky Kimura. (Bottom row) SiFu Andrew Kimura and SiFu Tsuyoshi Abe posing for a picture at the Inosanto Academy in Marina Del Rey. When the opportunity arises, Dan Inosanto and Taky Kimura visit one another to reflect and reconnect about their past and future, working together to keep their SiFu's flame alive.

SiGung Taky Kimura in martial pose with top student SiFu Tsuyoshi Abe. Also known as Taky Kimura's second son, SiFu Abe is the only student to have the honor of being both a Fourth Level under SiFu Taky Kimura and a Senior Full Instructor under Dan Inosanto. He is considered to be one of the most rounded martial artists in the teachings of Bruce Lee.

Taky & Max Tadman

Description of Photo

Me standing with one of my favorite people, Max Tadman, David Tadman's son. Upon my visit to Los Angeles with my son Andy, David and his family were nice enough to have me over for dinner and musings. There are moments when you meet people and you consider them family and for me, the Tadmans will always be an extended family of mine.

Father & Son Carry on Bruce Lee's Gung Fu Traditions

Description of Photos

From a very young age, Andrew Kimura was privy to the teachings of Bruce Lee's Jun Fan Gung Fu, taught to him by his father Taky. The close and loving relationship both father and son share has trickled down to the students past and present. The place of learning and teaching is like a temple that houses its children, protecting them, caring for them, teaching and preparing them for whatever might come. As Taky Kimura prepares his son Andy for the future in taking over the reins when that time comes, he also preaches love and tolerance to both his son and students, within the philosophies of his best friend, Bruce Lee.

Father and son together in Jun Fan Gung Fu pose for the camera, keeping the faith and tradition of the Wing Chun system, at the same time upholding the evolution of Bruce Lee's progressive idealism.

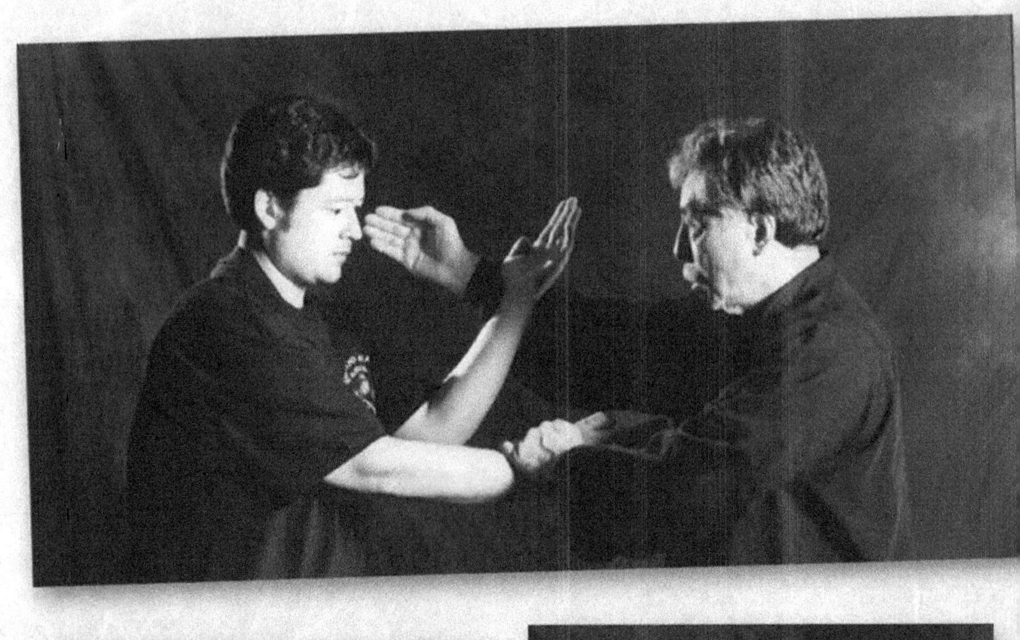
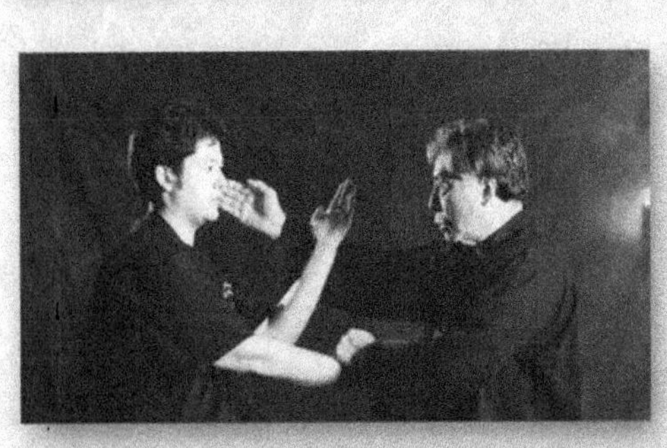

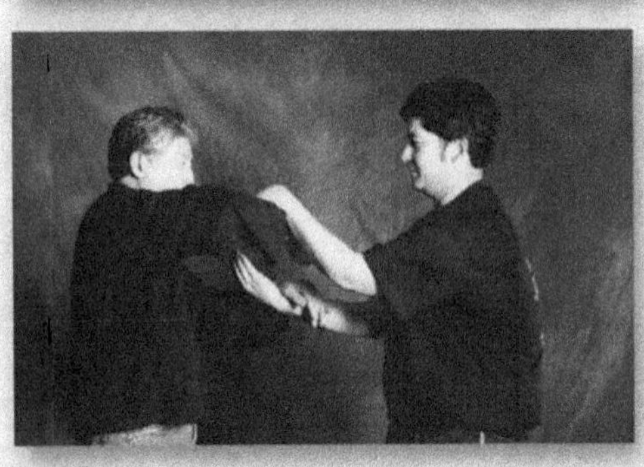
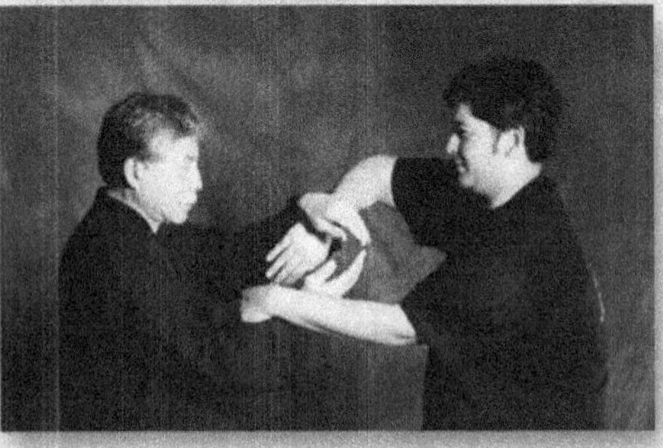

Taky Kimura & Dan Inosanto

Description of Photos

Early on when Bruce Lee stepped foot back on American soil, he quickly gathered students together to teach them his way of martial arts. Through the many students Bruce had, he chose only a few to help him represent his vision. Taky Kimura, James Lee and Dan Inosanto were not only students of the late Bruce Lee, but they became his appointed instructors who represented Seattle, Oakland and the Los Angeles Branches. When James Lee passed away, Bruce Lee told Taky Kimura and Dan Inosanto that they are the only ones left to see his vision through and that Dan Inosanto should understand that Taky Kimura is considered his senior when it came to the lineage of his teachings. As the years went on, Taky Kimura and Dan Inosanto became very close friends and confidants, and to this day, both Taky and Dan support and honor one another in the light of their SiFu and dearest friend, Bruce Lee.

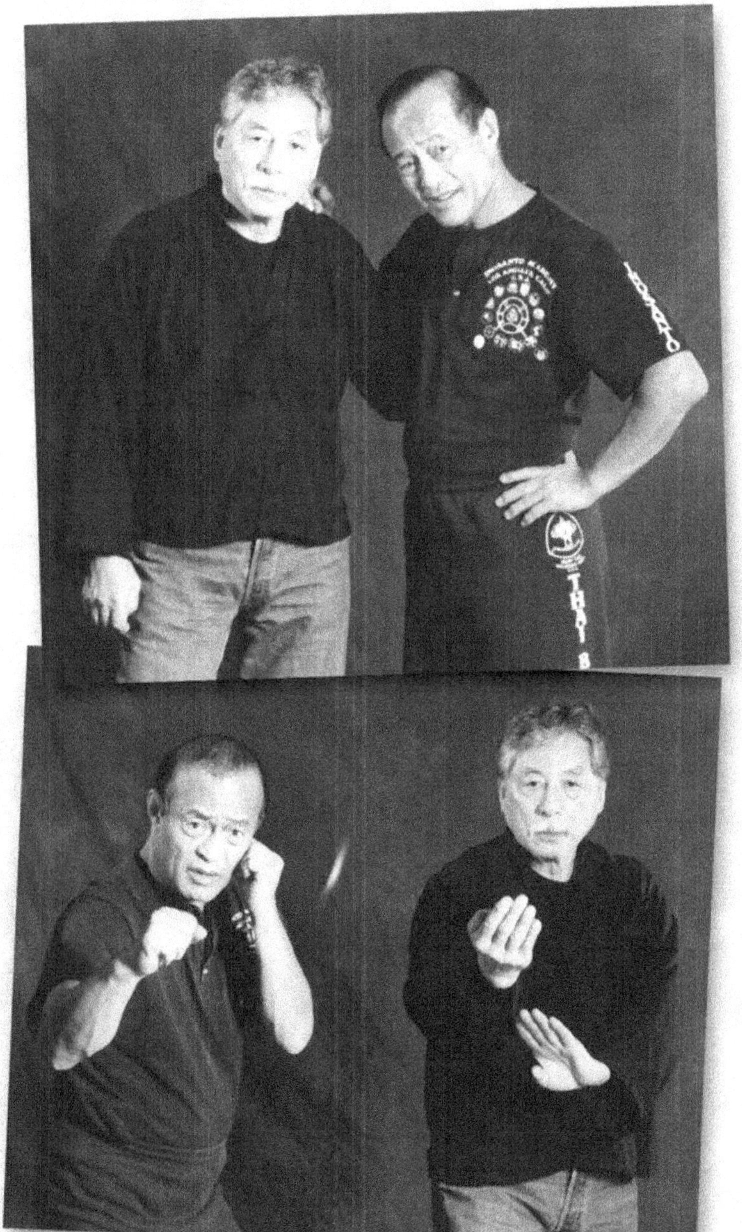

Taky Kimura and Dan Inosanto together again as friends and martial art students of the late and great Bruce Lee. As they pose together for the camera, one cannot deny the history on both sides of the coin.

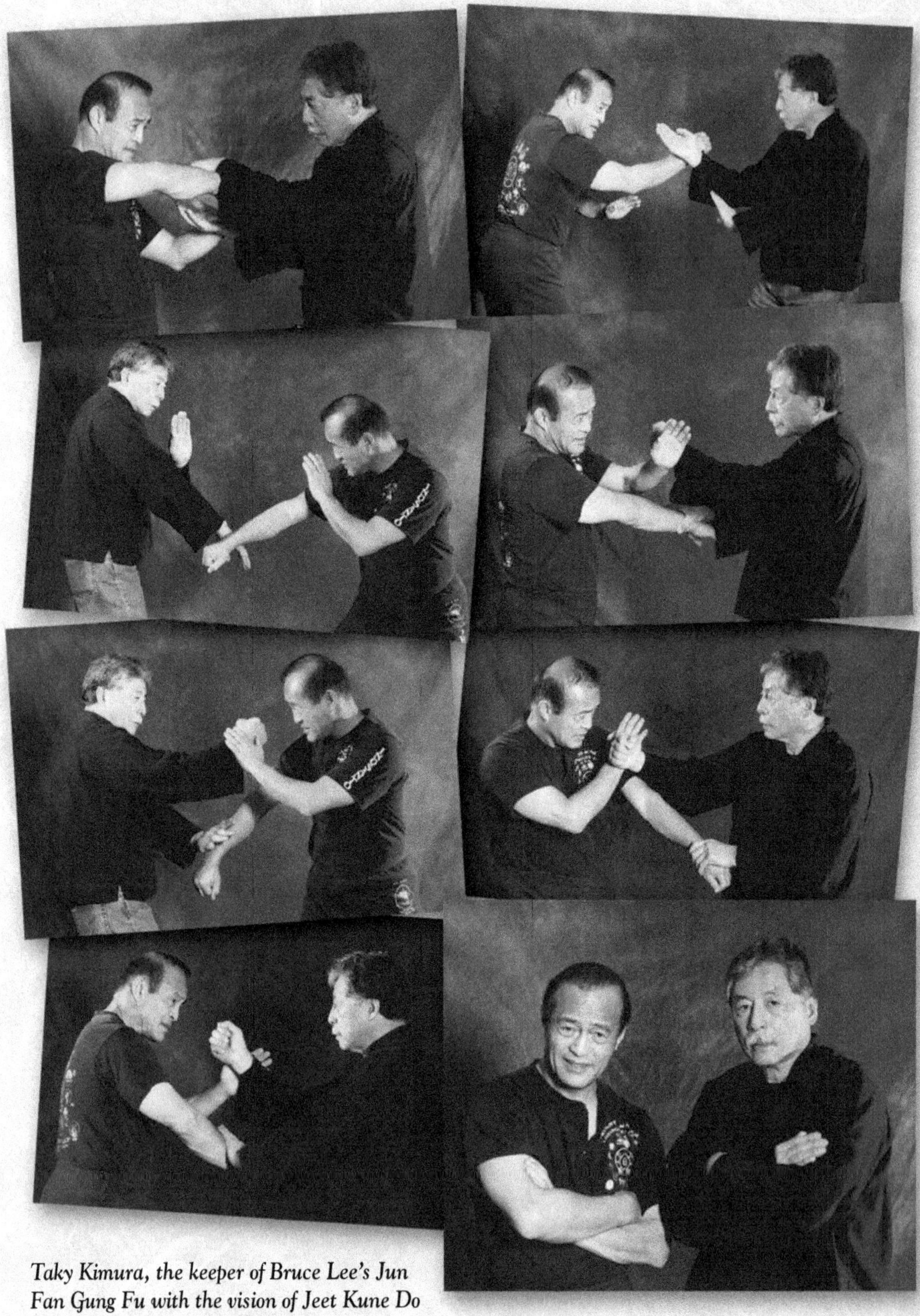

Taky Kimura, the keeper of Bruce Lee's Jun Fan Gung Fu with the vision of Jeet Kune Do and Dan Inosanto, the keeper of Bruce Lee's Jeet Kune Do with the base of Jun Fan Gung Fu. These two life long friends brought together by Bruce Lee honor and respect one another to this day in the tribute of their SiFu Bruce Lee.

Seattle Class, Then & Now

When potential students come to me for instruction, it is not always an automatic that I will take that individual in to our Institute. I have to talk with the individual and feel that person out, it has to be for the very right reasons. They must be sincere and want to learn for the right reasons. It is important for the individual to understand that the philosophical is just as important as the physical, more so, because it gives you a better understanding of the human condition. I pledged many years ago that I would not prosper from Bruce Lee's name and legacy and I feel I have kept to that promise all these years. So, therefore, when I choose the potential student, they must meet the criteria I feel Bruce would have wanted.

Our Institute is full of students from the past and present. We are all family there and share a common goal, to search for the path of self enlightenment, the journey, the quest. It has many names and has many meanings, but like a family, we have to thrive together, helping one another achieve the goal. My students can come to me and ask me anything. Sometimes my students get sidetracked and leave my instruction for a while, but they come back when time suits them well. The point is, not to point fingers, or not to judge, or to demand, it is to help one another achieve. Bruce had a saying and that was, "It is what it is"! This means, you take the good with the bad, the happy with the sad, the strong with the weak, you just are and it is what it is. This helps the individual except his or her position in their life and can take on anything that lies in front of them.

I am approached from people from all over the world who want to know more about Bruce Lee and what he was teaching, so I welcome them in to our world at the Institute and they become one of us and then the beginning starts. Until my last days on this earth, I will hold true to these convictions, not just for me, but for Bruce, my family, my students and the many friends I have encountered throughout the years.

The First Seattle Gung Fu Class

Description of Photos

Bruce had many students in his time, but the original group of guys in Seattle where more than just students, they were all friends as well. Bruce even roomed with many of the guys in a house located in inner Seattle on 6th and Cherry Ave. for an extended, stay right after living at Ruby Chow. The many guys who lived and frequented the house were Jessie Glover, his first acquaintance, James Demile, Ed Hart, Howard Hall, Pat Hooks, Leroy Garcia, Joe Cowles, Skip Ellsworth, Tak Miyabe, and some others whom I cannot recall at this time. In these pictures Bruce plays and stands proudly with some of his original group of Seattle students. From Jesse Glover and James Demile, to Ed Hart and Skip Ellswroth, Bruce loved playing the part of SiFu and we all loved being his students as well. Those were great times.

Bruce Lee and first student Jesse Glover practicing the art of Jun Fan Gung Fu at their place of residence 6th and Cherry Ave. in Seattle, Washington.

The Jun Fan Gung Fu Class

Description of Photos

The Jun Fan Gung Fu Institute class practicing in a car park located next to Ruby Chow. Those times were great, we all were like family. After the class, we would all go eat and exchange thoughts about our training as well as talks on Eastern philosophy.

Class Portrait

Description of Photo

Throughout the years, the Seattle Jun Fan Gung Fu Institute had many students come and go, but one thing was for sure; all the students were amazed at Bruce's martial arts prowess and when they saw him do his thing, they were instantly sold to his way of teaching. Though students came and went, it was always a family atmosphere and we all cared about one another. Looking back now, there is still a hand full of us original students who still have contact with each other and celebrate the man we called our SiFu. Even if you were a student for a short time, you always walked away with life lessons from Bruce. That's how I want to remember those days, like we were one big family unit being lead down the road of enlightement.

A gathering of teachers and students from the Seattle Jun Fan Gung Fu Institute. The more well known students can be seen in the top and bottom row and include James Demile third from picture left, Jesse Glover fifth, Bruce Lee, Doug Palmer. Bottom row, Taky Kimura second from left and Charlie Woo center.

SiFu Bruce Lee Teaches Class

Picture of SiFu Bruce teaching the Seattle Jun Fan Gung Fu Institute class. Me with Charlie Woo, Linda Emery is far right.

Bruce Visits the Seattle Class

Description of Photos

After a long absence, Bruce came to visit us in Seattle at his Institute in 1968, and while he was there, he updated the class on many things that he was working on and changed some of the things we were doing in class. I noticed that Bruce was becoming more and more philosophical and that the younger Bruce I had known was becoming a man with a mission so to speak. The old students were happy to see him, while the new students were full of anxiety in meeting their SiGung who was a rising star in Hollywood.

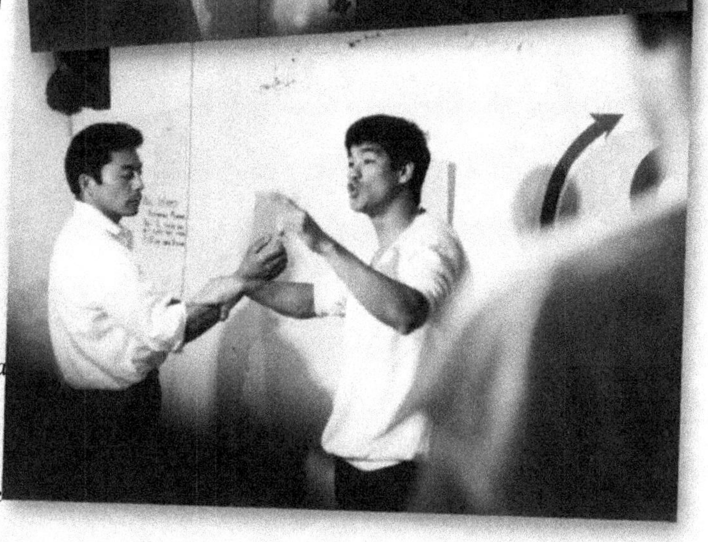

- *Bruce Lee explaining himself to a student at the Jun Fan Gung Fu Institute class upon his return to visit in 1968.*
- *Bruce Lee showing the importance of a proper stance with hand positioning through his top student and head Instructor at the Seattle Jun Fan Gung Fu Institute in 1968.*
- *-Bruce Lee and Taky Kimura showing students how to pull your opponent in to your centerline to execute a strike at the Jun Fan Gung Fu Institute in 1968, Seattle, Washington.*

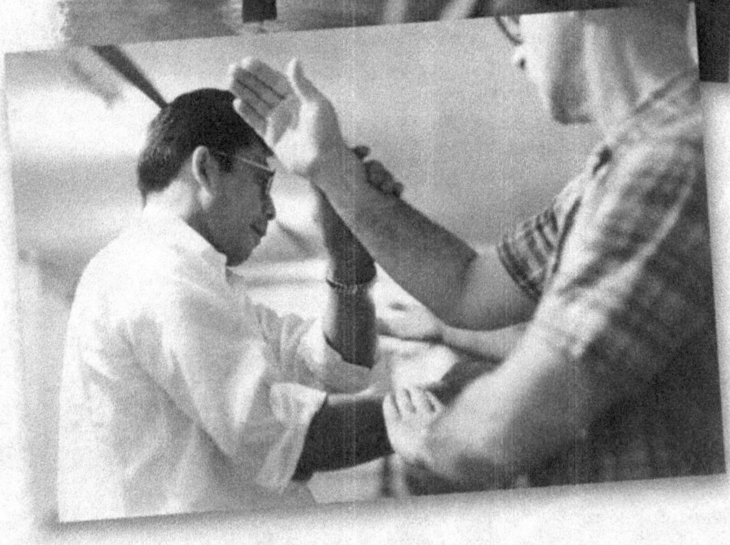

• Bruce Lee expressing the philosophies behind his new and approved way of fighting, his Jeet Kune Do.

• Taky Kimura demonstrating to the class a traditional Gung Fu sidekick upon Bruce Lee's visit back to Seattle for a visit in 1968.

• Taky Kimra showing the art of sticky hands (Chi Sao) with a student at the Seattle Gung Fu Institute upon Bruce lee's return to visit the school in 1968.

SiFu Taky Sharing the Knowledge

Description of Photos

- 85 year old 7th rank SiFu Taky Kimura cobra stretches along side his students at the Jun Fan Gung Fu Club in Seattle Washington.
- After a hard training session at the Seattle Jun Fan Gung Fu Club, the students are about to salute and bow in respect to their SiFu, Taky Kimura.
- A nightly workout ritual with the old and new students and instructors, at the Seattle Jun Fan Gung Fu Club.

Andy Kimura Demonstrates During Gung Fu Class

Description of Photo

5th rank instructor SiFu Andrew Kimura demonstrates with 4th rank instructor Michael Hilow the Jun Fan method during class at the Seattle branch Gung Fu Club.

Michael Hilow showing the Basics of the Jun Fan Method

Description of Photo

4th rank instructor Michael Hilow showing the basics of the Jun Fan method to students at the Jun Fan Gung Fu Club in Seattle.

Taky Kimura & Jose M. Fraguas

Description of Photos

Jose M. Fraguas – professional writer and a Jun Fan Gung Fu/Jeet Kune Do instructor – is a long-time close friend of the Kimura family. Fraguas publicly recognizes his admiration and respect for SiFu Taky Kimura, not only as a Martial Arts instructor but as an example of having outstanding human quality: "What we need in the modern society of Martial Arts is not admiration for the "tough fighters" around the world, but rather to look up to those individuals who display the flexible mind and strength to maintain high moral standards in daily life. Taky Kimura is an example of someone who trained himself to overcome hardship and develop a deep spirituality as a human being."

(Top) Fraguas posing in a traditional Jun Fan Gung Fu By-Jong, wearing Bruce Lee's original jacket used by the "Little Dragon" when he taught Gung Fu classes at the Seattle "Kwoon."

(Left) Jose M. Fraguas posing with SiFu Kimura during Taky's visit to Empire Books/Empire Media studios in Los Angeles.

The Kimura Legacy

Description of Photo

Like father like son, Andrew Kimura and son Brodie and a very proud father and grand-father, Taky Kimura, in pose for the camera at the Jun Fan Seattle Gung Fu Club 2009.

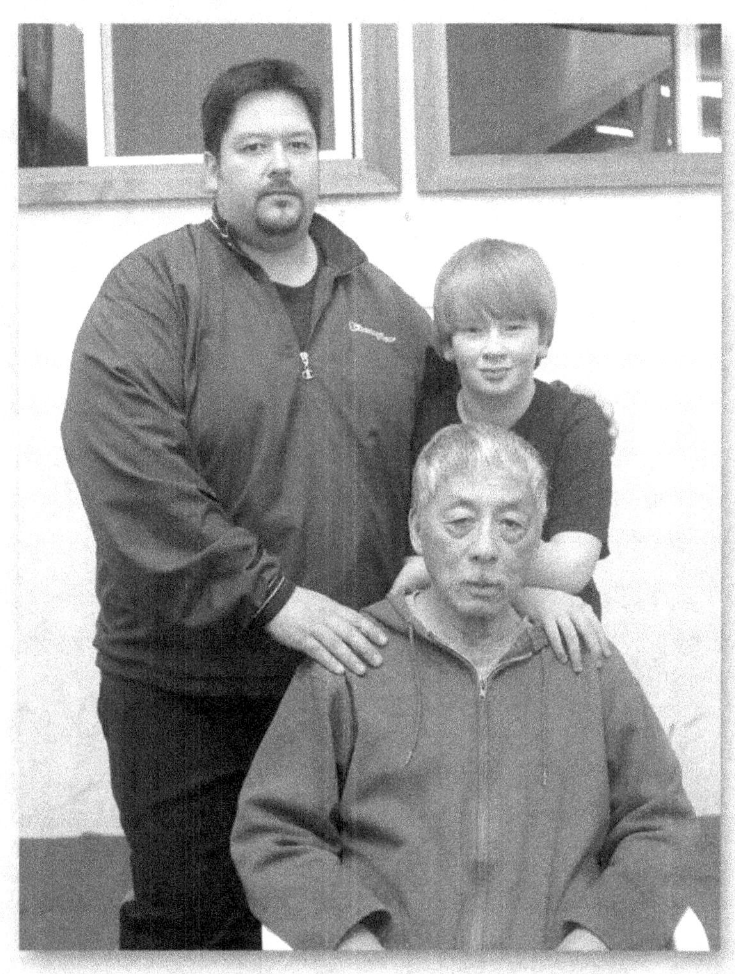

Senior Students

Description of Photo

- Left to right, Michael Hilow 4th rank, Abe Santos 4th rank, Andrew Kimura 5th rank, Scott Lindenmuth 4th rank and 7th rank SiFu Taky Kimura center at the Jun Fan Seattle Gung Fu Club.
- Top row left to right, 4th rank instructor Michael Hilow, 4th rank Instructor Abe Santos, 5th rank instructor SiFu Andrew Kimura, 4th rank instructor Scott Lindenmuth and 1st rank Chris Seung. Bottom row left to right, 3rd rank instructor Anne Harrington, 7th rank SiFu Taky Kimura and 3rd rank Julie DonTigny at the Jun Fan Seattle branch Gung Fu Club.
- SiFu Taky Kimura posing for the camera with 4th rank instructor Michael Hilow at the Jun Fan Seattle branch Gung Fu Club.
- Left to right, 3rd rank instructor Anne Harrington, 7th rank SiFu Taky Kimura and 3rd rank instructor Julie DonTigny at the Jun Fan Seattle branch Gung Fu Club.

Taky Strong at 85

Description of Photos

• SiFu Taky Kimura wearing his SiFu's original custom Gung Fu top at the Seattle Jun Fan Gung Fu Club playing the Mook Jung (wooden dummy) as was taught to him by Bruce Lee.

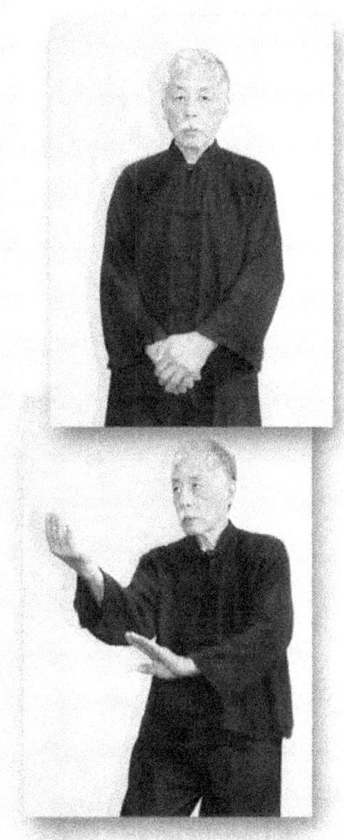

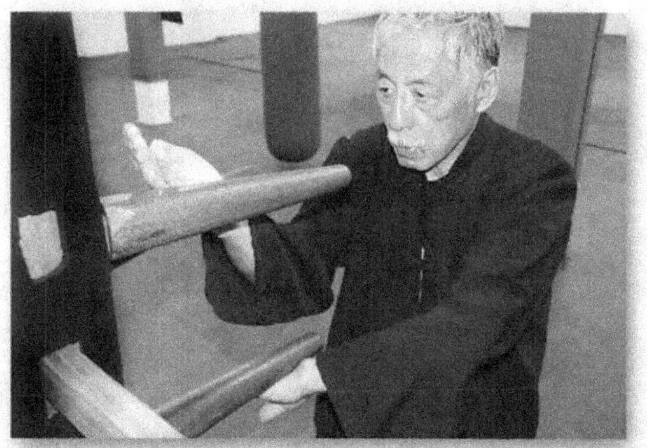

• SiFu Taky Kimura discusses Bruce Lee's philosophy with a student at the Jun Fan Gun Fu Club.
• SiFu Taky Kimura discussing the Jun Fan Gung Fu method with instructor Scott Lindenmuth at the Jun Fan Gung Fu Club.
• SiFu Taky Kimura posing stoically for the camera in one of his original Gung Fu tops he used to wear while demonstrating along side Bruce Lee.

The Jun Fan Gung Fu Institute Through the Years

Description of Photos

Throughout the years since Bruce Lee's passing, there have been many students who have seeked instruction in the Jun Fan Gung Fu method. From the moment I was appointed head instructor of the Seattle branch Institute, I took on a responsibility not only to my SiFu Bruce Lee, but also to the countless individuals who have walked through my door past and present. For me, it has been an honor and joy to be able to pass on to people what Bruce Lee taught me. To teach not only the physical, but also the philosophical and spiritual beliefs of SiFu Bruce, have been a task I have accepted with open arms. The individuals, from different walks of life, religion, different points of you, have taught me as

Early to mid-eighties Club.

2009 Group.

Early 1960's original group.

1988 group (25th anniversary).

1998 Group.

1993 Group.

well to be a better human being and I thank all my students past and present for being a part of my growth as well.

It has been 36 years since Bruce Lee passed away and much longer since the doors of the first Jun Fan Gung Fu Institute opened in the early 1960's, but for me, I treat every day like it is the first day, for there are the old and new students to teach and share my musings with.

It has been my privilege in doing my part, in keeping my best friend and SiFu's legacy alive and I know he is looking down upon not just me, but all of us who keep his flame burning, and he is smiling and motivating us all.

PRACTICAL KARATE
PRACTICAL KARATE
PRACTICAL KARATE
PRACTICAL KARATE
Mas Oyama's KARATE
SECRET FIGHTING ARTS OF THE WORLD
CONTEST JUDO
BODY AND MIND IN HARMONY
TAI CHI FOR
Secrets of Shaolin Temple Boxing
The Way of Karate
JUDO FOR YOUNG MEN
K. TOHEI
AIKIDO
THE ARTS OF SELF-DEFENSE
JUDO
TRAINING METHODS
Canon of JUDO

Bruce and his Books

From an early age, Bruce Lee had a deep interest in many subjects that torched on, religion, philosophy, humanity, art, poetry, cinema, music and what he is most known for, the martial arts. He studied these subjects, through the books he acquired from many different sources like new used bookstores. Bruce Lee wanted to be, and was successful at, being a well-rounded man, do in part because he was a well-rounded reader.

Incredibly, his book collection was in the thousands and even more incredible, he read each book he owned. Bruce Lee felt that knowledge is extremely important if we are to involve as human beings and there were two ways two experience such knowledge, through self discovery, or the material handed down through the generations for us to investigate, dissect, taking out what is not useful to us and leaving what was most important, so that we can use it as our own and add to it if need be.

Bruce Lee passed away at the age of 32, but his knowledge of life and art went far beyond his those thirty-two years. He loved his books and because of those books, he would define his own future. Within this section, you will get a glimpse at the books he read and studied and then passed on to me for my enlightenment.

From time to time, I take these books out and read through them, remembering the musings with Bruce about the subject matters. It is one thing to be blessed to have known Bruce, but it is certainly another blessing to have the books that he held dear that helped him with his own self-discovery, laying the path for greatness.

Book 1

Book Note 1

Bruce Lee dissected this book completely and like always, he added his own flavor to the techniques as can be seen within his Chinese notes in red upon on the pages.

From book cover left, to book page right, the notation reads in Chinese "KICK". Bruce is suggesting, yes use the head block and be aware of the follow up punch to the face from your opponent, but use a straight kick to the opponent's groin to prevent him from following through with his attack.

Book page bottom left, Bruce's note reads "STRAIGHT IN FROM THE SIDE" meaning when your opponent strikes, it is better to block the strike and deliver a kick coming in from a side stance.

A rare look at Bruce Lee wearing a karate / judo Gi while delivering a side kick to his opponent. Seattle, Washington 1960.

Book 2

Book Note 2

Another example of a book Bruce bought at a secondhand bookstore and added it to his library. He then gave it to me a few years later around 1967-68, as he wanted me to understand in where he was getting his information. Many of the books like this one were very old to start, but Bruce liked looking back at the origins of a specific style or movement to see its roots. Sometime, the beginning of a certain style or belief is where it's most simplicity lies and as it grows, sometimes it becomes distorted and a classical mess so to speak. This book in today's market is worth a lot, they are hard to find, but a precious one at that.

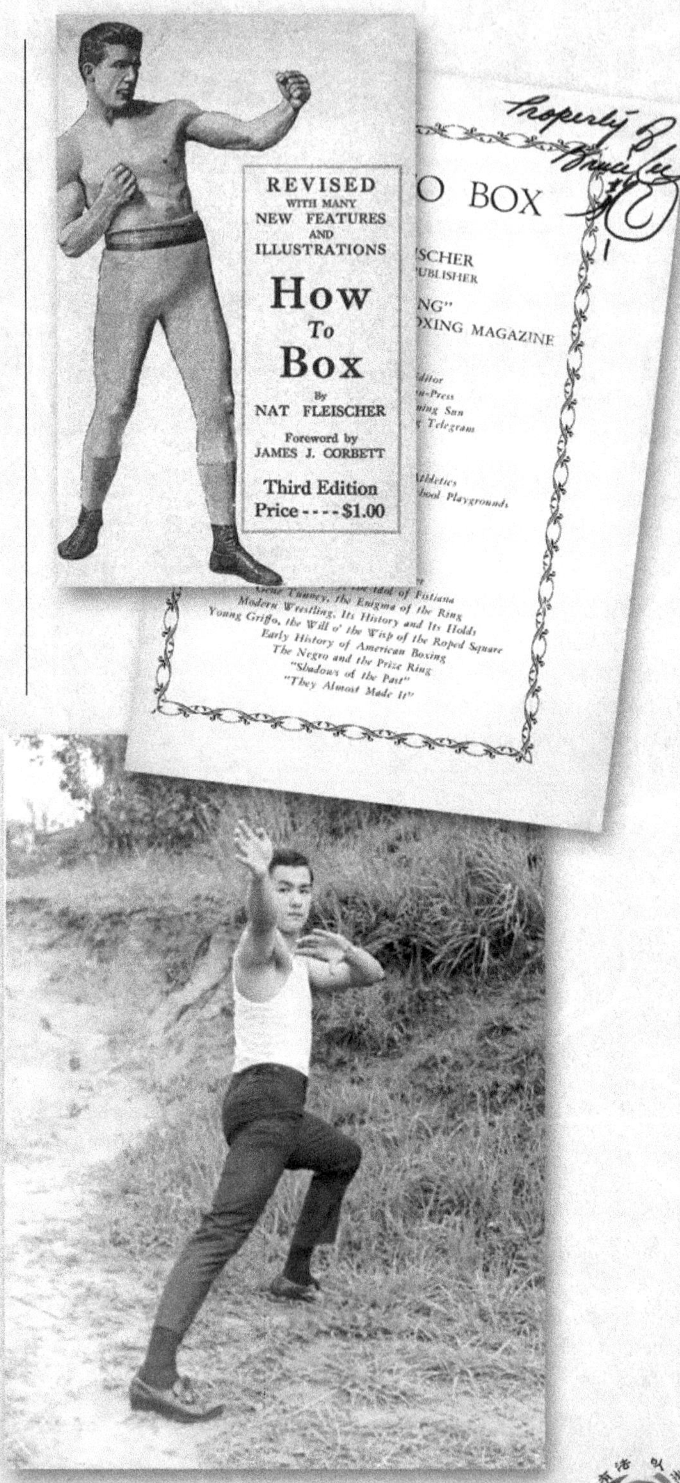

Bruce Lee in Hong Kong in 1963 as his younger brother Robert takes this picture. When Bruce went back to Hong Kong in 1963, he was discovering many of the different martial arts styles as well as brushing up on his Wing Chun with Master Yip Man. Here, Bruce is doing a traditional long arm movement that one can find in the system of Choy Lay Fut.

Book 3

Book Note 3

One of Brue Lee's personal boxing reference book guides he later on gave to me for my own personal studying! Bruce had many of these types of books and he read them all from front to back.

REVISED
WITH MANY
NEW FEATURES

TRAINING
for
BOXERS
by
NAT FLEISCHER
Foreword by
JACK DEMPSEY
Ninth Edition
Price $1.00

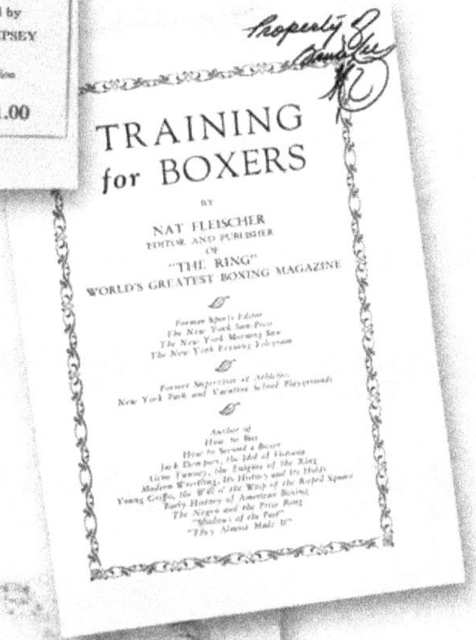

Property of Bruce Lee

TRAINING
for BOXERS
BY
NAT FLEISCHER
EDITOR AND PUBLISHER
OF
"THE RING"
WORLD'S GREATEST BOXING MAGAZINE

Bruce in traditional Wing Chun pose in 1963, upon his return home to Hong Kong to visit his family.

Book 4

Book Note 4

Bruce's personal note dedicated to me it reads;

TAKY, Simplicity is the last step of art, and the first step of nature (in Chinese it says "SIFU"). To my student and friend: Concentrate yet not cling to it

Best Wishes
and
good luck
Bruce

Bruce signed many books like this to me, but I hold this one dear to my heart. Bruce always expressed to me from his soul his deepest thoughts about philosophy and life, and when he expressed those thoughts by pen, he made them so simple to understand and right to the point.

Bruce looking sharp for the camera as brother Robert snaps the shot. This picture was taken in 1963, in Hong Kong at the family's 218 Nathan Road home.

Book 5

Book Note 5

The book page note reads from left to right, Break discipline, Follow discipline and Learn discipline. Bruce loved all types of books, secret combat / techniques by the CIA and anything that he could incorporate in his vision in a stealth manner that would let attackers know his martial art was not to be messed with. The head of the F.B.I., J. Edgar Hoover, indorsed this particular book and to Bruce that was a big deal.

Bruce looking like he came out of a James Bond spy novel, posing in front of his car in Seattle, Washington near the Gung Fu Institute.

Book 6

Book Note 6

Bruce Lee picked up this book when he went back to Hong Kong in 1963. His father Li Hoi Chuen was deeply into Tai Chi Chuan and it really struck up an interest in Bruce to investigate it further. Bruce knew that Tai Chi was a martial art that many older people studied and he was more of an intense martial artist, so it was not to later on that he appreciated the health and maintenance that Tai Chi could give to the practitioner. When Bruce was done with this book, he dedicated it to me and handed it over so I could study it and use its applications.

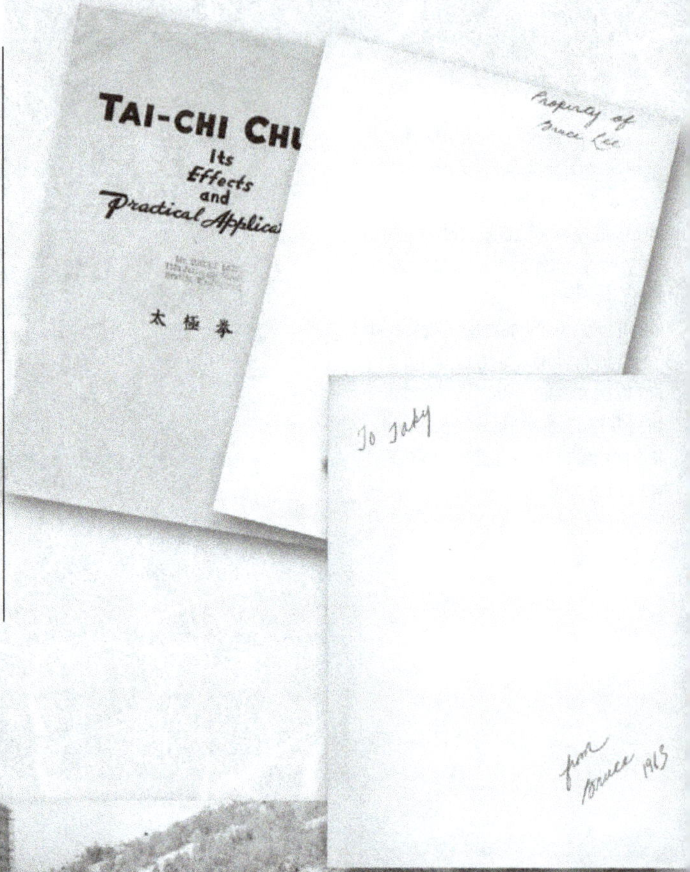

Bruce Lee standing next to his father in King's Park with his father's Tai Chi group that met every morning to practice. The men got a huge kick out of Bruce's martial arts skill and even tried to learn from him while he was there throughout those summer months. In the background, you can see they were building Queen Elizabeth's Hospital. It was like two worlds collide, Bruce is doing Wing Chun and his father and friends were doing Tai Chi.

Book 7

Book Note 7

"The Roar of the Crowd" by James L. Corbett was one of Bruce Lee's favorite books. This book was signed three times by Bruce and chopped with his Chinese stamp. I have never seen another book in where he signed it so many times, but I am very lucky that one of those signatures was dedicated to me.

Bruce Lee side-kicking Dan Inosanto in this image that was one of many meant for Bruce Lee's Fighting Method books.

Book 8

Book Note 8

Bruce brought this book with him from Hong Kong in 1959. Bruce writes on the cover; The Chinese twenty-four foot-fighting technique and signs his name Bruce Lee Siu Long, his Chinese name.

Bruce writes bottom left; this book deals mainly on foot techniques. He was always investigating the many styles of Gung Fu. The books on good footwork were important for him because without the footwork, one cannot defend himself properly.

Bruce used to write "Property of Bruce" Lee on all his books as well as his address, just in case if the books were misplaced, someone would return them. To Bruce, especially back then, money was hard to come by and he treasured every book he could get, these books were part of his being. When he left for Oakland and then LA, he gave me many as gifts as a friendship gesture and learning guide. He wanted me to investigate and explore what he knew.

Bruce Lee in Hong Kong, 1958, looking sharp for the camera as his sister Phoebe takes the picture.

Book 9

Book Note 9

Another example of Bruce Lee's investigations of different martial arts. Bruce picked this book up in Hong Kong in 1963. Bruce not only loved the many martial arts from China, but the philosophy and the imagery as well. Here, Bruce drew for me a Praying Mantis, one of the Gung Fu animal systems that were practiced within the different Gung Fu styles of China. Bruce was very interested in The Northern Mantis Clan style; it is a very elusive and agile system.

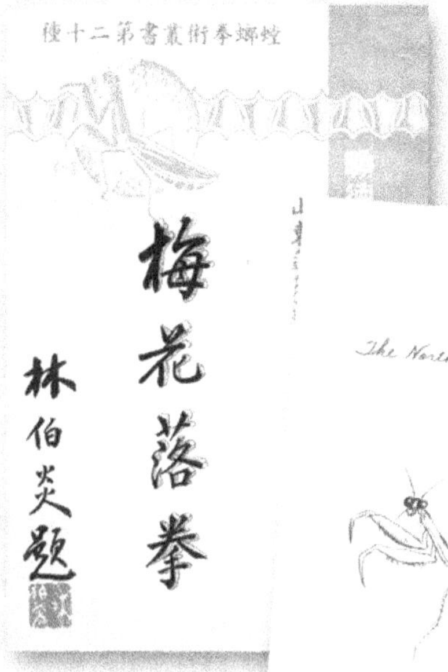

Bruce Lee in 1963 in Hong Kong at his 218 Nathan Road family home.

Book **10**

Book Note 10

Bruce Lee's notes in this book reads: "Iron Palm's Power", same as the title of the book. Bruce drew these illustrations of how the power of the Iron Palm training will lead you to extra ordinary strength, that would allow you to break through boards, chop wooden staffs in half and gauge out pieces of brick with your fingertips. Bruce constantly trained his knuckle and palm region of his hands. His belief was, the harder you train the hand it will slice through your opponent like butter. He was always picking up books like this / manuals to investigate many of the other training methods in the many diverse martial arts styles.

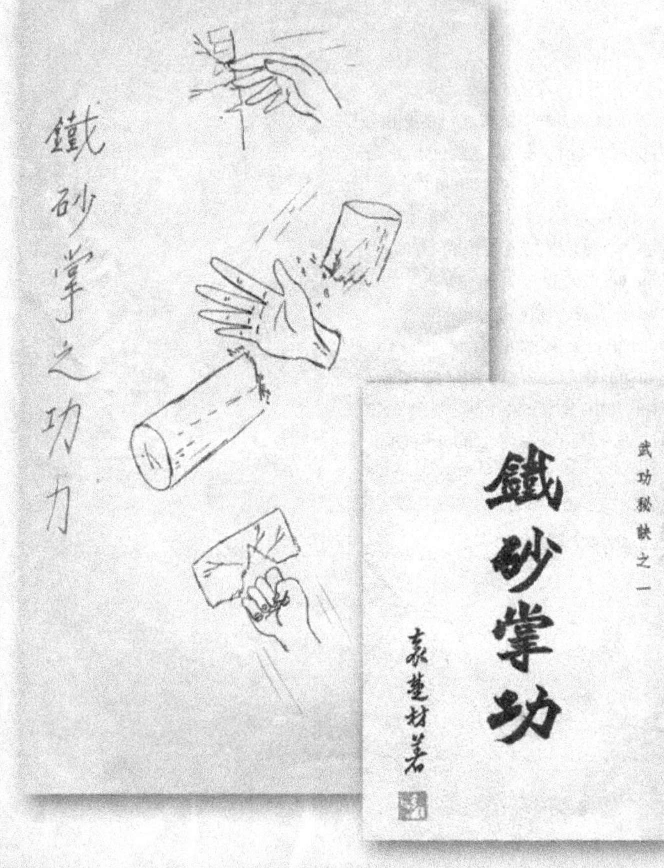

Bruce Lee demonstrating the Iron Palm technique on bricks, in Seattle, Washington.

Book 11

Book Note 11

Bruce kept his books dear to him and felt they were the learning guides to the world. He signed his name on all his books in various ways, but mostly signed them, "Property of Bruce Lee". This book also has the Jun Fan Gung Fu Institute crest on it.

This book reads in Chinese YING YI 5 WAYS STYLE.

Left to Right: Taky Kimura, Bruce Lee and friend and student Sue Ann Kay posing for the camera in Seattle, Washington on a cold winters day.

Book 12

Book Note 12

When Bruce Lee put together the Chinese Gung Fu book, he really did not know in how it would be perceived, or accepted. In the beginning, it seemed he was just putting this book together for family and friends and a learning guide for his students. Half way through the process though, he knew that this book would be an important one for him and he felt the energy around him from waiting onlookers to get their hands on one. This book was looked at as a mystical Chinese book of hidden secrets for many and for some; they wanted a secret way of fighting to destroy all their enemies. But to everyone's delight, when the book started to be passed around, it became an enjoyable learning tool that opened up the eyes to everyone about the foreign art of Gung Fu by Master Bruce Lee. I have many of this same book, signed by Bruce, but this one is my favorite in the way it was inscribed to me. BRUCE WAS THANKFUL FOR MY HELP, FRIENDSHIP, and LOYALTY since our first meeting in 1960.

Bruce wrote;

"To my dear friend Taky, thanks for everything starting from 1960," Bruce.

Here is the original and much wider and clearer picture for the cover of the "Chinese Gung Fu" book. Bruce was relentless in getting all the moves to look perfect for the camera and he took many to make sure he could choose a perfect one.

Book 13

Book Note 13

Though Bruce Lee had countless books on the martial arts, he also was an admirer of books about Chinese wisdom and philosophy. This book entitled "A Chinese Garden of Serenity" was given to me as a gift from Bruce. It's a very special book in which he underlined many of the passages within. When I read these philosophical Epigrams, my reflections of Bruce are very vivid and you can see by the many underlines passages he made that his mindset was a very deep and concentrated one.

The underline passage reads; *A Greedy man may be materially rich, but spiritually poor; a contented man may be materially poor, but spiritually rich. One who holds a high position may feel physically at ease, but mentally fatigued; one who has a low position may feel physically fatigued, but mentally at ease. Which of these is a gain and which a loss, which is real and which unreal, a man of insight can, of course, distinguish for himself.*

A Chinese Garden of Serenity

REFLECTIONS OF A ZEN BUDDHIST

Property of Bruce Lee

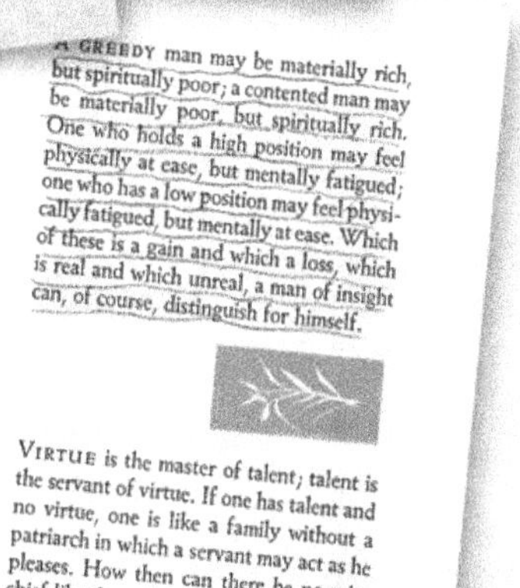

A GREEDY man may be materially rich, but spiritually poor; a contented man may be materially poor, but spiritually rich. One who holds a high position may feel physically at ease, but mentally fatigued; one who has a low position may feel physically fatigued, but mentally at ease. Which of these is a gain and which a loss, which is real and which unreal, a man of insight can, of course, distinguish for himself.

VIRTUE is the master of talent; talent is the servant of virtue. If one has talent and no virtue, one is like a family without a patriarch in which a servant may act as he pleases. How then can there be no mischief like that of an elf?

Bruce Lee looking sharp walking up stairs to his room above Ruby Chow's restaurant in 1961 after attending school.

Book 14

Book Note 14

Throughout Bruce Lee's investigation of the martial arts, he often mention in how the Akido masters could do amazing things with their Chi and how simple it was to throw a large and stronger man of his feet, flipping him across the room. But to Bruce, were these amazing feats, or a skilled learned in cooperation with teacher and student? Bruce often asked, "can the Aikido master choose someone off the street with no prior knowledge of the belief systems of that martial art and do the same things to him that he does to his student? What is a show and what is real? Does the student help the instructor throw him self across the room, or is this something very real?" The answer is yes to both. There are limits and beyond those limits lies choreography.

Bruce Lee signed this book, "Property of Bruce Lee" and below he writes,
Aikido,
From Sifu Bruce.

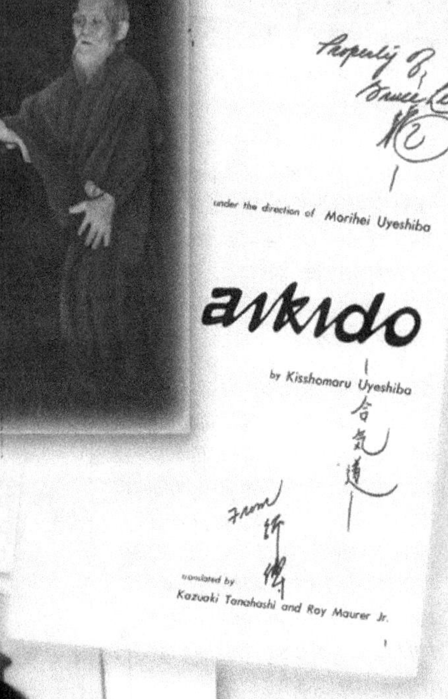

Bruce Lee with his mother Grace and son Brandon in the Commissary at TVB in Hong Kong, before Bruce went on to demonstrate in front of a large audience his skill as a martial artist with thousands watching him on television. This night was truly the beginning for his overnight success.

Interview with Shuzo Kato

When Bruce Lee first set ground in the States in 1959, he brought with him little money, street smarts and the martial arts training handed down to him by Professor Yip Man. Throughout his time in Seattle, Bruce Lee investigated many types of martial arts in which, was the beginning for him in adding and subtracting what he liked from those various styles and mentally incorporating them into the discipline he already knew. In the process of investigating Western Boxing, Wrestling and various other styles Gung Fu, he joined a Judo class at the University of Washington for a three-month period. Shuzo Kato was the instructor who taught Bruce Lee in those few months back in 1961. His recollections of "The Little Dragon" give us an insight in the times when Bruce Lee was in the early stages of self-investigation and discovery. Respect, honor and skill, Shuzo Kato talks about the time he taught a legend...

Shuzo Kato is left.

Shuzo Kato 3rd from left.

RFTD: Can you tell us about your background in Judo?

SK: I started training in Judo in 1937 in Seattle, Washington at 1510 Washington St. The place was called Seattle Dojo. I took lessons up until the time I was incarcerated in the relocation camps.

RFTD: How and when were you first introduced to Bruce Lee?

SK: I had a part time job at the University of Seattle. I taught a 3:15 class there for the purpose of teaching Judo to the students. The University graciously bought mats for the students as well as Judo Gi's (uniforms). I met Bruce Lee when he joined my class in 1961.

RFTD: What were your first impressions of Bruce Lee?

SK: He was very unpretentious and I really couldn't tell him from one guy to the next at first. He was very respectful to me and the other students in the class, but to be honest, I was kind of in awe with him as I read in the Seattle papers he was a master of Gung Fu as well as in the art of Cha Cha. At that time I was taking dancing lessons with my wife and I had seen many write-ups on him that he was very good in both areas. I was impressed with his professionalism and character.

RFTD: What kind of student was Bruce Lee?

SK: He was always respectful and he never pushed the fact he was a master of Gung Fu on me, or the other students. He always listened to my instruction. I passed out a booklet of Judo instruction to the class and he was very interested in it and thanked me for giving him one. He would ask me a lot about the certain movements we were doing in class, because he had such an interest in breaking them down and analyzing them for his study. He was really into the science of it all, which impressed me greatly.

RFTD: How long did Bruce Lee train with you?

SK: It was for only three months that I taught him and was his instructor.

RFTD: It was well known that Bruce Lee really appreciated the Japanese samurai films. Did he ever mention to you anything about this?

SK: Yes he did, and in fact, most of us back then loved them too. We used to go to the community theaters and watch the films, of course they were subtitled for all to enjoy, but I was really surprised to know that he truly appreciated them.

RFTD: Did you and Bruce Lee ever spend any time with one another outside your instruction?

SK: Only for brief periods of time. We would both discuss what was going on in our communities as Japanese and Chinese. We talked a lot about giving back to the our community. Bruce was already so popular with the rest of my students as they all read about him in the papers so they felt honored in having him there.

RFTD: When the three months ended and your instruction in teaching Judo stopped, did Bruce Lee have plans in sticking with your teachings outside the University?

SK: No, he just thanked me graciously for letting him train with the class and also thanked me for being his teacher in that small amount of time. Later on, I found out that Bruce was very close to Taky Kimura who I was in camps with during war time. Taky and I took Judo classes together while we remained in the horrible interment period. We became very close. I also taught one of Bruce's first students by the name of Jesse Glover. Over the years, I have had a fondness for Bruce because we are tied together in many ways through the friends we both had.

RFTD: Years later, when Bruce Lee became famous in the cinematic world, what were your thoughts about his screen performances?

SK: Well, I was totally amazed with his skill and screen presence. I thought he was amazing! I liked very much in how Bruce took the name Kato for his character in the "Green Hornet". From seeing him in class to watching him on screen was a huge difference, he was great.

Shuzo Kato 3rd from left.

Doug Palmer

Reflections of My Master

In 1961, Doug Palmer met Bruce Lee in Seattle, Washington. From their very first introduction, they hit it off and became friends. Doug would become one of Bruce Lee's very first students within the legendary Jun Fan Gung Fu Institute and would stay a loyal student for years and has kept Bruce's legacy alive to this day. Not only was Doug Palmer privy to the growth and evolution of the teachings of Bruce Lee, he also had a unique insight into who Bruce was a human being. When Doug stayed with Bruce and his family in Hong Kong in 1963, he got an insight into how the Eastern side of Bruce was an essential part of his life and how he was able to transcend that culture to the Western view.

Doug Palmer has graciously given us an interview about his memories of Bruce Lee and it is his hope that the old and new fans on the rise will get an insight into who Bruce Lee was as a teacher, friend and human being.

Doug Palmer in 1963 at Bruce's family's house in Hong Kong. Bruce in back making a funny face for the camera.

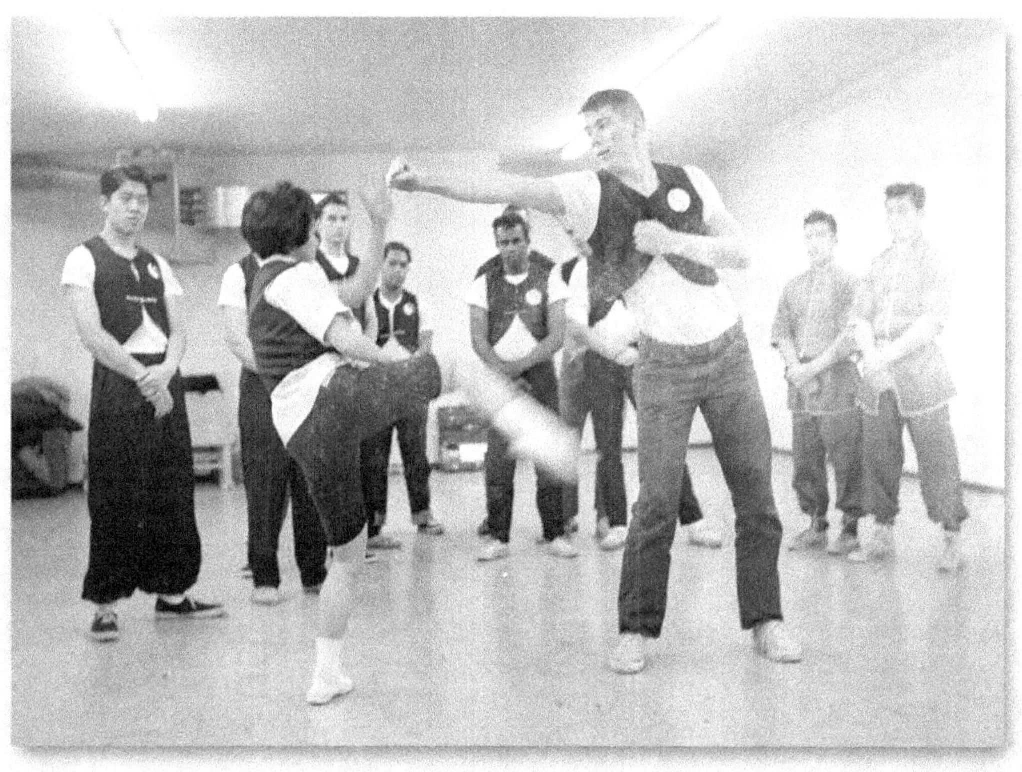

RFTD: Can you tell us how and when you first met Bruce Lee?

DP: In the summer of 1961, before my senior year in high school, I saw a Gung Fu demonstration given by Bruce and some of his students at a festival in Seattle's Chinatown. At that time I had boxed for some 6-7 years and was fairly proficient, and had seen demonstrations of Judo and Karate, but had never seen anything like Bruce's Gung Fu. I was mesmerized.

In talking to friends in the Chinese community, I found out that the younger brother of one of my friends was currently taking lessons from Bruce, and I said that I'd like to take lessons, too. A week or so later, while milling around in the crowd at another festival, sponsored by Seattle's Japanese community (called Bon Odori), I felt a hand on my shoulder. I turned around and Bruce was standing there. He looked at me appraisingly and said, "I heard you were looking for me." I stuck out my hand and we shook hands. I told him that I had seen his demonstration in Chinatown and was interested in learning Gung Fu. Bruce told me to drop by one of the workouts and watch. If I was still interested, we would talk. I attended the next class (held in a yard outside the house of one of one of the students, Roy Garcia, as I recall), and when I told him afterwards that I still wanted to join the class, he said OK.

RGFTD: What were your first impressions of him?

DP: His obvious physical abilities were the first thing that struck me - his blinding speed, extreme flexibility, grace and mastery of several different Gung Fu schools, and evident strength and power. The next impression

was one of great confidence in his own abilities, a strong personality, a keen sense of humor, and a willingness to share his knowledge with anyone (regardless of background) that was interested in learning.

RFTD: Did you have a Martial Arts background prior to meeting Bruce Lee?

DP: As mentioned above, I had boxed for 6-7 years, once a week religiously, and had won several bouts, including one as part of a group that visited the State Reformatory to box the team of inmates there.

RFTD: Can you tell us how Bruce's classes were structured?

DP: All his classes would start with the bow-in and salutation (he at the front of the class, the rest of us facing him), and then he would have someone lead us in exercises (which consisted of exercises to stretch the tendons (behind the knees and at the elbows); loosening exercises; exercises to strengthen various parts of the body, like the wrists, or frog-jumps in a big circle; exercises to harden the bones or muscles in the forearm, like alternate strikes on each others' forearms in a sequence that hardened three different sides of the forearm; and finally a few minutes of "meditation" - a breathing technique while in the horse stance). Then we'd form two lines facing each other and practice various techniques - side kick, front kick, paak sao, laap sao, chaap choi/gwa choi, straight punches - each side alternating offense and defense. (For instance, if one side was doing the side kick, the other side blocked the kick.) After that he would usually gather everyone around and demonstrate a new technique, or a counter to one we already knew, and sometimes talk for awhile about the mental, or psychological, aspects of Gung Fu. Then we'd usually spar with each other. Bruce would move from couple to couple, correcting our moves and often sparring with each of us for awhile. With the more advanced students he would do Chi Sao (sticking hand). At some point, after an hour and a half or so, he called a halt and we would all line up and bow out, and do the salutation again. (At this time, virtually all the techniques were Wing Chun).

RFTD: What kind of teacher was he?

DP: He was patient, open (he'd answer any question), thorough and fairly informal (except for the bow and salutation at the beginning and end of each session, the only other formality he required was that we address him as SiFu (Teacher) during the class (outside of class, he was "Bruce").

He was also pretty easy-going. I remember one class I was practicing chaap choi/gwa choi with a big guy - I was then 6'-2" and 160-170 lbs. or so, and I'd guess the other guy was in his late twenties or early thirties and at least 230 and a bit taller. I was practicing the offense, which consisted of moving in with a right-handed chaap choi, or knuckle fist, to the rib area. The other guy was supposed to block the chaap choi with a sweeping downward block, after which the person on offense would execute a gwa choi, or back fist, to the head. It could be delivered either with a regular full backfist, or with the knuckle of the index finger, aimed at the temple. In either case, the person on defense was supposed

to block the backfist with his palm in a particular manner. The other guy was apparently a black belt in Judo who considered himself a real martial artist, but who gave the impression that he wasn't convinced that there was anything special to Gung Fu. When I came in with the chaap choi/gwa choi, he would block in a particularly awkward way that made it impossible for me to execute the backfist with the snap that we were supposed to make. I tried to correct him a few times, but he wasn't really trying to do it right, and it almost seemed he was going out of his way to tangle up my backfist before I could even get it off, instead of letting me snap it into his palm held a few inches from his temple. Finally, I got frustrated because I couldn't get the gwa choi off, so I decided to move in even faster and try to avoid his entangling arm. When I did, however, his head was closer than I thought - perhaps he was off balance when his arm-block met no resistance - and I tried to slow my backfist down. I ended up snapping my knuckle against his right temple. Thinking I had just grazed him, I started to apologize, but he immediately went to his knees. We had to help him up and for a long time he was leaning up against the wall, holding his temple, drooling, with his eyes unfocussed and crossing each other. I was pretty scared. Bruce ambled over while the guy was leaning against the wall and asked what had happened. When I told him, he thought for a moment, then nodded and said, "Be careful," then ambled off again.

RFTD: Was Bruce a perfectionist?

DP: Definitely. Whatever he was interested in doing, he wanted to be exceptional at it. This included not just the martial arts, and acting in and directing his movies, but also in things like Cha-Cha (he was an excellent dancer, and invented a number of moves himself), and in the clothes he wore (he was meticulous in describing to his tailor in H.K. exactly what he wanted in terms of pocket style, etc., and sometimes drew pictures - like of the angle and shape of the pocket flap, for instance). He was also an excellent artist.

RFTD: When Bruce was teaching you and the other students in Seattle, he was progressing in his Martial Arts almost on a daily basis. Can you tell us what kind of philosophy Bruce preached to his students at that time?

DP: Bruce stressed the mental aspects of martial arts as well as the physical, as noted above. Much of that he drew from Taoist Philosophy, much of the ideas and imagery of which he would apply to Gung Fu. He would talk about this (and other things) during class, and sometimes I took notes. I remember one mental exercise that was very useful in quieting the mind so that a movement was not telegraphed. In paak sao, or slapping hand, one simultaneously used the left hand to slap the opponent's right forearm aside, while coming in with a straight right punch. Many students would telegraph their punch in various ways (by starting to slap before the punch, or moving the body first, or pressing forward slightly with the arm before starting the punch). Bruce told us to imagine the mind as the surface of a smooth pond, and to explode with the punch (and slap) only when the mind (and the image of the pond) was completely still. It worked - at least for me! I was much better able to exe-

Bruce Lee and Doug Palmer enjoying a night out on the town with the Lee family friends. Bruce's second mother Eva Tso sits to Bruce's right (picture left).

cute the move without the opponent being able to block it when utilizing such technique. Bruce also had many other stories which illustrated how the mental aspects of the martial arts were as important (if not more so) than the physical.

RFTD: Did Bruce teach each individual different depending on their physical and psychological make up?

DP: I don't recall anything specific regarding him changing his teaching to accommodate different psychological makeups, but I recall him talking about how some techniques were more or less suitable depending on not only your own physical attributes, but your opponent's. E.g., if you were shorter, with shorter arms than your opponent, other things being equal you should probably not be trading punches and kicks from a distance, but should find a way to get inside.

RFTD: Did you get to see Bruce's transformation from his Jun Fan Gung Fu, to his Jeet Kune Do?

DP: Only in discontinuous steps. When I took lessons continuously my senior year of high school (1961-62) and throughout the summer of '62, it was all Wing Chun. But when I came back from college (I went back East) for Christmas breaks and summer vacations, I noticed that he always had something new to show me or talk about. For instance, at one point he got into watching old boxing films - Jack Dempsey, Sugar Ray Robinson, Archie Moore, among others. Sometimes he would play one of the films and comment on a particular move he liked. Another time, as I recall, he demonstrated something I think he called "broken timing," a way of punching in a manner that threw your own timing off,

so you blocked where you expected his punch to be and he then floated it in after your hand fanned the air. It was something like a feint, to draw the block, but more subtle than that. Every time I saw him it seemed as if he had taken everything he knew before and added something entirely new to it in an organic way, so that his previous techniques were all still valid and worked, but were now just a part of an even greater whole, a greater paradigm. Kind of like Newtonian physics being subsumed as a special case of Einstein's relativity.

RFTD: In the Martial sense, what was the most amazing thing you saw Bruce do?

DP: Maybe his "one inch punch." He was a great showman, and could get any crowd eating out of his hand by setting that up right. I remember one demo I watched at Garfield H.S. (the Seattle inner city high school I graduated from, as did Linda the year after). He was asked by a teacher to talk to his class, and for some reason I went along - maybe I was on vacation, since my recollection is this was the year after I graduated.

Anyway, the class had a bunch of big, brawny football and basketball players who were lounging in their chairs in the back of the room, giving theatrical yawns and exchanging amused glances with each other as Bruce started out talking about Gung Fu and the "three different punches." He demonstrated a "karate" punch from the hip that was pretty snappy, then a straight Gung Fu punch (more from the solar plexus), also pretty snappy. Then he mentioned the "one inch" punch, which he talked about and then demonstrated in the air. In the air, of course, it doesn't look like much, and there were a number of eye rolls from the class. Then he said he really needed to demonstrate it, and called for a "volunteer," picking out the biggest guy he could spot in the back of the room, with the biggest attitude. The guy couldn't very well refuse, so he reluctantly made his way up to the front, trying to strut nonchalantly. Bruce had him stand in front of the class facing him, and got in position for his one-inch punch, with his arm straight out and the palm of his hand only an inch from the kid's chest. Everybody in the class is grinning and watching expectantly, and the volunteer is trying to act cool. Then Bruce stops and holds up a finger like he just thought of something. He runs around behind the kid and grabs a chair and positions it about five feet behind him, then runs back to his original position. "Just in case," he says, then proceeds to position his palm again in front of the kid's chest for the "punch." Now the class is sitting up straighter, expectant tittering, the volunteer is looking over his shoulder at the chair placed behind him and surreptitiously shifting his legs a bit to brace himself against the "one inch punch." Bruce asks if the kid is ready and after bracing himself some more, but not so much as to indicate that he's taking it too seriously, he nods. Bruce's arm shimmers (it is already extended, and he doesn't cock it back) and the palm closes the inch to the kid's chest. The kid literally flies backwards off his feet and is dumped into the waiting chair, which he overturns ass over tea kettle, sliding on past the chair into the wall. Bruce makes a big show of running over to the kid as the class lets out a collective gasp, apologizing

and helping him up, dusting imaginary dust off his shirt as he escorts the kid back to the front of the class, then proceeds without pause to continue talking about Gung Fu. Needless to say, he has the whole class on the edge of their chairs, with rapt attention, even when he starts to talk about Taoist Philosophy.

RFTD: You had more than just a teacher student relationship with Bruce, can you tell us what your friendship was like?

DP: We "hung out" (as the kids say these days), going out to eat, talking about all kinds of things, telling jokes, kidding around, etc. We also double-dated once or twice.

RFTD: Did Bruce ever show you any techniques that he did not share with the rest of the students?

DP: Not that I know of. He was very open about sharing his knowledge, and secure in his own mastery of the martial arts. He never evidenced any behavior that I saw as "hoarding" knowledge, or withholding any "secret techniques." In addition, he was constantly growing and searching himself, and his whole philosophy was opposed to the idea that there

Bruce practising Gung Fu with Palmer in Hong Kong, 1963.

was some one school or technique that was the "ultimate," and thus (it would seem to me) the logical extension of his philosophy (which was consistent about everything I saw him do or say) was that it was counter-productive and stagnating to try to keep certain techniques secret, and thus almost by definition static. Only by opening oneself up to the dynamic of the open exchange and sharing of knowledge could one evolve.

RFTD: You were a witness to Bruce and Taky Kimura's close friendship. Can you tell us what that special relationship was like between them?

DP: One of Bruce's gifts was his ability to interact as a friend with people who were quite a bit older than he was (like Taky), or younger (like me - I was four years younger). Taky and Bruce were already close when I came along, and stayed close. No doubt a large part of their special relationship was Taky's unwavering loyalty over a long period of time, which has continued after Bruce's death by his efforts to maintain the original school and Bruce's legacy, with no particular financial reward. The school in Seattle was run as a private club, with no advertising other than word-of-mouth, for only nominal dues to cover costs, in the basement under Taky's store. I never heard Taky complain or say or imply anything remotely negative about Bruce. I remember one time Bruce was demonstrating some technique to the class with Taky. Usually Bruce's control was perfect - he could snap a punch at full speed and power to within a millimeter of someone's nose under any conditions. But this time Bruce was talking to the class and had his head turned toward the class as he executed a straight punch; he wasn't concentrating as much as he usually did, and apparently forgot that Taky was wearing glasses. His punch, which was the normal millimeter or so from Taky's face, unfortunately blasted into Taky's glasses, shattering one of the lenses. At the time, it seemed like some of the shards flew into Taky's eye, and he was holding his eye for quite awhile. In retrospect, maybe Taky blinked in time, and none of the shards actually hit his retina, and only lodged in his eyelashes. At any rate, it was quite dramatic and scary for everyone who was watching, but Taky never said a word. Of course, Taky was a tough dude - as I recall, he walked around with a burst appendix for a few days before finally going to see a doctor.

RFTD: Can you tell us what kind of conversations you and Bruce had regarding the Martial Arts, outside class?

DP: As mentioned above, every time I saw him after being away awhile, he had new ideas and an expanded approach to the martial arts that he was eager to share. He could go on for hours about whatever his latest vision or addition was. He was also an entertaining storyteller, and had numerous stories about his martial arts encounters when he was younger in H.K., and the few he had in the States after he arrived here. When I saw him for the last time, in Hong Kong a year or so before he died, I remember him describing the various martial artists he had invited to H.K. to be in one of the movies he was making. He wanted great martial artists in his movies, to make the best martial arts scenes possible, and

didn't care if they had any acting experience. One of the martial artists he had invited was a Korean practitioner, who by reputation was a real master. Bruce expressed a great deal of disappointment, however, because he did not think the Korean, once he arrived in H.K., was as good as he was led to believe, and that the scenes they filmed were thus not as great as he had hoped for. He also described the filming of his scenes with Kareem Abdul Jabbar, which had taken place not long before.

RFTD: You had the opportunity to go to Hong Kong with Bruce in 1963. Can you tell us how this came to be?

DP: After studying gung fu my senior year of high school, it was hard to go back East to college. But one of the reasons I chose Yale was because it was well-known for its Asian language classes, and I wanted to study Chinese. I had wanted to study Asian languages for a couple of years, but Bruce's influence solidified that. While at Yale my freshman year, I studied Mandarin (Cantonese, the dialect spoken in H.K., was not taught). Probably when I was home at Christmas, Bruce told me he was going home for 6 months or so the following spring and summer, and broached the idea of me going over to H.K. for the summer. Another friend from high school, a Chinese-American named Lanston Chinn, who had started taking Gung Fu that year, was also planning to go, and we talked about sharing an apartment. However, sometime in the spring (of '63) Lanston suddenly started having periodic seizures, and the doctors were in the process of giving him a battery of tests to try to diagnose

Doug Palmer practicing Wing Chun in Hong Kong, Kowloon side in 1963, Bruce to his right practicing Tai Chi with his father Li Hoi Chuen. Doug was Bruce's guest and stayed with him at his family's house in those very hot summer months.

the cause and bring the seizures under control. As a consequence, Lanston was unable to go. At that point, since it was just me, Bruce's family invited me to stay with them, to which I readily agreed.

RFTD: The Hong Kong trip was the first time Bruce went back, from the time he left in 1959. Can you tell us what that was like for Bruce on a personal level?

DP: It appeared to be a time of renewing many of his friendships and other relationships. He had a number of close friends in the Cantonese movie business, whom he spent time with and introduced me to. He spent time working out with his teacher, Yip Man. No doubt Bruce, who had left Hong Kong for the first time at the age of 18 or so, had matured quite a bit away on his own, and his relationships were re-established on a different level than before.

RFTD: What did you and Bruce do in Hong Kong on a daily basis?

DP: The day would often start with Bruce ironing the clothes he planned to wear that day (he was a fastidious dresser, and didn't think the maid who did the ironing did a good enough job). We did a lot of things together, shopping (visiting the tailor or buying stone chops to have personal seals carved), visiting friends at their homes or at the movie studio, going to street fairs, often going to a steam bath for a bath and massage, etc. Bruce loved the massages, which were legitimate massages given by men, whom Bruce considered to be stronger and able to give better massages than women. The bath house also had the added benefit of enabling us to get really clean. That summer, H.K. had a water shortage, and the water pipes in the family apartment could only be turned on for a few hours every fourth day or so. As a result, the bath tub and every bucket and pail and other receptacle in the place was used to store water. To bath, we took a bucket of water and a sponge and gave ourselves a

Bruce Lee and Doug Palmer dressed up in Gung Fu pose for the camera in 1963, while vacationing in Hong Kong.

sponge bath in a curtained-off corner of the veranda overlooking the street. Since H.K. summers are hot and unbelievably muggy, I was often sweaty again within minutes of finishing my sponge bath. So the bath houses filled a very real function that summer as a place to get thoroughly clean. We also usually ate at least one meal a day, either lunch or dinner. The food in H.K. was fantastic and very reasonable. We usually ate Chinese food (Cantonese, Chiuchow, Shanghainese), but we went a number of times to a particular Russian restaurant that Bruce liked, too. But many dinners were eaten at home, too, and mealtime was a time for family gathering, exchanging news for the day, sometimes playing games after the meal. Two quick anecdotes: At my first meal with Bruce's family, after they picked me up at the airport, I was on my best behaviour. The first course was a soup, and I went out of my way to empty each spoonful into my mouth without slurping, just as my mother had always admonished. After a little bit, during which everyone seemed to be watching me, Bruce leaned over and said in a horse-whisper, "Make a little noise." I later learned that it was polite in H.K. to slurp a little when eating soup or noodles, to show that you were enjoying the food. After that, I loosened up and had no problem at all showing my appreciation! After dinner one evening the family played a board game. The game was very simple, involving a die and a board with a path you had to advance along. Spaces along the path contained different animals, which corresponded with animals on each face of the die. You advanced on the board by being first to yell out the name of the animal that was rolled with the die. It was pretty simple, but I had just learned the animals' names in Cantonese, so I was at a slight disadvantage and was surging with adrenalin, concentrating on what animal ended face up when the die came to rest, trying to mentally translate it into Cantonese and yelling it out before anyone else did. One of the animals was a shrimp, pronounced "haai" in Cantonese. In my excitement, when the shrimp came up I would yell it out quickly with a high pitch. I knew that Cantonese was a tonal language, having more tones than the Mandarin that I had studied for the past year, but I didn't think that much about it when the family members, especially some of the women, would titter when I yelled out "Shrimp!" at the top of my lungs. Finally Bruce leaned over, and told me quietly that "haai," with a lower tone, meant shrimp, and that "hai" with a higher tone meant a "woman's sex organ." I was mortified, and quite tongue-tied for the rest of the game whenever the shrimp came up.

Sometimes Bruce and I went our separate ways, too - on dates, for instance. Bruce had many girls he knew, and introduced me to some. If Bruce was off on a date (or working out with Yip Man or something else), I would often spend time with Robert (who was then 14) and his cousin, Anthony Lai, and friend, Tsoi-Jai. We made many excursions together all over H.K., including to the beach and to an amusement park. At the amusement park, there was one game booth where you could win prizes by flipping a coin so that it landed in and stayed in a saucer. There were a number of saucers arranged in rows over a screen or wire-mesh of some sort, with plenty of space between each saucer. If a flipped coin missed a saucer completely, it would disappear through the

screen (which had wide openings). If it landed on a saucer, the saucer was small enough that it would inevitably bounce off and disappear through the screen. The only possible way to keep the coin in a saucer seemed to be to bounce it off one saucer so that it landed and came to rest in a second one, but we never saw anyone pull this feat off. However, the first row of saucers seemed to be within arm's reach for me, with longer arms than anybody else in the crowd. When the game operator's back was turned, standing in the aisle between the rows of saucers and the narrow counter that separated the booth from the crowd, I reached over the counter and placed a coin in a first-row saucer. As soon as I had done so, I melted back behind Robert and Anthony and Tsoi-Jai, who yelled that they had successfully flipped a coin into a saucer and demanded their prize (as I recall, a pack of cigarettes - they didn't smoke, but they could sell them).

The first time, the operator appeared quite surprised (to land a coin in a first-row saucer, without any bounce from another saucer, was virtually impossible) and then puzzled, but he paid off. A few minutes later, when his back was turned again and he heard Robert and Anthony and Tsoi-Jai once more making a din, he was quite suspicious, but again he paid off, this time more slowly. When it happened the third time, he finally spotted me behind them in the crowd and put two and two together. He paid off, but then removed the first row of saucers and put an end to our fun.)

If I had a date, Bruce would coach me as to H.K. dating etiquette, and even give me tips on how to initiate "moves" on my date in a movie theater. He would actually choreograph a move and have me practice it on him or Robert ahead of time.

Bruce was also big on practical jokes, and he dreamed a few up that we would pull off together. One of them involved the H.K. police, whom Bruce detested (he felt they were corrupt, and bullies). If a policeman had a red marker on his uniform (as I recall on his epaulette), he supposedly spoke English. But the level of English was not that high, so Bruce would have me go up to a cop with the red marker and ask, "Excuse me, can you tell me the way to the Canton Theater?" There was a Canton Road, but no Canton Theater, and the cop would frown and say, "Canton Road?" I would then launch into very fast gobbledy-gook about meeting a friend at the Theater, etc., etc. and the cop would repeat, "Canton Road?" After a few rounds of this, as the cop became more flustered, I'd say, in Cantonese: "Lei ngee-ngee-ngum-ngum jo mat yeh?" - loosely translated as "What the hell are you mumbling about?" Bruce would walk up just then and ask if he could help; I'd say I was trying to find Canton Theater, he'd say he was going that way, and we'd walk off, leaving the cop standing there. Another routine involved a mock fight, which we'd stage on an elevator just as the door opened and a bunch of people were about to get on. We'd finish a mock argument, I'd take a roundhouse swing which he'd block, then hit me in the stomach, folding me up. The crowd would watch this with big eyes, seeing this much smaller Chinese guy dispatch a huge foreigner. As you can see, Bruce's sense of humor did not entail anybody ever knowing that they were the butt of a joke. He told many stories of the fights he used to have before he left H.K., with British sailors, etc. One sailor he dispatched by pretending to be very awkward, blocking the sailor's blows with clumsy, uncoordinated movements and then incapacitating him with a backhanded flick to the groin that appeared to be a fluke. He then swished away, tittering. I asked him why he didn't let the guy know he'd messed with the wrong guy, and he replied: "If someone gets beat by someone who is obviously stronger or better, he can accept that; but if he's beaten by someone who he thinks is a spastic, by mistake, he'll be pissed off for the rest of his life."

RFTD: Did Bruce introduce you to the legendary Yip Man? If so, what were your impressions of him?

DP: Bruce introduced me to Yip Man and I watched them work out (mostly Chi Sao, as I recall) in Yip Man's apartment, in a high-rise. Before we went there, Bruce told me that Yip Man did not know he was teaching Gung Fu to non-Chinese, and so I had to just watch them work out and pretend I didn't know anything. (Teaching Gung Fu to non-Chinese was taboo in H.K. at that time, and indeed in Chinatowns all around the world.) Yip Man spoke no English, but was very polite and gracious, and had no problem with me sitting there and watching. He and Bruce stripped to their undershirts to work out. My recollection is that Yip Man was a bit shorter than Bruce, but he seemed younger than his age and very fit.

RFTD: Did you and Bruce train at all in Hong Kong?

DP: Not much. It was super-muggy, and there was nowhere to really work out. In addition, we were both "on vacation."

RFTD: If you were to say the one thing in Hong Kong that you and Bruce truly enjoyed doing, what would that be?

DP: Besides, dating, it would have to be eating. We both loved good food, and H.K. had the best Chinese food in the world at that time (and probably still). Some favorites: Shanghai-style fried rice and oyster sauce beef. But we had a lot of more exotic stuff, too, especially at banquets.

RFTD: After Seattle Bruce moved to Oakland and then Los Angeles. What was it like to see Bruce evolve in his Martial Arts ability along with his physical prowess?

DP: It was fascinating and awe-inspiring, to think that he had a developed system that was the best possible, and then to see him at a next meeting some months or more later show how he had extended it, with the old system being now just a part of a greater whole.

RFTD: When Bruce was achieving his goals in television and film, did you both keep in contact?

DP: We kind of lost contact when he went down to L.A. After college (I graduated in '66 in Chinese Studies) I went to law school (having gotten married my last year in college), and then, after spending the summer of '69 in Seattle my wife and I moved to Tokyo, where I had a job.

While I was overseas, I knew he was in the "Green Hornet" series and was trying to break in to Hollywood, but we had no direct contact. Then, about a year or so before his death, I went down to H.K. on business, taking along my wife. As far as I knew, he was still in L.A. I wanted to look up his family, however, and went to the old apartment on Nathan Road where I had spent the summer. The apartment was being used as a nursery school, and no one seemed to know the Lee family or where they might have gone. I looked up Anthony Lai and Robert and every relative's name I could think of in the phone book, and had some fruitless conversations in Cantonese with old ladies on the telephone, but was unable to find anyone. Towards the end of our stay in H.K., I had a meeting with a Chinese accountant who had helped set up a H.K. company for a client. After the meeting, I told him that I was trying to find the family of a good friend, a fellow named Bruce Lee; that the friend was in the States, in L.A., but I thought his family would still be in H.K.; that the friend's father's name was Lee Hoi-Chuen, then deceased but well-known in his day as a Cantonese opera star - maybe he had heard of him? The accountant looked at me strangely, and said, "You say you're a good friend of Bruce Lee?" I said yes, but he was in L.A., I was really looking for his family, that I hadn't seen since 1963 but who had all been generous and overflowing with hospitality to me. He said,

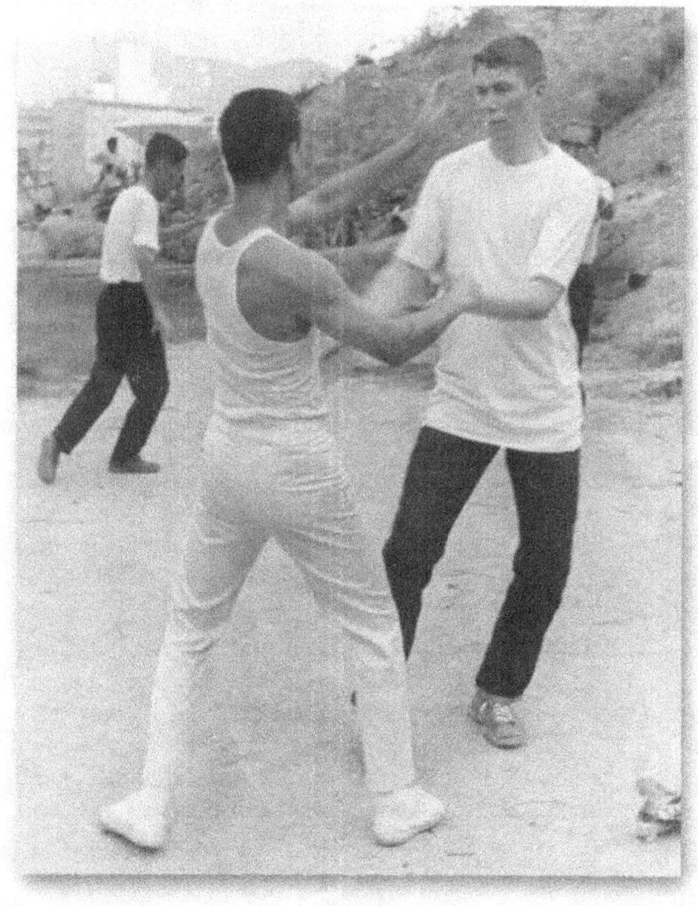

"He's not in L.A.; he's here in Hong Kong. You're good friends with him, and you didn't know that?" When I expressed surprise, he picked up a newspaper that was sitting on a table in his office and flipped to the movie section. There was a full-page ad of Bruce's latest movie, showing him doing a flying kick.

There was actually one person listed in the phone book with the name Bruce Lee. I called him, but he told me (politely, but with the air of someone who had to do it often) that he was not the Bruce Lee I was looking for. Finally, I hit on the idea of having a Cantonese-speaking friend call Bruce's movie studio, saying that an old friend was trying to get ahold of him. Whoever fielded the call would not give out Bruce's number, but said they'd take a message and pass it along to Bruce. I said, "Tell him that Baak Ma Dak called," and left the phone and room number of my hotel. Within five minutes, the phone rang and Bruce was on the line. "You son of a gun," he said, "let's get together." (Baak Ma Dak was the name Bruce had given me - "Dak", pronounced "duck" and meaning "virtue," being chosen because it sounded like "Doug," and "Baak Ma," meaning "white horse," being chosen as an approximate pronunciation of Palmer.)

Linda and Bruce picked us up for dinner and then gave us a tour of the movie studio, where he was filming what turned out to be his last movie. He also showed us one of his movies in a private theater at the studio - as I recall, it was the first one made after his return to H.K., shot in Thailand - "The Big Boss" or something like that. Then he took us to his new house, still under construction in Kowloon Tong. He was dressed much more casually than he dressed in 1963 - jeans and a sweatshirt, but he was obviously known by everyone in H.K. If we were stopped at a light, the cabbie stopped alongside would start up a conversation. When we went into a restaurant for dinner, without a reservation, the waiters cleared away a table despite a long line that was waiting and gave it to us. We had more waiters circulating around our table than all the other tables put together.

We talked about the possibility of my coming down to H.K. after my stint in Tokyo was up and helping him with his legal and business interests. We stayed in touch after I returned to Tokyo, but then suddenly he was gone. I was in shock when a friend in Tokyo told me, who had heard the news on a U.S. armed forces radio broadcast in Tokyo.

RFTD: When you first saw Bruce Lee on screen for the first time, what were your thoughts about the man you called teacher and friend, expressing himself on film?

DP: I think I had actually seen a Cantonese film that Bruce was in as a child, that came through Seattle's Chinatown. And then I had seen a few "Green Hornet" episodes. But the first film I saw with him in it as an adult, where he could really express himself, was the one he showed us in H.K. when we toured the movie studio. He was not totally happy with the film (as I recall, he was not the director, and came in fairly late in the film - I think that experience made him want to control more of the films after that), but I was impressed by his ability to express his sense of humor and natural magnetism through that media, and to por-

tray realistic yet dramatic fight scenes. (By contrast, the few scenes he was allowed as Kato in the "Green Hornet" were lame, presumably because he did not choreograph them, and they did not want him upstaging the "Green Hornet".)

RFTD: After all these years, what can you say were the fondest memories you had of Bruce Lee?

DP: Probably remembering his sense of humor, both his corny jokes (which he told with infectious enthusiasm) and practical jokes, as well as his generosity.

RFTD: If you were to describe Bruce Lee in three words, what would they be?

DP: Genius, generous, and perfectionist. Also self-confident. To elaborate: He was genius in the way he looked at the martial arts from a new perspective; he was not content with limits set by any particular system, questioned the underlying principles, and tested all theory against the practice. He was generous in many ways - with his time and his assistance, both in terms of personal effort and also financially. No doubt he got that from his parents, who were both kind and generous. When I spent the summer in H.K., I arrived with a bad knee, which I had torn six months before during Freshman year and which had been diagnosed as a torn meniscus cartilage, that would require an operation if it didn't heal on its own. I hobbled around during the summer, and Bruce's family asked me if I was interested in having a Chinese herbal doctor that they knew, and who was good with sprains and tears in joints, etc., try his hand at treating the problem. I said sure - nothing to lose, and it was fairly cheap. So this guy came by each morning to their apartment and treated me. He heated up a poultice made of various herbs, that looked like a mud-pack, on a little charcoal brazier he brought with him, and applied it directly to my knee. When it cooled off, he would heat it up again and repeat the process. After a half hour or so of that, he'd rub some kind of oil into my knee. After a few weeks, I ran out of money and so was going to discontinue the treatments. Bruce must have told his father, because he came to me on the last day and asked if the treatments were helping. If they were, Bruce said, his father had offered to pay for the treatments. I was embarrassed, and said I thought they were helping, but that I didn't want them to pay for it. His father waved my protestations aside, and I had another week or so of treatment before we had to leave. By that time, the knee was fully healed - I could snap a front or side kick with full strength and speed, etc. and I've never had a problem since.) Bruce himself was no less generous. I remember when I last saw him in H.K.; we were at the house he was building and Linda showed him a letter that had arrived, from an old friend in Oakland. I had met the person one time I was in Oakland with Bruce, many years before, and Bruce told me he was dying of cancer. When he finished the letter, he turned to Linda and quietly told her (in a voice I am sure I was not meant to hear) to send the old friend a substantial sum of money.

RFTD: In closing, what can you say about Bruce Lee the teacher and friend, who took a hold of the world with his magic called Jeet Kune Do and left a legacy that keeps his energy and memory alive to this day?

DP: One of the things that I respected most about Bruce, and also was a measure of his self-confidence and genius, was his total open-mindedness, and willingness to teach anyone - of any race, gender, age or socioeconomic background - if they wanted to learn. While in H.K., as long as Yip Man was alive, out of respect he did not flaunt that fact. But outside of H.K., he observed no restrictions. His classes, even before I joined, were mini-United Nations. When we left H.K. at the end of the summer in 1963, after stopping off in Tokyo for a few days, we stopped in Honolulu. Among other things there, he was asked to give a demonstration to a Gung Fu school. He asked me to accompany him, and we gave the demo together. I was mostly the dummy, of course, but it was obvious that I had had some training. There must have been at least 100 students and teachers in the crowd, all Chinese. In Hawaii then, the Chinese studied Gung Fu and the Japanese studied Karate, there was no mixing. After the demo, Bruce was of course surrounded by a group who had all sorts of questions; but a number of people came up to me, too, out of Bruce's earshot, asking, "Is he teaching you Gung Fu?" It was clear that what they really meant was, "Is he teaching Gung Fu to non-Chinese?"

One of the instructors pestered Bruce with questions, asking him how he would block a straight kick. Bruce asked the guy to kick, and then blocked it with a standard open-palm slap on the instep. After blocking the kick, Bruce raised his hands in some sort of gesture to illustrate what he was saying. The guy, however, had kept his leg extended, half up in the air. As soon as Bruce raised his hands, the guy kind of flicked his foot a couple of inches and said, "See, I could have gotten you." I could tell Bruce was steaming, but he just kept talking as if nothing had happened. He started talking about various ways of tying someone up, and threw a straight punch at the guy's face, slow enough so he could block it. As soon as he did, Bruce executed a quick laap sao (pulling hand), effectively trapping both his hands. The guy had been smoking, with a cigarette hanging in his mouth, and Bruce jerked his arm so abruptly the guy's cigarette went flying out of his mouth. Bruce then proceeded to go on for several minutes, holding the guys two hands trapped with one of his firmly enough that the guy couldn't move, but with Bruce's other hand free to wave around and underline his various points. The guy had no choice but to stand there looking like an idiot, with both hands tied up, until Bruce finally released him. Bruce hadn't hurt him, and hadn't said anything about the guy's feeble "kick," but everyone who was watching got the point and understood that Bruce was in total control.

Charlie Woo posing for the camera, demonstrating the Jun Fan Gung Fu basics at the University Way Institute.

Sue Ann Kay, Taky Kimra and Charlie Woo posing for the camera in Seattle, Washington after Gung Fu class.

Special Dedication

By Charlie Woo

I had the pleasure of meeting Charlie Woo during the era of my post internment camp situation, as our family had relocated in Seattle after four years of incarceration.

I had joined a Seattle Judo Dojo prior to my good fortune of meeting Bruce Lee. Charlie was a second-degree Judo Champion and he and I commonly did "Randori", a competitive like sparring practice in which he kicked my butt the majority of the time.

We became instant friends and this culminated in our joining the original group of guys that Bruce Lee had been teaching that included Jessie Glover, his first acquaintance, James Demile, Ed Hart, Howard Hall, Pat Hooks, Leroy Garcia, Joe Cowles, Skip Ellsworth, Tak Miyabe, and others whom I cannot recall at this time, in which I apologize profusely.

Bruce, even at that young age was a stern no nonsense teacher who put us through unrelenting paces, but we enjoyed it immensely.

He keenly observed the mental as well as the physical talent of each of us, the stages of natural, athletic and mental capabilities of how quickly we showed in assimilating each and every facet of what he demonstrated.

Bruce was a unique personality in that he could be kicking butt during practice, then open our minds to a change of pace with a mental philosophical statement that just opened our minds to an exciting level.

He loved to stop and tell us a mind boggling philosophical story that uniquely gave us a second breather and allowed us to go with a renewed second wind.

He was a keen observer of potential and natural athleticism as that was one of his unique God given talents. He could observe you doing something and his unique mindset would allow him to add it to his curriculum much more perfectly than you, even though you may have been practicing it for years.

I am honored to say that Charlie Woo stood by me and along side Bruce Lee during those early years. He was a good man, an honest man, a man with dignity and integrity. There is no doubt that if Charlie were with us today, he would have been one of the great Jun Fan Gung Fu practitioners. So, I dedicate this book not only to Bruce Lee, but also to all our fallen brothers like Charlie, who supported Bruce Lee's vision and that were down for the cause.

• *Charlie Woo posing in fun, outside the Jun Fan Gung Fu Institute in Seattle, Washington.*

• *Taky Kimura and Charlie standing next to the Jun Fan Gung Fu Symbol and creed at the University Way Institute.*

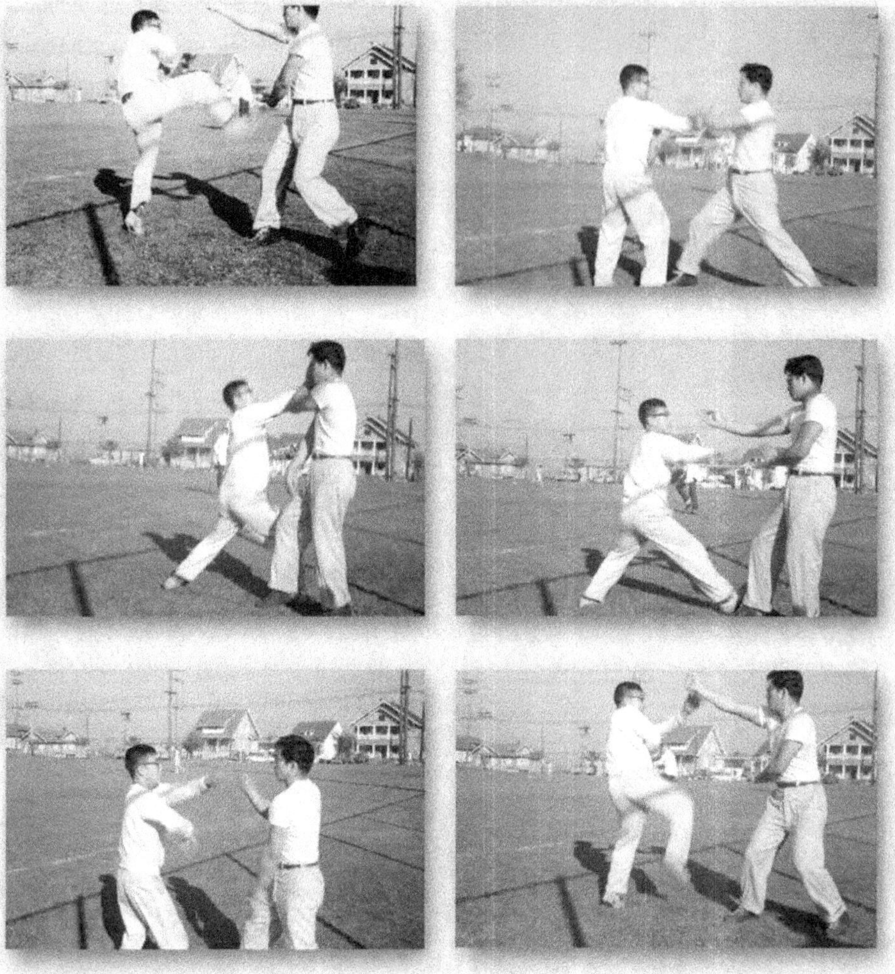

Bruce Lee taking pictures of Taky Kimura and Charlie Woo, practicing the Jun Fan Gung Fu method at Jefferson Park on Beacon Hill. Bruce used to love training there on the weekends and then going to eat afterwards with his students. Pictures like this were either going to be used for book publication or personal reference for Bruce and his students.

Diploma of Graduation
Clallam Bay High School
Cape Flattery School District, Clallam Bay, Washington
This Certifies that
Takauki (Taky) Kimura
Diploma

Taky Kimura Graduation

By Julie DonTigny

We had contacted the school to see if Taky could graduate, but no one could have scripted what he was to receive in return. Taky was excitedly recognized everywhere he went, people said they were coming to the graduation just because of him. An old classmate apologized for not being aware that Taky had never received his diploma and apologized for not doing something sooner. He tearfully told the story of the day Taky was taken - how they cried at the 1942 graduation because he wasn't there. It was wrenching. We had always focused on what Taky had lost and didn't consider what his classmates went through in losing him.

The ceremony was incredible. The entire crowd erupted in cheers when Taky entered and they included him in nearly every piece. They found an old class photo of Taky when he was 15 or so and bought him a Washington State University sweatshirt, where he was to go to school on scholarship. The speeches of the salutatorian and valedictorian were both dedicated to what they had learned from Taky's story – perseverance, positive attitude, forgiveness and humility. About 14 members of the Makah Nation came up and said their uncle was good friends with Taky and how much he had cherished that friendship. They had many gifts for him including an eagle feather and a hand-carved canoe paddle, then sang a traditional gift-giving song reserved for the most reverent of occasions. Taky took the microphone and tried to thank them and everyone in the community, but he was overwhelmed with emotion.

The final speaker was a member of the school board, Greg Colfax. He began, "Mr. Kimura, I do not accept your thanks, your gratitude, for honoring you today.... Instead, we thank you. We thank you for the humiliation and suffering you endured all these years - that teaches all of us the meaning of democracy; the meaning of civil rights; the meaning of calling those of another race brother and sister." It was an incredibly moving and powerful speech that reminded us all of what had been stolen from Taky and so many Japanese-Americans.

The crowd went wild when his name was called for his diploma; we believe he had 3 standing ovations in all. The work the graduates and the school did, the warm welcome from the entire community, it was unbelievable. We're still stunned. It was so much bigger than a diploma; it was a chance for Taky and the community to heal.

Honoring a U.S. Citizen

By Gregory Colfax,
School Board Member of Cape Flattery School District

June 12, 2009 at the Graduation of Clallam Bay High School

It is with honor and humility that we, today, confer on Mr. Kimura the High School diploma he so long waited for. His graduation, interrupted by World War II, and his internment in the camps of isolation, resulted in losing not only his right to an education, but his right to freedom. We can only surmise his loss and pain from that experience as one of a sad chapters in United States History.

President Roosevelt said: "The only thing we have to fear, is fear itself." This act of internment of Japaneses-Americans was fear not fully stood up to. The United States fell backward, lost its footing and rushed to judge a whole race as suspect, as un-American. The ethos of the time displayed how ignorance can become government policy.

Mr. Kimura, I do not accept your thanks, your gratitude, for honoring you today with this long in coming graduation certificate from Cape Flattery's High School. No, we can not accept your "thank you". Instead, we thank you. We thank you for the humiliation and suffering you endured all these years- that teaches all of us the meaning of democracy; the meaning of civil rights; the meaning of calling those of another race brother and sister.

Your exclusion from our communities during the war is a great humiliating definition of democracy. We must thank you for teaching all of us, that one race's suffering, one race's denial of their fundamental right to live with respect and honor from all the other races- that make the United States, the United States, comes into sharp focus because of your experience in the internment camps.

We thank you this evening for returning to our community, because we must think, we must contemplate the very meaning, the definition, of being a citizen of the United States of America. We must ask ourselves hard questions with answers that go beyond our living rooms, our communities, our cities, and our state. We must strive for planetary answers.

We must approach fear, our racial fears, our religious fears, our economic fears, our fear of global annihilation, with your experience, Mr. Kimura as, not a backdrop to our questions, but as a lighthouse in a darkened sea of worry.

Democracy is as powerful in its singular individual as it is in its plurality. During World War II we lost the individual in favor of a select plurality. Our challenge today, the 21st Century, is to remember and honor the individual in an unavoidable plurality.

We are humbled by your presence this evening Mr. Kimura. We thank you with this diploma, and more than that, we thank you for teaching us about the soul of humanity, the heart of democracy, and the passion for justice.

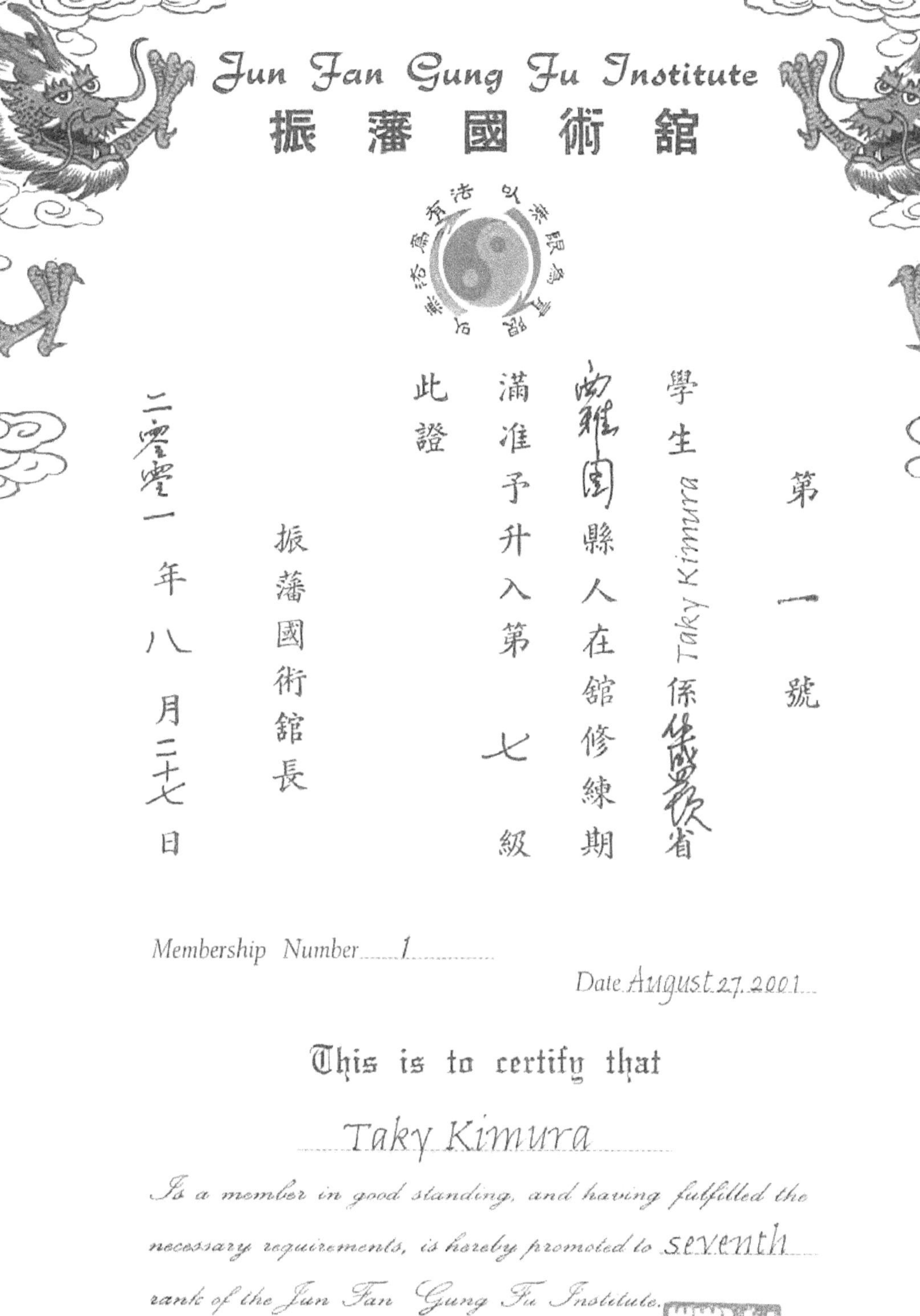

Jun Fan Gung Fu Institute

振藩國術館

以無法為有法 以無限為有限

第一號

學生 Taky Kimura 係華盛頓省西雅圖縣人在館修練期滿准予升入第七級

此證

振藩國術館長

二零零一年八月二十七日

Membership Number 1

Date August 27, 2001

This is to certify that

Taky Kimura

Is a member in good standing, and having fulfilled the necessary requirements, is hereby promoted to seventh rank of the Jun Fan Gung Fu Institute.

李小龍之妻

Linda Lee

INSTRUCTOR.

By direction of my husband, Bruce Lee

PRESIDENT.

In Closing

To fill a book about my experience with Bruce Lee as my dear friend and Sifu, would be a never-ending story that could fill 1000 thousand books or more. The hours, days, months and years during and after the passing of my dear friend are an endless journey of heartfelt musings. When I ventured out in doing this book, I tried to describe the moments and feelings captured by the letters, notes and images within that Bruce and I shared together on many levels.

If you read this book, or in the process of doing so, you have chosen this book because you either are a huge fan of Bruce Lee, or you have an interest in knowing more about a man who broke many barriers and accomplished many goals. Whether or not you're a martial artist or student of philosophy, actor, musician or artist in any way, Bruce Lee stood for the understanding of one's self and the journey one takes to accomplish your desired fate. He stands for what all of us try to achieve, he is the lesson taught, the journey on going, the praise we all can accomplish by hard work and a soft and stern stance in who we each are in the equation of life. Bruce Lee was and is more than just a man, he was and is an ideal that we all strive for, he is our push to do better, our yearning to be. So whether or not you find this book to be your cup of tea, there is one point that cannot be argued, we are all here in celebration of a man who has, or will, change us forever more.

In the end, I will leave you with a quote that Bruce Lee used to say. May it resonate within your mind and be a guiding tool for you, and may it also help you in your own journey in finding who you are and what you want out of life.

With Love and Appreciation to you all,

Takayuki Kimura

"Ever since I was a child I have had this instinctive urge for expansion and growth. To me, the function and duty of a quality human being is the sincere and honest development of one's potential."

Bruce Lee

For further authentic information on Bruce Lee or the art and philosophy of Jun Fan Jeet Kune Do®, please contact:

BRUCE LEE FOUNDATION

11693 San Vicente Blvd., Suite #918

Los Angeles, CA 90049

www.bruceleefoundation.org

The Bruce Lee Foundation, a California 501(c)(3) public benefit corporation, seeks to preserve, perpetuate, and disseminate Bruce Lee's life example, philosophies, and art of Jun Fan Jeet Kune Do ® through inspirational events, educational programs, martial arts instruction, and the Bruce Lee Museum. We believe that the Bruce Lee Foundation can enrich lives, open minds and break down barriers through the active proliferation of Bruce Lee's legacy of undaunted optimism in the face of adversity, unwavering humanism, mental and physical perseverance, and inspirational presence of mind toward the betterment of our global community.

www.ingramcontent.com/pod-product-compliance
Lightning Source LLC
Chambersburg PA
CBHW080729300426
44114CB00019B/2520

* 9 7 8 1 9 3 3 9 0 1 4 5 9 *